*The Oxford Guide to Library Research*

# The Oxford Guide to Library Research

THIRD EDITION

*Thomas Mann*

OXFORD
UNIVERSITY PRESS

2005

# OXFORD
UNIVERSITY PRESS

Oxford University Press, Inc., publishes works that
further Oxford University's objective of excellence
in research, scholarship, and education.

Oxford   New York
Auckland   Cape Town   Dar es Salaam   Hong Kong   Karachi
Kuala Lumpur   Madrid   Melbourne   Mexico City   Nairobi
New Delhi   Shanghai   Taipei   Toronto

With offices in
Argentina   Austria   Brazil   Chile   Czech Republic   France   Greece
Guatemala   Hungary   Italy   Japan   Poland   Portugal   Singapore
South Korea   Switzerland   Thailand   Turkey   Ukraine   Vietnam

Published by Oxford University Press, Inc.
198 Madison Avenue, New York, NY 10016
www.oup.com

Oxford is a registered trademark of Oxford University Press

Library of Congress Cataloging-in-Publication Data
Mann, Thomas, 1948–
The Oxford guide to library research / Thomas Mann. — 3rd ed.
p. cm.
Includes bibliographical references and indexes.
ISBN-13: 978-0-19-518997-1 (hardcover)

ISBN-13: 978-0-19-518998-8 (pbk.)

1. Library research—United States.
I. Title.
Z710.M23 2005
025.5′24—dc22
2005006087

Printed in the United States of America
on acid-free paper

*For*
*Jack Nabholtz*

# Contents

Particular importance of Congressional hearings — Archives, Manuscripts, and Public Records

# *Preface*

This book will answer two questions above all. First, what significant research resources will you miss if you confine your research entirely, or even primarily, to sources available on the open Internet? And second, what techniques of subject searching will you also miss if you confine yourself to the limited software and display mechanisms of the Internet? As I will demonstrate, bricks-and-mortar research libraries contain vast ranges of printed books, copyrighted materials in a variety of other formats, and site-licensed subscription databases that are not accessible from anywhere, at anytime, by anybody on the Web. Moreover, many of these same resources allow avenues of subject access that cannot be matched by "relevance ranked" keyword searching. One can reasonably say that libraries today routinely encompass the entire Internet—that is, they will customarily provide terminals allowing free access to all of the open portions of the Net—but that the Internet does not, and cannot, contain more than a small fraction of everything discoverable within library walls.

If you wish to be a good researcher you have to be aware of the trade-offs between virtual and real libraries. While the former apparently overcome the *where* restrictions of bricks-and-mortar facilities, they do so only at the unavoidable cost of imposing other significant and inescapable restrictions of *what* and *who*. Internet providers must limit *what* they make available to begin with (unregulated copyright-free material); or, if they mount copyrighted sources and hope to profit from them, they must then impose major restrictions on *who* has access (those who pay fees at the point of use, or who pay special fees or assessments to become part of defined and password-restricted user groups). Membership fees, in some instances, are covered by

local taxes within a defined geographic area, or by tuition in academic set-
tings; but researchers outside these paying communities will not have the
same overall access as those inside, and the range of coverage paid for by
subscription fees can itself vary greatly from one community to the next.

In the overall universe of information records there are three considerations that are inextricably tied together:

1. copyright protection;
2. free "fair use" of the records by everyone; and
3. access limitations of *what*, *who*, and *where*.

It is not possible to combine (1) and (2) without restricting at least one
element of (3). "Free" cyberspace access (that is, without point-of-use
charges) always entails barriers of either *what* is searchable to begin with,
or *who* can view it.

The overall point is this: the only way to overcome the barriers of
cyberspace, and to provide *free* access even to people who don't pay local
taxes or tuition, is to impose a *where* restriction within library walls. Within
those walls, libraries can make any information records, including both copyrighted print sources and expensive subscription databases, freely available to
all visitors, whether or not those users live in the immediate area, and whether
or not they pay any monetary support for the library's operation. Those who
regard "access within walls" as the weakness of real libraries have the situation exactly backwards: it is precisely this restriction that *enables* libraries to
make all information, both public domain and copyrighted, freely available to
anyone at all who comes in the door. This is a genuine strength of real libraries, one that cannot be matched by the Internet. (Long-term preservation, another such strength, lies beyond the scope of the present book.)

Printed books and journals, as physical objects whose contents cannot be
broadcast, have built-in *where* restrictions that enable them to be offered for
free use within library walls. This restriction itself, however, is mitigated by
several additional considerations. First, much printed material can be checked
out and used in other locations at any time of the day or night. Second,
materials unavailable in one locale often can be freely borrowed from another. Finally, publicly accessible libraries are dispersed in many different
geographic areas. You cannot get "everything" freely online from your home
or office; but most readers of this book will nonetheless have convenient

access to local libraries that do indeed provide free access to vast stores of resources not accessible via Google, Yahoo, or Amazon.com.

Another significant difference between real and virtual libraries lies in the formats of material they are capable of offering. Very few people can stand to read book-length narrative or expository texts—say, 150 pages or so—on computer screens. Nor do they like the point-of-use expense of printing reams of individual sheets. Even the cyberprophets who predict the end of real libraries often make their predictions, ironically, in printed and copyrighted books, which are freely available to everyone only in the real libraries they belittle. Nor, after more than a decade of fervent hype, do e-books show any signs of significantly encroaching on the territory of real books.

Format is a real and important consideration because it is significantly linked to a kind of hierarchy in the world of learning:

1. *Data* are the unorganized, unfiltered, and unevaluated raw materials of thought, comparable to sense experiences.
2. *Information* reflects an organization of data to the point that statements can be made about it, either true or false, and coherent or incoherent with other information.
3. *Opinion* is a level of thinking with an added weight, either of confidence or of approval/disapproval, attached to a belief, prior to or apart from objective confirmation.
4. *Knowledge* reflects a still higher level of organization to the point that truth or falsity can be assessed by tests of correspondence to, and coherence with, the world of experience and of other ideas. This level entails discernment of patterns within information and the making of generalizations that are accessible to, and acceptable by, other people.
5. *Understanding* is a higher level of thought in that it comprehends not just patterns and generalizations, but the *causes*, *reasons*, or *stories* behind them. An understanding of physical causes gives one a measure of predictability, the hallmark of the sciences. The humanities, on the other hand, are grounded on the assumption of the non-illusory nature of free will and the reality of chosen (not merely unconscious) goals as motivating factors; their hallmarks are philosophical justification by reasons (not just physical causes), and narrative integration of experience in explanatory sequences of beginnings and middles

leading to ends. (The social sciences mix both scientific and humanistic criteria of explanation.)

*Wisdom* is the final goal of learning; its function lies in assessing the worth of all of these levels according to ultimate criteria of truth, goodness, and beauty. It accomplishes this within overarching frameworks or philosophies of what counts as evidence, or what counts as an explanation to begin with. Such frameworks necessarily assume some *ultimate* stopping point or ground of explanation, which, when reached, finally suffices in justifying a sequence of thought. Wisdom also entails ethical virtue in a way that precludes its simple ranking as number 6 in the hierarchy; it is more of a penumbra enveloping the other levels than a top step itself (see the Appendix).

Wisdom, of course, is difficult to come by. We are on simpler ground with the more hierarchical levels of learning such as knowledge and understanding. These are not generally attainable in high degree by people with brief attention spans, especially in the areas of the conventional academic disciplines that are the main focus of this book. Achievement of the higher levels of thought requires written texts in narrative or expository forms that are of substantial length, spelling out both the complexities and the interrelationships of relevant considerations.

It is here that we run into what appears to be a significant difference between screen displays and books: while both can *contain* texts of any length, it is becoming more apparent that readers much more readily absorb lengthy texts via book formats. Format of presentation changes the degree and quality of access to what is presented, and the advantages that e-books offer in keyword-search capabilities for specific information seem to be substantially outweighed by the greater barriers they erect against readers' overall understanding of their lengthy texts as connected wholes. The difference is somewhat like the contrast between water in liquid and frozen states; identical chemical composition does not make chewing ice satisfying to thirsty people. Why this is so, I will leave to psychologists; I have simply noticed, repeatedly, that the large majority of people who advocate the replacement of real libraries by virtual ones have themselves seldom read any book-length narratives or expositions in the format they would so cavalierly impose on everyone else.

I think it is reasonable to conclude that there is an inherent bias in screen-display formats toward the pictorial, the audio, the colorful, the animated, the instantaneous connection, the quickly updated, and the short verbal text —qualities which most readily engender learning at the levels of data, information, opinion, and (to a lesser extent) knowledge. The level of understanding, however—which is ultimately inseparable from lengthy verbal narratives and exposition—is still conveyed, and attained, more readily through the different medium of book formats.

A concern for the maintenance of real libraries that provide *free* access to *books* is thus not in the least "sentimental"; rather, it reflects a justifiable and serious concern that our culture not lose its higher levels of thought. Simply making book-length texts *available* electronically by no means assures that they will actually be understood as well in online formats as they would be in codices—hence one of the reasons for the continuing need for real, rather than exclusively virtual, research libraries. (Further reasons will be given in Chapters 3 and 5.)

This book maps out nine major roads, and some important side paths, that will lead you efficiently into the full range of humanity's accumulated thought records—both online and offline. Its emphasis, frankly, will be first of all on books, and then on other resources that cannot be freely tapped into from anywhere, at any time, by anybody—but which can indeed be freely consulted by anyone who steps within the walls of a research library. The present volume, then, unlike most other contemporary guides to research, centers on the resources available within research libraries—including print, microform, and manuscript sources, as well as site-licensed databases. In the context of this book, the open Internet forms the next circle out, rather than occupying the center itself.

Most guides to research are organized either by subject ("These are the resources for education, these for history, these for nursing," and so on) or by type of literature (Web sites, commercial databases, encyclopedias, handbooks, directories, etc.). Such guides continue to be important and useful. This one, however, is different. Although it makes use of both these traditional schemes, this guide is primarily structured around nine different *methods* of subject searching:

- Controlled vocabulary searching
- Use of subject-classified bookstacks for general or focused browsing
- Keyword searching
- Citation searching

- Related record searching
- Use of published subject bibliographies
- Boolean combination searching (with some other computer manipulations)
- Using the subject expertise of people sources
- Type of literature searching

Each of these methods is potentially applicable in *any* subject area; each has strengths and weaknesses, advantages and disadvantages; and each is capable of turning up information that cannot be reached by the other eight.

I have found through experience that this scheme simply works better, as an overall model, than the traditional alternatives. (It does not abandon them, however; rather, it encompasses them.) My own background includes work as an academic researcher at the doctoral level, as a private investigator, as a graduate student in library science, as a freelance researcher, as a reference librarian at two universities, and as a general reference librarian for over twenty years at the largest library in the world. A second forming element derives from my having closely observed and worked with tens of thousands of other researchers over a quarter century. Taken as a whole, my experience has taught me that most people unconsciously work within a framework of very limited assumptions about the extent of information that is easily and freely available to them, especially in libraries; indeed, most researchers, nowadays, have only very hazy notions of anything beyond general Internet searches.

It strikes me, too, that previous writers on this "research" subject who are not librarians have overlooked some fundamentally important steps and distinctions in telling their audiences how to proceed; many have even perpetuated harmful notions. On the other hand, some librarians who have written on the subject have not placed the weight and emphasis on certain matters that scholars and other investigators require; indeed, many research guides offer little more than lists of individual printed and electronic sources with no overall perspective on methods or techniques of *using* them. And the proliferation of guides focused exclusively on the Internet tends to dumb down the whole process by suggesting, or even stating, that "everything" is available online—thereby confining researchers' views, right from the start, to only one galaxy of sources within an information universe that is truly much larger. Moreover, very few writers of any sort give concrete examples of what to do—or of what not to do, which may be the more instructive.

Much of what I've discovered over the past thirty years I have had to learn the hard way, and I especially hope to save the reader from some of the more egregious mistakes and omissions I've been guilty of myself at one time or another. Unlike many people whom I've helped, I have had the fortunate (although painful) experience of gaining feedback from these mistakes, due to their being brought to my attention by the several shifting professional perspectives I've had on the same types of problems. The insight of "Oh! There's a way to *do* that! I wish I'd known that before" has come to me in many unexpected ways over the years. This experience, I think, has made certain patterns in the orientations of other researchers more evident to me, specifically:

- Patterns in the types of questions they ask, and in how they ask them
- Patterns in the usually unconscious assumptions they hold about the range of options available to them
- Patterns in the bad advice they are sometimes given by teachers, employers, and colleagues
- Patterns in the mistakes and omissions that routinely reduce the efficiency of their research.

Viewed collectively, these patterns tend to suggest the areas in which most people need the most help; and it is on this group of concerns that I wish to concentrate. I hope especially to give readers a sense of the principles and rules involved that are applicable in any situation, not just an annotated list of particular subject sources. I also hope that through the examples I've come across in my own research projects and in helping others (from which I've sometimes created composite examples for this book), this guide will give readers a sense of the trade-offs that are always involved in choosing one research option rather than another. I especially hope to provide a perspective of how the different trade-offs balance and compensate for each other in the total information system.

I wish to thank all of my colleagues at the Library of Congress—staff and readers alike, past and present—from whom I have learned more than I can convey here. In addition to those individuals thanked in previous editions of this book, I wish especially to thank the following for their direct or indirect input into the current revision, or simply for the questions they asked that forced me to stretch in unexpected ways: Jane Blevins, Kenneth

Kitchell, Judy Krone, Edward Luft, Jim McGovern, Lawrence Marcus, Josephine Pacheco, Gary Price, James Reston, Jr., Stephen Rhind-Tutt, Chris Sherman, Judith Roach, Marian Taliaferro, Anne Toohey, Virginia Wood, and The League of Extraordinary Gentlemen (Joel Achenbach, Tony Cantu, Mike Dirda, Bob Edgar, Herb Levine, Irvin Matus, Doug Owsley, Mike Weimer, and Martin Winkler). I am most grateful to Art Emerson and Patricia Andrasik for helping with the illustrations. A special thanks goes, as usual, to Colleen Hoppins, for her encouragement and inspiration; and to the memory of the late D.W. Schneider, who got me started as a librarian. The editors and staff of Oxford University Press, especially Elda Rotor, Cybele Tom, and Helen Mules, have done a wonderful job of shepherding the manuscript through production; I am grateful to all of them, and to Rick Balkin, agent extraordinaire, who has done his usual fine job of making the whole process run smoothly. I also wish to acknowledge a debt to the editors of *Library Quarterly*; some of the examples that I use in Chapter 3 appeared earlier in an article I wrote for them.

A note to library catalogers: the first edition of this work appeared in 1987 as *A Guide to Library Research Methods*; the second edition (1998) was published under the current title.

While the book assembles the insights of many people, its shortcomings are attributable only to myself. I am most conscious of its omissions; in trying to convey a sense of the overall universe of knowledge records and the range of options for getting into them, one is reminded of the fable of the six blind men of India, each of whom tried to describe a whole elephant from the limited the part he could directly touch. Undoubtedly, with the continuing proliferation of resources, there are parts of the research library (and Internet) "elephant" that are not described here; the best I can say is that this book's overall "methods of searching" framework for organizing such resources is reasonably stable, is not too complex to be grasped as a whole, and has proven its utility in extensive practice. The principles underlying this model will remain useful despite continual changes of individual resources.

I hope all readers will learn enough from this book that the prospect of research will be as exciting for them as it has proven to be for me.

*Washington, D.C.*					T. M.
*January, 2005*

*The Oxford Guide to Library Research*

# 1

## Initial Overviews: Encyclopedias

The best way to start many inquiries is to see if someone has already written an overview article outlining the most important facts on the subject and providing a concise list of recommended readings. This is precisely what a good encyclopedia article does. Unlike most Web sites, encyclopedia entries have usually gone through a process of editorial review and fact checking by reputable publishers; in addition, the selection of encyclopedias by libraries is in itself another hurdle of review. One of the main problems with Internet searching is that it often generates so many results that, in spite of elaborate algorithms for ranking the retrieved pages, researchers are left without any coherent overview of the information they need. This problem, so intractable on the Net, is often solved quickly and easily by use of encyclopedias.

Unfortunately, the misuse of encyclopedias tends unnecessarily to limit their effectiveness—both for the student writing a term paper and for the business executive, professional, or independent learner that student will become after leaving the classroom. This misuse comes in a number of forms: (1) in expecting the best encyclopedias to be readily and freely available online (most are not); (2) in expecting an encyclopedia to be the beginning *and end* of a complex inquiry; and (3) in expecting the general encyclopedias that everybody knows about to provide a level of detail found only in the specialized encyclopedias that very few people know about. When students get inadequate results from the general sets (either online or printed), they frequently tend to change their overall assumptions about the future use of all such sources.

The first important point, then, is that encyclopedias should be regarded as good starting points for nonspecialists who need a basic overview of a subject or a background perspective on it—not as compendiums of all knowledge that will make further specialized research unnecessary. Nor should one expect much up-to-the-minute information from such sources—it is the newspaper, the journal article, or the Web site, and not the encyclopedia, that one should turn to for current events. (Encyclopedias by their very nature seek to summarize knowledge that is more or less "established" and not subject to rapid change.) Part of the problem is that educational institutions often leave students with only hazy notions of what *other* sources lead quickly to the more specialized or current information, and so researchers often don't perceive encyclopedias as starting points within a clear context of what lies beyond. (This book will provide that context.)

The second point needing emphasis is that a deeper level of specialized information is indeed available within encyclopedias, if one looks beyond the familiar *Britannica, Americana, World Book,* or *Collier's.* Thousands of more specialized encyclopedias exist, some of them one-volume works. These valuable resources are "specialized" in the sense of concentrating on certain subject areas, not in the sense of being written in specialist jargon. The very purpose of most encyclopedias is to provide an overview orientation to someone who is not already conversant with the subject being discussed. An expert will usually not need an introductory article within his or her own field, but may well require one in many other areas.

Sometimes, however, experts will indeed require a large overview of recent or technical developments within their own fields; but the sources providing these perspectives are not introductory, and they are written in a way that assumes the reader already knows the basics. For this kind of overview the researcher will turn to review articles, not encyclopedias (see Chapter 8).

Readers of any sort, however, will usually get farther into a subject initially by using specialized rather than general encyclopedias. People seeking introductory articles in the sciences, for example, will often be better served by the *McGraw-Hill Encyclopedia of Science and Technology,* 20 vols. (McGraw-Hill, revised irregularly), which is the standard set in its field, rather than the *Britannica, Americana, Collier's,* or *World Book.* Similarly, those in the social sciences will frequently be better off turning to the authoritative *International Encyclopedia of the Social & Behavioral Sciences,* 26 vols. (Elsevier, 2001). Students in the arts, too, should consult the specialized works in these areas, among them the excellent *Encyclopedia of*

*World Art*, 17 vols. (McGraw-Hill, 1959–87); the *Dictionary of Art*, 34 vols. (Grove, 1996); and the *New Grove Dictionary of Music and Musicians*, 29 vols. (Grove, 2001). (Don't be misled by the term "dictionary"; in library and publishing terminology, it refers simply to the alphabetical arrangement of articles without regard to their length, and thus is often synonymous with "encyclopedia.")

Note also a particularly important point: while several general encyclopedias are now available either online or in CD-ROM format, the bells and whistles of the electronic versions—such things as moving images and sound bites of speech or music—should not distract you from the fact that their content remains at a relatively general level. Much deeper levels of subject content can be found in the specialized encyclopedias; and the large majority of these appear in print format only, to be consulted in real rather than virtual libraries.

Among the thousands of relatively little-known specialized encyclopedias, the above titles are especially good; other works that are considered standard in their fields include the following:

*American National Biography,* 24 vols. (Oxford U. Press, 1999)
*Dictionary of American History,* 10 vols. (Charles Scribner's Sons, 2003)
*Dictionary of Scientific Biography,* 16 vols. (Scribner's, 1970–80)
*Dictionary of the History of Ideas,* 5 vols. (Scribner's, 1973–74)
*Dictionary of the Middle Ages,* 13 vols. (Scribner's, 1982–89)
*Encyclopedia of Philosophy*, 8 vols. (Macmillan, 1967; one-volume supplement, 1996)
*Routledge Encyclopedia of Philosophy,* 10 vols. (Routledge, 1998)
*New Catholic Encyclopedia,* 15 vols. (Catholic U. of America Press, 2003)
*The Anchor Bible Dictionary,* 6 vols. (Doubleday, 1992)
*New Palgrave Dictionary of Economics*, 4 vols. (Stockton Press, 1998)
*Encyclopedia of Education,* 8 vols. (Macmillan Reference, 2003)
*Encyclopedia of Psychology,* 8 vols. (Oxford U. Press, 2000)
*Encyclopedia of Religion,* 16 vols. (Collier Macmillan, 1993)
*Grzimek's Animal Life Encyclopedia,* 17 vols. (Gale, 2002–2004)
*Encyclopedia of Sociology,* 5 vols. (Macmillan Reference, 2000)
*Oxford Dictionary of National Biography* [British], 60 vols. (Oxford U. Press, 2004)

Although the above sets are certainly important, they by no means exhaust the field. The following is a list of selected representative titles; it only scratches the surface of the range of sources available in research libraries:

*Biographical Dictionary of American Labor* (Greenwood Press, 1984)

*Biographical Dictionary of American Mayors, 1820–1980* (Greenwood Press, 1981)

*Biographical Dictionary of the American Left* (Greenwood Press, 1986)

*Blackwell Encyclopedia of Management* (a series of one-volume works on Accounting, Business Ethics, Finance, Human Resource Management, Marketing, etc.; Blackwell, 1997–99)

*Companion Encyclopedia of the History and Philosophy of the Mathematical Sciences,* 2 vols. (Routledge, 1994)

*Corsini Encyclopedia of Psychology and Behavioral Science,* 4 vols. (Wiley, 2001)

*Dictionary of American Communal and Utopian History* (Greenwood Press, 1980)

*Dictionary of Art Titles: The Origins of the Names and Titles of 3,000 Works or Art* (McFarland Publishers, 2000)

*Dictionary of Concepts in Literary Criticism and Theory* (Greenwood Press, 1992)

*Dictionary of Literary Biography,* 300+ vols., ongoing (Gale Research, 1978–)

*Dictionary of the Literature of the Iberian Peninsula,* 2 vols. (Greenwood Press, 1993)

*Dictionary of Mexican American History* (Greenwood Press, 1981)

*Dictionary of Named Effects and Laws in Chemistry, Physics, and Mathematics* (Chapman and Hall, 1980)

*Dictionary of Statistics and Methodology: A Nontechnical Guide for the Social Sciences* (Sage Publications, 1999)

*Encyclopaedia Judaica,* 16 vols. (Encyclopaedia Judaica, 1972)

*Encyclopedia of Islam and the Muslim World,* 2 vols. (Thomson/Gale, 2004)

*Encyclopaedia of Islam, New Edition* (in progress; Brill, 2000–)

*Encyclopaedia of Religion and Ethics,* 13 vols. (Charles Scribner's Sons, 1925–32)

*Encyclopedia of Accounting Systems,* 2 vols. (Prentice Hall, 1994)

*Encyclopedia of Aesthetics,* 4 vols. (Oxford U. Press, 1998)
*Encyclopedia of African-American Culture and History,* 5 vols. & supplement (Macmillan Reference USA, 1996–2000)
*Greenwood Encyclopedia of African American Civil Rights* (Greenwood Press, 2003)
*Encyclopedia of Aging,* 4 vols. (Macmillan Reference USA, 2002)
*Encyclopedia of Agricultural Science,* 4 vols. (Academic Press, 1994)
*Encyclopedia of the American Constitution,* 6 vols. (Macmillan Reference USA, 2000)
*Encyclopedia of American Cultural & Intellectual History,* 3 vols. (Scribner's, 2001)
*Encyclopedia of American Economic History,* 3 vols. (Scribner's, 1980)
*Encyclopedia of American Foreign Policy,* 3 vols. (Scribner's, 2002)
*Encyclopedia of American Political History* (CQ Press, 2001)
*Encyclopedia of American Religious History,* 2 vols. (Facts on File, 2001)
*Encyclopedia of American Social History,* 3 vols. (Maxwell Macmillan International, 1993)
*Encyclopedia of American Spy Films* (Garland Publishing, 1990)
*Encyclopedia of Applied Ethics,* 4 vols. (Academic Press, 1998)
*Encyclopedia of Applied Plant Sciences,* 3 vols. (Elsevier Academic, 2003)
*Encyclopedia of Asian History,* 4 vols. (Collier Macmillan, 1988)
*Encyclopedia of Asian Philosophy* (Routledge, 2001)
*Encyclopedia of Bilingualism and Bilingual Education* (Multilingual Matters, 1998)
*Encyclopedia of Biodiversity,* 5 vols. (Academic Press, 2001)
*Encyclopedia of Bioethics,* 5 vols. (Macmillan Reference USA, 2004)
*Encyclopedia of Cancer,* 4 vols. (Academic Press, 2002)
*Encyclopedia of Contemporary Literary Theory* (U. of Toronto Press, 1993)
*Encyclopedia of Crafts,* 3 vols. (Scribner's, 1980)
*Encyclopedia of Crime & Justice,* 4 vols. (Macmillan Reference USA, 2002)
*Encyclopedia of Crime and Punishment,* 4 vols. (Sage Publications, 2002)
*Encyclopedia of Cultural Anthropology,* 4 vols. (Henry Holt & Co., 1996)
*Encyclopedia of Democracy,* 4 vols. (Congressional Quarterly, 1995)
*Encyclopedia of Drugs, Alcohol, and Addictive Behavior,* 4 vols. (Macmillan Reference USA, 2001)

*Encyclopedia of Earth Sciences* (an ongoing series of one-volume encyclopedias covering Atmospheric Sciences, Geomorphology, Hydrology, Oceanography, etc.; Reinhold/Kluwer, 1996–2003)

*Encyclopedia of Education in Antebellum Pensacola* (Patagonia Press, 1999)

*Encyclopedia of Educational Research,* 4 vols. (Maxwell Macmillan International, 1992)

*Encyclopedia of Environmental Issues,* 3 vols. (Salem Press, 2000)

*Encyclopedia of Higher Education,* 4 vols. (Pergamon Press, 1992)

*Encyclopedia of Environmental Analysis and Remediation,* 8 vols. (Wiley, 1998)

*Environment Encyclopedia,* 11 vols. (Marshall Cavendish, 2001)

*Encyclopedia of Ethics,* 3 vols. (Routledge, 2001)

*Encyclopedia of European Social History: From 1350 to 2000,* 6 vols. (Scribner's, 2001)

*Encyclopedia of Fluid Mechanics,* 10 vols. & 3 vol. supplement (Gulf Publishing Co., 1986–90, 1993–94)

*Encyclopedia of Food and Culture,* 3 vols. (Scribner's, 2003)

*Encyclopedia of Food Science and Technology,* 4 vols. (Wiley, 2000)

*Encyclopedia of Forensic Sciences,* 3 vols. (Academic Press, 2002)

*Encyclopedia of Forest Sciences,* 4 vols. (Elsevier, 2004)

*Encyclopedia of Genetics,* 4 vols. (Academic Press, 2002)

*Encyclopedia of Historic Places,* 2 vols. (Facts on File/Mansell, 1984)

*Encyclopedia of Historic and Endangered Livestock and Poultry Breeds* (Yale U. Press, 2001)

*Encyclopedia of Historical Treaties and Alliances,* 2 vols. (Facts on File, 2001)

*Encyclopedia of Holocaust Literature* (Oryx Press, 2002)

*Encyclopedia of the Holocaust,* 4 vols. (Macmillan Publishing Co., 1990)

*Encyclopedia of Human Emotions,* 2 vols. (Macmillan Reference USA, 1999)

*Encyclopedia of Human Biology,* 9 vols. (Academic Press, 1997)

*Encyclopedia of the Human Brain,* 4 vols. (Academic Press, 2002)

*Encyclopedia of Human Nutrition,* 3 vols. (Academic Press, 1999)

*Encyclopedia of Information Systems,* 4 vols. (Academic Press, 2003)

*Encyclopedia of Language and Linguistics,* 10 vols. (Pergamon Press, 1994)

*International Encyclopedia of Linguistics,* 4 vols. (Oxford U. Press, 2003)

*Encyclopedia of Latin American History and Culture,* 5 vols. (Charles Scribner's Sons/Simon & Schuster, 1996)

*Encyclopedia of Law Enforcement,* 5 vols. (Sage Reference, 2004)

*Encyclopedia of Leadership,* 4 vols. (Sage Publications, 2004)

*Encyclopedia of Library and Information Science,* 4 vols. (Marcel Dekker, 2003)

*Encyclopedia of Microbiology,* 4 vols. (Academic Press, 2000)

*Encyclopedia of Microscopy and Microtechnique* (Van Nostrand Reinhold, 1973)

*Encyclopedia of Nationalism,* 2 vols. (Academic Press, 2001)

*Encyclopedia of Neuroscience,* 2 vols. (Elsevier, 1999)

*Encyclopedia of Ocean Sciences,* 6 vols. (Academic Press, 2001)

*Encyclopedia of Physical Science and Technology,* 18 vols. (Academic Press, 2002)

*Encyclopedia of Prisons and Correctional Facilities,* 2 vols. (Sage Publications, 2004)

*Encyclopedia of Psychological Assessment,* 2 vols. (Sage Publications, 2002)

*Encyclopedia of Recorded Sound* (Routledge, 2004)

*Encyclopedia of the Renaissance,* 6 vols. (Scribner's, 1999)

*Encyclopedia of Rose Science,* 3 vols. (Academic Press, 2003)

*Encyclopedia of Social Theory,* 2 vols. (Sage Publications, 2004)

*Encyclopedia of Southern Culture* (U. of North Carolina Press, 1991)

*Encyclopedia of Special Education,* 3 vols. (Wiley, 2000)

*Encyclopedia of Spectroscopy and Spectrometry,* 3 vols. (Academic Press, 2001)

*Encyclopedia of Strange and Unexplained Physical Phenomena* (Gale Research, 1993)

*Encyclopedia of Terrorism* (Sage Publications, 2003)

*Encyclopedia of Terrorism* (Facts on File, 2002)

*Encyclopedia of Themes and Subjects in Painting* (N. H. Abrams, 1971)

*Encyclopedia of U. S. Foreign Relations,* 4 vols. (Oxford U. Press, 1997)

*Encyclopedia of the U.S. Supreme Court,* 3 vols. (Salem Press, 2001)

*Encyclopedia of the United Nations and International Agreements,* 4 vols. (Routledge, 2003)

*Encyclopedia of Violence, Peace, and Conflict,* 3 vols. (Academic Press, 1999)

*Encyclopedia of White-Collar and Corporate Crime,* 2 vols. (Sage Reference, 2004)

*Encyclopedia of Women and Gender,* 2 vols. (Academic Press, 2001)

*Encyclopedia of World Cultures,* 10 vols. (G. K. Hall, 1991–96)

*Encyclopedia of World Geography,* 24 vols. (Marshall Cavendish, 2002)

*Facts on File Dictionary of Chemistry* (Facts on File, 1999)

*Facts on File Dictionary of Classical and Biblical Allusions* (Facts on File, 2003)

*Facts on File Dictionary of Mathematics* (Facts on File, 1999)

*Facts on File Dictionary of Numerical Allusions* (Facts on File, 1986)

*Feminist Encyclopedia of Spanish Literature,* 2 vols. (Greenwood Press, 2002)

*Gale Encyclopedia of Alternative Medicine,* 4 vols. (Gale Group, 2001)

*Gale Encyclopedia of Medicine,* 5 vols. (Gale Group, 2002)

*Gale Encyclopedia of Science,* 6 vols. (Gale Group, 2001)

*Gale Encyclopedia of U.S. Economic History,* 2 vols. (Gale Group, 1999)

*Great Soviet Encyclopedia,* 32 vols. (Macmillan, 1973–83)

*Guide to American Law: Everyone's Legal Encyclopedia,* 12 vols. & 6 vol. supplement (West Publishing Co., 1983–85, 1990–95)

*Harper Encyclopedia of Military History from 3,500 b.c. to the Present* (HarperCollins, 1993)

*Historical Dictionary of Reconstruction* (Greenwood Press, 1991)

*Historical Dictionary of the New Deal* (Greenwood Press, 1985)

*International Encyclopedia of Communications,* 4 vols. (Oxford U. Press, 1989)

*International Encyclopedia of Dance,* 6 vols. (Oxford U. Press, 1998)

*International Encyclopedia of Education,* 12 vols. (Elsevier Science, 1994)

*International Encyclopedia of Statistics,* 2 vols. (Free Press, 1978)

*International Military and Defense Encyclopedia,* 6 vols. (Brassey's [US], 1993)

*International Wildlife Encyclopedia,* 22 vols. (Marshall Cavendish, 2002)

*Kodansha Encyclopedia of Japan,* 9 vols. (Kodansha, 1983)

*Legal Systems of the World: A Political, Social, and Cultural Encyclopedia,* 4 vols. (ABC-CLIO, 2002)

*McGraw-Hill Encyclopedia of Astronomy* (McGraw-Hill, 1993)

*Macmillan Encyclopedia of Architects*, 4 vols. (Collier Mcmillan, 1982)

*Macmillan Encyclopedia of Native American Tribes* (Macmillan Library Reference USA, 1999)

*Macmillan Encyclopedia of World Slavery*, 2 vols. (Macmillan Reference USA, 1998)

*Macmillan Health Encyclopedia*, 9 vols. (Macmillan Reference USA, 1998)

*Medieval Iberia: An Encyclopedia* (Routledge, 2002)

*A Milton Encyclopedia*, 9 vols. (Buckness U. Press, 1979–83)

*Modern Encyclopedia of Russian and Soviet History*, 60 vols. & supplement (Academic International Press, 1976–2000)

*Mrs. Byrne's Dictionary of Unusual, Obscure, and Preposterous Words*[1] (Carol Publishing Group, 1994)

*New Grove Dictionary of American Music*, 4 vols. (Grove's Dictionaries, 1986)

*New Grove Dictionary of Jazz* (Grove's Dictionaries, 2001)

*New Grove Dictionary of Musical Instruments*, 3 vols. (Grove's Dictionaries, 1984)

*New Grove Dictionary of Opera*, 4 vols. (Grove's Dictionaries, 1992)

*New Palgrave Dictionary of Economics and the Law*, 3 vols. (Stockton, Press, 1998)

*Oxford Companion to Philosophy* (Oxford U. Press, 1995)

*Oxford Encyclopedia of Ancient Egypt*, 3 vols. (Oxford U. Press, 2001)

*Oxford Encyclopedia of the Reformation*, 4 vols. (Oxford U. Press, 1996)

*Philosophy of Law: An Encyclopedia*, 2 vols. (Garland Publishing, 1993)

*Routledge Encyclopedia of Language Teaching and Learning* (Routledge, 2001)

*Routledge International Encyclopedia of Women*, 4 vols. (Routledge, 2000)

*Van Nostrand's Scientific Encyclopedia* (Van Nostrand Reinhold, 2002)

*Women's Studies Encyclopedia*, 3 vols. (Greenwood Press, 1993)

*World Education Encyclopedia: A Survey of Educational Systems Worldwide*, 3 vols. (Gale Group, 2002)

*World Encyclopedia of Peace*, 8 vols. (Oceana Publications, 1999)

*World Encyclopedia of Political Systems and Parties*, 3 vols. (Facts on File, 1999)

*World Press Encyclopedia*, 2 vols. (Gale, 2003)
*Worldmark Encyclopedia of Cultures and Daily Life*, 4 vols. (Gale, 1998)
*Worldmark Encyclopedia of the States* (Gale Group, 2001)

None of these sources is freely available on the open Internet. Many of the subjects suggested here are covered by several other specialized works, too; and hundreds of additional encyclopedias exist for still other topics.

There are several ways to determine whether a specialized encyclopedia covers your area of interest. Note, however, that a particularly important factor in the search process is that you *begin by assuming that such a source exists, even when you don't know that it does*. Reference librarians know that proceeding on this assumption always makes the discovery more likely, as it provides the motive for venturing into uncharted waters.

Several particularly good shortcuts are provided by a few subscription Web sites and printed reference books:

- *Reference Universe*. This is a subscription database from Paratext Electronic Reference Publishing (www.paratext.com) of articles in over 5,000 specialized encyclopedias. It does not provide the full texts; for those you still have to go into a library. *Reference Universe*, however, indexes not just the titles of individual articles, but also the very detailed back-of-the-book indexes from all of the sources. It thus provides an unusually deep level of access into these valuable overview articles. The database is continually growing; new sources are added every two weeks. Coverage of encyclopedias published after 1990 is particularly thorough, but earlier works are indexed as well.
- *First Stop: The Master Index to Subject Encyclopedias*, by Joe Ryan (Oryx Press, 1989). This is a cumulative keyword index to the titles of individual articles in 430 specialized encyclopedias (and some other reference sources, such as the Cambridge history series). The articles indexed here must be at least 250 words in length and must also include a bibliography. (These encyclopedias are also covered by *Reference Universe*.)
- *Subject Encyclopedias: User Guide, Review Citations, and Keyword Index*, by Allan N. Merwis (2 vols.; Oryx Press, 1999). This is a supplement to *First Stop*; it lists 1,129 specialized encyclopedias and indexes articles from the 98 titles that rank the highest according to the

author's rating system. (These sources, too, are indexed in *Reference Universe*.)

- *Xreferplus* (www.xreferplus.com) is a subscription-based, full-text database offering articles from over 160 dictionaries, encyclopedias, quotation books, and so on, from dozens of publishers. The articles you will find here are not lengthy; they are all from single-volume, short-entry sources. A somewhat comparable subscription service is *Oxford Reference Online* at www.oxfordreference.com, which provides brief articles from more than 100 dictionaries and reference books, all published by Oxford University Press.

One of the virtues of these sources is that they greatly facilitate cross-disciplinary research. A single topic can be treated from many different perspectives. For example, articles on "Vietnam" or "Vietnamese" appear in all of the following sources:

*American Folklore: An Encyclopedia* (Garland Publishing, 1996)
*Cassell's Encyclopedia of World Literature* (Cassell, 1973)
*Countries of the World* (Gale Research, annual)
*Dictionary of American History* (Charles Scribner's Sons, 1976 [new ed., 2003])
*Encyclopedia of American Journalism* (Facts on File, 1983)
*Encyclopedia of Drugs and Alcohol* (Simon & Schuster, 1995)
*Encyclopedia of Religion* (Collier Macmillan, 1993)
*Encyclopedia of Social Issues* (Marshall Cavendish, 1997)
*Encyclopedia of the American Presidency* (Simon & Schuster, 1994 [new ed., 2004])
*Encyclopedia of the Third World* (Facts on File, 1992)
*Encyclopedia of the United Nations and International Agreements* (Taylor and Francis, 1985 [new ed., Routledge, 2002])
*Encyclopedia of Violence* (Facts on File, 1993)
*Encyclopedia of World Art* (McGraw-Hill, 1959–87)
*Europa World Year Book* (Europa, annual)
*Far East and Australasia* (Europa, annual)
*International Encyclopedia of Education* (Pergamon, 1985 [new ed., Elsevier, 1994])
*International Encyclopedia of Higher Education* (Jossey-Bass, 1978)

*New Catholic Encyclopedia* (McGraw-Hill, 1967–74 [new ed., Catholic U. of America Press, 2003])

*New Grove Dictionary of Music and Musicians* (Grove, 1980 [new ed., 2001])

*Oriental Art: A Handbook* (Rizzoli, 1980)

*The Oxford Companion to Politics of the World* (Oxford U. Press, 1993 [new ed., 2001])

*The Oxford Companion to the Supreme Court* (Oxford U. Press, 1992)

*Princeton Encyclopedia of Poetry and Poetics* (Princeton U. Press, 1974 [new ed., 1993])

*Women and the Military* (ABC-CLIO, 1996)

*World Christian Encyclopedia* (Oxford U. Press, 1982 [new ed., 2001])

*World Encyclopedia of Political Systems and Parties* (Facts on File, 1987 [new ed., 1999])

*World Press Encyclopedia* (Facts on File, 1982 [new ed., Gale, 2003]

*Worldmark Encyclopedia of the Nations* (John Wiley, 1984 [new ed., Gale, 2001])

*World's Coastline* (Van Nostrand Reinhold, 1985)

Articles from all of these encyclopedic works will be brought to a researcher's attention just from a consultation of *First Stop* and *Subject Encyclopedias*. A search for "Vietnam" or "Vietnamese" as title words in all of the encyclopedia articles covered by *Reference Universe* turns up a listing of over 200 articles from a very wide range of disciplines; searching the same terms as back-of-the book index words generates over 400 additional references.

A procedure that I have found very useful is to use these sources to identify relevant articles, and then, when looking for them in the actual reference collection, *to browse around for similar encyclopedias nearby*. For example, in helping one researcher who wanted overview information on "Montague grammar," a system of describing natural language in a rigorous manner, I looked in *Reference Universe*, which listed what turned out to be an eleven-page article (with an extensive bibliography) in the one-volume *Concise Encyclopedia of Philosophy and Language*. One shelf to the left, however, was the four-volume *International Encyclopedia of Linguistics*, which has a more concise three-page article; and next to that was the ten-volume *Encyclopedia of Language and Linguistics*, which provided an earlier version (by the same author) of the article from the *Concise* volume, but added a two-page biographical article on Montague himself. (A comparison of the bibliographies from the *Concise Encyclopedia* and the *International Encyclopedia* showed that they overlapped on only two titles—which gave a rough indication that those two sources, at least, were considered "standard" in the field; and so the researcher, had he wished to pursue the subject, could thus have determined which two books, out of the dozens listed, he should start with for further reading. Comparing bibliographies from different encyclopedia articles is always a good technique to zero in on the best sources quickly.)

Other good resources for identifying specialized encyclopedias are the following:

- *Guide to Reference Books* (American Library Association, revised irregularly). The current print-format edition of this venerable source is usually referred to as "Balay," after Robert Balay, its editor. (Plans are underway for a subscription-based online version.) It is a comprehensive list of reference sources in all subject areas and languages, categorized by types of literature, including dictionaries and encyclopedias.
- *Dictionary of Dictionaries and Eminent Encyclopedias*, by Thomas Kabdebo (2nd ed.; Bowker-Saur, 1997). This is a critical guide to more than 6,000 dictionaries and encyclopedias; works discussed can be monolingual, bilingual, or multilingual as long as English is one element. It will often tell you the *best* source in an area, and compare it to other sources. It has a very good index.
- *Kister's Best Encyclopedias: A Comparative Guide to General and Specialized Encyclopedias*, by Kenneth Kister (2nd ed.; Oryx, 1994). This provides detailed descriptions and comparisons of more than 160 general and 400 specialized English-language encyclopedias; a few foreign-language sources are also briefly covered.
- *ARBA Guide to Subject Encyclopedias and Dictionaries*, edited by Susan C. Awe (2nd ed.; Libraries Unlimited, 1997). This provides annotated descriptions of 1,061 sources.
- *Dictionaries, Encyclopedias, and Other Word-Related Books*, by Annie M. Brewer (2 vols.; 4th ed.; Gale Research, 1988). This is a listing of about 30,000 works arranged in the order of Library of

Congress Classification numbers, with an index of subjects and titles. Entries reproduce non-evaluative library catalog records.

- *Catalog of Dictionaries, Word Books, and Philological Texts, 1440–1900*, compiled by David E. Vancil (Greenwood Press, 1993). A good source for historical research, this in an inventory of the Cordell Collection of Dictionaries at Indiana State University; it is the world's largest, with more than 5,100 pre-1901 imprints plus several thousand more for the twentieth century. Indexes are by date, by language, and by subject. Entries are not annotated.
- *Anglo-American General Encyclopedias: A Historical Bibliography: 1703–1967*, by S. Pedraig [James Patrick] Walsh (R. R. Bowker, 1968). Another good source for a historical overview; its 419 entries are extensively annotated. Indexes are by Editors and Publishers/Distributors; there is also a chronological listing of titles.

None of these sources is computerized, although the *Guide to Reference Books* soon will be. A problem common to all of the above finding aids is that, once published, they become dated. On the other hand, it is important to realize that becoming dated does not necessarily mean becoming *out*-dated, especially since encyclopedias aim to summarize knowledge that is regarded as reasonably "established" to begin with.

If you wish to check continually updated finding guides to determine if new encyclopedias have appeared, there are two in particular to consult (in addition to *Reference Universe*). The first is *American Reference Books Annual*, or *ARBA* (Libraries Unlimited, 1970–), which lists, with evaluative annotations, most of the English-language sources published in the U.S. and Canada within the past year (accessible by a subject index). It includes electronic encyclopedias available as Web sites or CD-ROMs. The second is your library's computer catalog, which is another continually updated source. Specialized encyclopedias, both old and new, will usually be listed under one of these forms of heading:

**[Subject heading]–Dictionaries**
**[Subject heading]–Encyclopedias**
**[Subject heading]–[Geographic subdivision]–Dictionaries**
**[Subject heading]–[Geographic subdivision]–Encyclopedias**

The important thing to note is that either of the subdivisions, **Dictionaries** or **Encyclopedias**, is capable of turning up a good source. (The several ways to find the right subject heading in the first place—especially the crucial first element in the string—will be discussed in the next chapter.)

The utility of specialized encyclopedias is often discovered by researchers writing short papers. Here are a few examples.

- An art history student needed to study the concept of "Gesamtkunstwerke," having to do with a total work of art combining several different art forms. The thirty-four volume *Dictionary of Art* (Grove's, 1996) provided a substantive two-page article with a bibliography of eighteen readings.
- A social-studies researcher interested in the idea of "community" in Nazi Germany found an article on precisely that topic, outlining the different concepts involved, in *The Encyclopedia of the Third Reich*, 2 vols. (Macmillan, 1991). The article included numerous cross-references within the set to other aspects of the subject ("Volk Community," "Front Experience," "Family," "Education," "Führer Principle").
- A researcher interested in "how blind people perceive colors" found that the concept of "Synaesthesia" was directly related; and on that topic she found a three-page article in the *Encyclopedia of Aesthetics*, 4 vols. (Oxford, 1998), and an eight-page article in the *Encyclopedia of Creativity*, 2 vols. (Academic Press, 1999).
- A student looking for initial orientation on the topic of "U.S. relations with Guatemala" found a good three-page article in the *Encyclopedia of U.S. Foreign Relations*, 4 vols. (Oxford, 1997).
- A humanities student interested in "Metaphor" could find only very brief articles in the *Britannica, Americana,* and *World Book* sets; but the *Encyclopedia of Aesthetics*, 4 vols. (Oxford, 1998) provided a seventeen-page article. Additional lengthy treatments could be found in the *Routledge Encyclopedia of Philosophy*, 10 vols. (Routledge, 1998); the *Encyclopedia of Philosophy*, 8 vols. (Macmillan, 1974); the *Dictionary of the History of Ideas*, 5 vols. (Scribner's, 1974); the *International Encyclopedia of Communications*, 4 vols. (Oxford, 1989); the *New Princeton Encyclopedia of Poetry and Poetics* (Princeton, 1993); and in the various *Linguistics* encyclopedias mentioned above.

In emphasizing specialized encyclopedias, I do not mean to suggest that the general sets are unimportant. Indeed, there are some surprising features within these sets that are particularly useful. The *Encyclopedia Americana*, for example (unlike other encyclopedias), sometimes prints the full texts of historic documents in addition to providing information about them. When you look up "Declaration of the Rights of Man and the Citizen" or "Mayflower Compact," or "Washington's Farewell Address," for instance, you get not just a summary, but actual texts. *Americana* also has articles on each individual century (e.g., on the Fifth Century or the Nineteenth Century) that are useful, and also articles on each book of the Bible, as well as on many individual works of art, literature, and music (the *Winged Victory* statue, the novel *Middlemarch*, the ballet *The Firebird*, etc.).

The *Britannica* set covers philosophy particularly well, including a book-length article "Philosophies of the Branches of Knowledge," which no other encyclopedia offers. The annual *Britannica Book of the Year* supplement is very good in its presentation of statistical data on political, social, demographic, and economic conditions in the countries of the world; and it provides them in two sections, the first by country and the second by subject, so that comparisons can be readily made among countries. The *Macropaedia* (long article) section of the *Britannica* also does something the other sets don't—it clusters what would otherwise be many alphabetically separated small articles within larger theme articles, often of book length. Thus "Musical Instruments" gathers in one place articles on percussion, stringed, keyboard, wind, and electronic instruments; and the article "Transportation" includes sections on history, motor vehicles, railroads, aircraft, ships, pipelines, urban mass transportation, traffic control and safety, and so on. The *Micropaedia* (short length) section of the set offers articles that often serve as overviews of the longer treatments in the *Macropaedia* section. The set's one-volume *Propaedia* is a fascinating classification of all of the articles in the entire *Britannica* in a logical order, showing relationships and linkages not apparent from the alphabetical sequence of the articles themselves. (This outline is entirely omitted from the online version of the encyclopedia. I much prefer the printed set myself, especially since its articles are so long.)

*Collier's* is particularly good for articles that give practical "how to" tips on dealing with problems of childhood and child development, on buying insurance, or interior design or sewing techniques. Its index is also excellent.

The *World Book* is exceptionally good in providing quick, "look it up" type information—on flags, state flowers, first aid, gardening instructions, symptoms of illnesses, metric-conversion tables, football rules, summaries of Shakespeare's plays, on so on.

General foreign-language encyclopedias are often particularly good in turning up biographical information on obscure figures who played roles in the histories of various countries. Their illustrations are also sometimes more useful than those in the English-language sets. These sources, however, are overlooked much too often.

Many encyclopedias focus specifically on biographical information. For an overview of research options in this area, see Chapter 14.

When you need an article on a particular subject (a substantive but less than book-length source), five possibilities should occur to you:

1. An encyclopedia article (generally written as an overview for non-specialists)
2. A "state of the art" review article (generally written as an overview for specialists)
3. A journal/periodical or newspaper article
4. A Web site on the topic
5. An essay in a book anthology

Each of the latter four forms is accessible through sources that will be discussed later. For an encyclopedia article, however, you should start by assuming there is a *specialized* encyclopedia covering your area of interest and then look for it.

## Note

1. The editor's introduction to *Mrs. Byrne's Dictionary*, by her ex-husband, is famous among bibliophiles: "Working alone and without government support (or even comprehension) she managed to assemble the six thousand weirdest words in the English language. Nobody asked her to do it because nobody thought such a thing was possible. In fact, I asked her *not* to do it."

# 2

## *Subject Headings and the Library Catalog*

A library's online catalog lists the book holdings of the institution; it may also list non-book formats such as manuscripts, sound recordings, videos, maps, photographs, and so on. The titles of journals held by the library will also be recorded, but as a general rule, the catalog will not enable you to search for the individual articles that appear within journals. (For those you will need separate databases and indexes, discussed in Chapters 4 through 8). Each entry in the catalog will provide you with a call number enabling you to locate the desired volume on the shelves.

The most frequent, and most serious, problem that people have in looking for books in the catalog is determining the right subject headings to use. For example, if a reader wants books on morality, should she look under "Morality" or under "Ethics"? Or must she try both? Or perhaps, with a more focused topic in mind, she should look directly under "Ethical relativism"? Similarly, if another reader wants information on sentencing criminals to death, should he look under "Death penalty" or under "Capital punishment"? And how does he know that he's thought up all of the right terms? Perhaps he should look under "Execution" or some other synonyms as well. Note that these three terms fall into quite different sections of the alphabet.

Reference librarians frequently deal with people having problems in this regard. One student, for example, became frustrated in looking for material under "Moonshining" because it is not entered under that heading. In a standard library catalog, works on this subject are recorded under **Distilling, illicit**. Another researcher wanted books on "Corporate philanthropy"; before asking for help she hadn't found anything because she was looking under "Philanthropy" rather than under the proper heading **Corporations— Charitable contributions**. Similarly, researchers who want "Multinational corporations" often make the mistake of searching under that term, when the proper heading is actually **International business enterprises**; and those searching for "Test-tube babies" usually fail to search under the proper heading, **Fertilization in vitro, Human**.

Not only the choice of words but also their order may be confusing—for example, should one look under "Surgical diagnosis" or "Diagnosis, surgical"? Under "Heavy minerals" or under "Minerals, heavy"? Under "Fraudulent advertising" or under "Advertising, fraudulent"? Inverted forms are not used consistently, so there is much room for error.

There are, however, systematic steps to take that will solve most of these problems. Specifically, there are four ways to find the right subject headings for your topic—to get *from* the terms you think of *to* the often different ones used by the library catalog. Two of these ways are available through an annually revised, multivolume list of terms called *Library of Congress Subject Headings (LCSH)*; two others are available through the library's catalog itself. Before looking at the four ways, however, it is important to consider three principles governing the compilation and use of the *LCSH* list: uniform heading, scope-match specificity, and specific entry.

## Uniform Heading

Uniform heading is the principle that addresses the problem of synonyms, variant phrases, and different-language terms being used to express the same concept (e.g., "Death penalty," "Capital punishment," "Todesstrafe") and whose appearances may be scattered throughout the alphabet. Librarians who create systematic catalogs choose *one* of the many possible terms, in such cases, and enter all relevant records under that single category term, rather than repeat the same list of works under each of several terms at different alphabetical positions. Since the full list of relevant books (or other records) appears under only one of the terms, the catalogers will insert *cross-references* at several of the other possible places in the alphabet to steer readers to the one main grouping.

For example, books on the subject of "Cockney dialect" have titles such as *Ideolects in Dickens, Bernard Shaw's Phonetics, Fraffly Well Spoken*, and

*The Muvver Tongue*. No one researching this topic would think up all of these unusual keywords. Catalogers, however, round up all such books by assigning to them the same (uniform) heading, **English language—Dialects—England—London**. The researcher who finds this one term, alone, can thereby retrieve all of the disparate title records to which it is attached.

Similar scattering shows up in just about any other subject area. Here, for example, is only a brief sampling of the many variant book titles that are cataloged under the heading **Capital punishment**:

*The Ultimate Coercive Sanction*
*To Kill and Be Killed*
*A Life for a Life*
*Executing the Mentally Ill*
*Hanging Not Punishment Enough for Murtherers*
*Habeas Corpus Issues*
*In Spite of Innocence*
*The Unforgiven: Utah's Executed Men*
*Until You are Dead*
*Fatal Error*
*Philosophy of Punishment*

Hundreds of other keyword-variant titles could be listed—and in scores of languages other than English. Without the creation and assignment of the artificial point of commonality (the *LCSH* term **Capital punishment**) to each record, a researcher looking for what the library has to offer on this topic would miss most of these works. Their natural-language keyword terms are simply too diverse to be rounded up systematically by Internet algorithms (which rank rather than categorize terms); nor could they be even guessed at with any efficiency.

A uniform heading also serves to round up the different *aspects* of a subject through the use of subdivisions of the lead term in the string. (This is an area in which *LCSH* differs from other thesauri, or lists of controlled indexing terms, in an important way.) In the "Cockney" case, the proper heading not only indicates the subject of the books to which it is assigned, it also appears in the library catalog's *browse display* in such a way as to show that it is *related to other aspects of the topic*. The following is a brief sample of the hundreds of subdivisions that show up under **English language—Dialects**:

English language—Dialects—Africa, West
English language—Dialects—Alabama
English language—Dialects—Australia
English language—Dialects—Bahamas
English language—Dialects—Bibliography
English language—Dialects—England—Berkshire
English language—Dialects—England—Bibliography
English language—Dialects—England—Cambridge
English language—Dialects—England—Cornwall (County)
English language—Dialects—England—Dorset
English language—Dialects—England—Lake District
English language—Dialects—England—London [the "Cockney"
  heading]
English language—Dialects—England—Norfolk
English language—Dialects—England—Penrith
English language—Dialects—England—Phonology
English language—Dialects—England—Suffolk
English language—Dialects—England—Wessex
English language—Dialects—Indiana
English language—Dialects—Ireland
English language—Dialects—New England
English language—Dialects—New York (State)
English language—Dialects—Social aspects
English language—Dialects—South Africa
English language—Dialects—United States
English language—Dialects—United States—Bibliography
English language—Dialects—Wales
English language—Dialects—West (U.S.)

Sometimes people wonder why a heading like **English language—Dialects—England—London** is used rather that a simpler form such as "Cockney dialect." The reason is that the former string appears, as in this example, *within a larger context* of other relevant headings. In this case, a researcher interested in the Cockney dialect may well discover, through such a browse display, several other aspects of English dialectology that might be of interest, but which he hadn't thought of. Browse displays of the many aspects of a topic enable researchers to recognize what they could not specify in advance; and the larger a library's collection, the more readers need such *menus* to serve as road maps into the range of available, but unexpected, resources. (The creation of browse displays is one of the main differences between a library catalog and a mere *inventory* of holdings; the latter does not display either subject categories or contexts. Library catalogers who create subject headings have to be mindful not just of the meaning of any individual term they assign to a catalog record, but also of the "browse" position in which the chosen form of heading will appear in relation to other headings.)

The creation of uniform terms with standardized subdivisions serves yet another purpose in relating a library's books to each other. The many possible subdivisions of a single term (e.g., —**Bibliography**, —**History**, —**Law and legislation**, —**Study and teaching**) may serve to direct researchers to entirely different call-number areas in the bookstacks, scattered throughout the classification scheme. For example, works under the *LCSH* term **Small business** usually get classed (and shelved) in HD (Economics) or KF (U.S. law) areas; but if the books being cataloged are assigned the subdivision, they switch to HF (Commerce) classes instead. If they receive the —**Finance** subdivision, they are usually classed in HG (Finance); and if they are on the bibliographical aspect of the topic (**Small business—Bibliography**) they are classed in Z7164.C81 ("Business bibliography"). All of these different class designations, while *scattered in the bookstacks*, nevertheless appear *together in the catalog* under the one heading **Small business**. Thus, when catalogers choose one heading form over another, they have to think not just of the meaning of the string, and not just of its contextual display in a browse list, but *also* of which classification number may be tied to the string that is created. (There is not a one-to-one relationship between all *LCSH* headings and specific classification numbers; but there are more than enough formal linkages that *the subject headings in the catalog effectively function as the index to the classification scheme in the bookstacks*. Good catalogers are fully aware of this linkage—which provides yet another important distinction between a library catalog and a simple inventory list.)

Uniform headings thus round up, in one place, both *variant titles* for the same subject that are alphabetically scattered throughout the catalog, and *variant classification numbers* for aspects of the same subject that are scattered throughout the bookstacks. (Scattering of *subject* aspects in the classification scheme will be discussed further in Chapter 3.)

The uniform-headings system serves an important collocation function. Users don't have to think up unpredictable ranges of keyword synonyms and variant phrases (or variant class numbers) for the same topic. This subject grouping is brought about by the intellectual work that catalogers do: first they *create,* and then they *add to,* each bibliographic record the artificial, standardized point of commonality (the *LCSH* subject heading) that enables keyword-variant (and class-number variant) records to be retrieved together. This point of commonality would not be retrievable, and indeed would not exist in the first place, if catalogers merely recorded or transcribed existing data from the books' title pages or tables of contents. (Note again the range of title phrases that are collocated by the headings **English language—Dialects—England—London** and **Capital punishment.**)

The emphasis in library catalogs on collocation, via uniform subject headings, points up a major problem with Internet search engines: no matter how sophisticated their relevance-ranking algorithms may be, they are still ranking only the keywords that you type in to begin with. If those terms are not the best ones in the first place, their mere ranking will not serve to point out the existence of entirely different words. *Relevance ranking*, in other words, is not at all the same as *categorization* and *collocation*. The latter functions are missing in Web searches (although there are some unsystematic linkages provided by features like "Customers who bought this book also bought these"). This is a major difference between online library catalogs and Internet search engines. The former, constructed on the principle of uniform heading, enable you to *recognize*, within a retrieved subject set, a whole host of relevant works whose variant keywords—such as those above—you could never have specified in advance. The crucial element of serendipity or recognition on the retrieval end of library searches is a direct function of keyword-transcendent *categorizations* having been created by librarians at the input (cataloging) end of the operation. Cataloging is thus not at all the same as merely transcribing existing data from title pages or tables of contents. It is a process of *adding* terms that are *standardized* "on top of," or in addition to, the words provided by the book itself. These standardized elements serve to collocate the widely varying expressions used by many different authors in talking about the same subject. And these category terms themselves, unlike title (or other) keywords, can be identified through predictable and systematic means (discussed below).

## Scope-Match Specificity and Its Modifications

Prior to the advent of computer catalogs, books, as a general rule, were seldom assigned more than two or three subject headings. This limitation was an important consideration in the era of card catalogs, because filing individual cards for each book under a half dozen or more terms at different places in the alphabet would result in a catalog that was physically very bulky. The fewer category groups to which any book was assigned, in other words, the fewer cards had to be filed, and the more manageable was the size of the overall physical file—a consideration of considerable importance in research libraries holding millions of books.

Another important consideration—still relevant even in the age of computer catalogs—is the volume of work that catalogers have to do. Although the number of books published every year is increasing, almost all libraries are chronically underfunded; and so catalogers who have to create records for dozens of books each day don't have the time to figure out ten or twelve headings for each one. (Again, cataloging is not simply a matter of transcribing words from tables of contents—nor is it simply a matter of employing existing headings from the *LCSH* list. It is also a matter of extending the list, creating new headings, and—the difficult part—integrating all of the new terms into an intricate web of cross-references by specifying hierarchical relationships both to and from the existing terms. Considerations of the best *form* of heading to create—and how that form will show up in relation to other terms in browse displays—are also important, as are considerations of how new forms may be linked to classification numbers, which may also have to be created at the same time. The intellectual work involved, when done well, is quite intricate and challenging.)

Considerations such as these affect scope-match specificity. In the card-catalog era, catalogers would usually assign the minimum number of headings that indicated the subject content of a book *as a whole*—i.e., they would not assign a standardized term for each individual chapter or section of the book. Thus a book about **Oranges** and **Grapefruit** would have both terms assigned to its catalog record, because in combination they covered the whole scope of the work. If another book dealt with these two fruits plus **Limes**, a third subject heading would be assigned. However, if a book dealt with **Oranges**, **Grapefruit**, **Limes**, and **Lemon**, in traditional cataloging it would not receive all four headings. Rather, a single generic heading representing all of the subtopics comprehensively would be assigned—in this case, **Citrus**. While that is indeed a generic term, it is nevertheless the most specific one that covers the book *as a whole*. Catalogers traditionally aimed for this level of coverage in the card-catalog era. If there was not a single term that expressed the subject of the book as a whole, the goal was to sum up the book in as few headings as possible—usually about three.

The advent of computer-based catalogs has eliminated the need to worry about card catalogs bursting with too many cards in too little space to contain them, so computerized catalog records often receive more than three subject headings. Records created prior to the 1980s, however, are still in online catalogs with what today would be considered nearly minimal subject headings on them. So, if you need to search for early books, remember that you do not have as much leeway in your choice of headings as you may have in searching for more recent books.

The current *Subject Cataloging Manual* of the Library of Congress, which is more or less the standard for catalogers in all large libraries in the English-speaking world, allows for a "20 percent rule"—that is, a heading may be assigned for any topic that takes up 20 percent of a book's content. The manual further notes that "generally a maximum of six [headings] is appropriate. In special situations more headings may be required."

I say the *Manual* is "more or less" the standard because many libraries today have chosen to produce records at a less rigorous level, called "core cataloging." At this level, two subject headings per book are usually deemed appropriate.[1] Some libraries choose this lower level of cataloging because of the increasing volume of book publication, coupled with the decreasing number of trained catalogers. Indeed, traditional cataloging is a subject no longer required in some library schools. Additionally, most libraries do "copy cataloging" as much as possible, which means that they strive to find, in various computer networks, catalog records already created by some other library—*any* other library—and simply import them into their own catalogs, usually with minimal review or quality control of the copied subject terms.

The "core" standard can create problems that researchers need to be aware of. For example, a book published twenty years ago, in 1984, with the title *Censorship and Interpretation: The Conditions of Writing and Reading in Early Modern England* received a generous set of headings:

**Censorship—England—History—16th century**
**Censorship—England—History—17th century**
**Books and reading—England—History—16th century**
**Books and reading—England—History—17th century**
**English literature—Early modern, 1500–1700—History and criticism**
**England—Intellectual life—16th century**
**England—Intellectual life—17th century**

A similar book published in 2001, however, *Press Censorship in Jacobean England*, received only two headings:

**Freedom of the press—England—History—16th century**
**Press—England—History—16th century**

There are a couple problems here. The first is that the cataloger of the second work mistakenly assigned "16th century" rather than "17th" for the Jacobean period. And here it must be admitted that cataloging is as much an art as a science; despite its many rules designed to bring about uniformity and standardization, the rules are only as good as the person using them. The more serious problem is that the first book, *Censorship and Interpretation*, is widely considered the standard work in its field— but a researcher who looked in a library catalog under any of the headings used for *that* book would not have found the later 2001 work, which covers much of the same ground from a different perspective. The scant two headings given to the later volume were simply not adequate to put it in any of the same categories in which the first book appears. The problem in this case was solved by a "guerilla cataloger" who, once the difficulty was pointed out, simply ignored the "core cataloging" standard and added to the 2001 record several more headings which overlap with those of the 1984 book.

Not all such problems, however, can be solved by guerilla catalogers who will ignore the rules they are told to work with, and do better work than the core standard requires. This means, unfortunately, that the "uniform" part of the principle of "uniform heading" has been diluted in the library profession in recent years; and so researchers need to be aware of the ways to compensate for decreasing standardization (discussed below).

## Specific Entry

This is by far the most important principle that researchers need to be aware of. It means that, given a choice between using specific or general headings for a book, catalogers will usually choose the most specific possible headings for the book as a whole, *rather than the more general headings* available in the *LCSH* list.

For example, if you are looking for material on nightmares, you should not look first under **Dreams** or **Sleep** but under **Nightmares** specifically. Similarly, if you want books on Siamese cats, you should look under the specific heading **Siamese cat** and *not* under the general heading **Cats**. One researcher, looking for material on Jewish children, mistakenly assumed the proper heading would be **Jews**. It isn't. It's **Jewish children**. Works under this more specific heading are *not* listed under the more general heading **Jews**.

Another reader looking for information on recreation rooms searched under **Homes**. The right heading is **Recreation rooms**.

A reader looking for information on archons (chief magistrates) in ancient Greece searched under **Civilization, ancient**. The right heading is **Archons**.

A reader looking for information on emblem books searched under **Iconography**. The right heading is **Emblem books**.

A reader looking for information on the problems that alcoholic parents create for their children wasted a lot of time after being inundated with records under **Alcoholics**. The right heading is **Children of alcoholics**; and there is also an even more specific term, **Adult children of alcoholics**. Again, books listed under the narrower terms are *not* listed under the general heading—you have to find the most specific headings *rather than* (not in addition to) the general terms. Still another reader, this one interested in the effects of divorce on children, made the usual mistake of looking under the general heading **Divorce** rather than under the specific heading **Children of divorced parents**. (And there is also a heading for **Adult children of divorced parents**.) Predictably, the search proved frustrating. The choice of *which* term(s) to use, when several levels of generality are possible, is made on the basis of the principle of specific entry.

This is not to say that the general headings aren't used; of course they are. If a book is about **Divorce** in general, then it will receive that heading, because in that case the general heading is indeed the *tightest fit* for the scope of that book. The problem is that most people search under general headings when they really have something more specific in mind; they *mistakenly* assume that the general categories "include" the more specific topics. The rule for researchers, then, is to start with the most specific terms from the *LCSH* list, and *then* "go general" only if you cannot find narrow terms that match your specific topic exactly.

Note that this rule runs directly against the grain of what students are usually told: "Start with a broad idea and then try to narrow it down as you go." While this may be very good advice in other situations, *you should do the exact opposite when you are using a library catalog.*

The problem for researchers who start with general terms is that they usually do find a few sources that appear to be in the ballpark—but they simultaneously miss most of the best material without knowing it, and *they usually stop with their initial pool of general sources.* The researcher who looks under **Divorce**, for instance, may indeed find a few books that have sections discussing the effects of divorce on children—but if she stops there (and most people do stop at the first level that seems at all relevant), she will miss all of the works under **Children of divorced parents**, which are *whole books* (rather than just chapters or section) on that topic.

There are two good reasons for specific entry. First, the segregation of different levels of specificity prevents any of them, broad or narrow, from becoming overloaded with irrelevant clutter. For example, the heading **Decoration and ornament** is quite general; but linked to it are 125 more specific terms such as:

**Airplanes, Military—Decoration**
**Antiques**
**Balloon decorations**
**Bars (Drinking establishments)—Decoration**
**Book covers**
**Bronzes**
**Cattle—Housing—Decoration**
**Church decoration and ornament**
**Decoupage**
**Driftwood arrangement**
**Embroidery**

**Floral decorations**
**Garden ornaments and furniture**
**Heraldry, Ornamental**
**Illustration of books**
**Lattice windows**
**Majolica painting**
**Nose ornaments**
**Railroad stations—Decoration**
**Ship decoration**
**Textile design**
**Vase painting**
**Wedding decorations**

If all of these narrower terms were included within the scope of the general heading, then researchers who wanted only the general-level books on **Decoration and ornament** would not be able to find them without having to wade through, at the same time, all of the hundreds of records for the much narrower topics.

Second, when there are several possible levels of relevant headings available in *LCSH*, it is the principle of specific entry alone that makes the choice of which level to use *predictable*. Works on blue crabs, for instance, could conceivably be cataloged under **Crabs**, **Crustacea**, or **Chesapeake Bay**, or even under **Ecology**, **Estuaries**, **Invertebrates**, **Marine biology**, **Marine invertebrates**, **Coastal fauna**, **Oceanography**, **Arthropoda**, or any of two dozen other terms—all of which appear as valid general headings in the *LCSH* list. The problem is that when you look in the direction of generality there is no logical or predictable stopping point, because all of the general headings could potentially apply. You could never tell which one would be the best to use. The solution is that when you search in the direction of specificity, there is indeed a predictable stopping point: the heading that is the tightest fit for what you want. The right term to stop at in the *LCSH* list, here, is **Blue crab**. It is the predictability of the rule that creates the "control" of the controlled vocabulary—without the specificity convention, users could not know in advance which level of term to choose, and the problem of guesswork among variant headings would remain, in spite of the existence of the thesaurus list. Without the rule, the list itself would be uncontrolled.

Although, as mentioned, there is an unfortunate tendency in library catalogs nowadays to lose the sharpness of their subject categorizations (due to the acceptance of inadequately reviewed copy cataloging), there is still more than enough substance to the principle of specific entry that you should make use of it: *as a rule*, look in the direction of cross-references leading to specific headings, and stop only at the level of terminology that provides the tightest fit for your topic, rather than the general levels above it. Look for general levels only *after* you've *first* tried to be as specific as possible, rather than vice-versa. If you match your retrieval technique to the rules the catalogers are supposed to follow, your results will be much more on target.

## Four Ways to Find the Right Subject Headings

So, then, how exactly do you find the right headings for your topic? There are four techniques. Two involve using the *LCSH* list of subject headings; the other two involve the use of the library's catalog directly.

**1.   Follow cross-references in the *Library of Congress Subject Headings* list, especially the NT (Narrower Term) references.**   As noted above, the *LCSH* list is an annual, multivolume set that lists the terms approved for use as subject headings in library catalogs; it is often referred to as "the red books" because of the color of the binding of its volumes. The list also includes words or phrases that are not used, with cross-references from them to the proper terms. Thus if you look up "Morality" you will find a note to "USE **Ethics**." Similarly, "Surgical diagnosis," which is not used, will tell you to USE the acceptable form, **Diagnosis, surgical**.

Once you find the proper term, the *LCSH* books will also give you a list of other subject headings that are related to it, so that you can systematically search either slightly different aspects of the topic or different levels of generality. Thus "Death penalty," which is not used, refers you to **Capital punishment**; and under this term you will find a list of other headings that are preceded by different code designations. These codes are very important. They are UF, BT, RT, and NT. (See Figure 1.)

UF means Used For; thus, in Figure 1, **Capital punishment** in boldface type is *used for* "Death penalty" or "Death sentence." In other words, if

**Capital punishment**   *(May Subd Geog)*
  ₁*HV8694-HV8699₁*
   UF  Abolition of capital punishment
       Death penalty
       Death sentence
   BT  Criminal law
       Punishment
   RT  Executions and executioners
   NT  Crucifixion
       Death row
       Discrimination in capital punishment
       Electrocution
       Garrote
       Hanging
       Last meal before execution
       Stoning
  — **Religious aspects**
  — — **Baptists, ₁Catholic Church, etc.₁**
  — — **Buddhism, ₁Christianity, etc.₁**
**Capital punishment (Canon law)**
   BT  Canon law
**Capital punishment (Germanic law)**
   BT  Law, Germanic
**Capital punishment (Islamic law)**
   *(May Subd Geog)*
   BT  Islamic law
**Capital punishment (Jewish law)**
   BT  Jewish law
**Capital punishment (Roman law)**
   BT  Roman law
**Capital punishment in literature**
   *(Not Subd Geog)*

---

*Fig. 1*

terms are preceded by UF, do not use them. They are not acceptable forms; instead, use the boldface heading above them.

BT means Broader Term(s); these *are* valid headings that you can search under (Criminal law, Punishment). These terms are not printed in boldface here, where they appear as cross-references; but they will be in boldface where they appear as headings in their proper alphabetical places in the *LCSH* list.

RT means Related Term(s). RT references are also valid headings (Executions and executioners).

NT means Narrower Term(s); these, too, are valid headings (for example, Death row, Discrimination in capital punishment, Electrocution, etc.).

There are two crucial points here, neither of which is intuitively obvious. The first is that the BTs, RTs, and NTs are *not subsets or subdivisions* of the boldface term above. They are *not included* in the coverage of the boldface term; if you want any of these subjects, *you must look for them directly.* Thus **Death row, Hanging,** and **Punishment** are not included in the coverage of the term **Capital punishment;** if you want any of these topics you must search for them individually and directly.

The second point is that the NT cross-references are by far the most important ones to pursue. They are usually the specific entry terms that you need to start with. And they may lead to other, even more specific terms. Thus, within the *LCSH* list, **Divorce** does not provide a direct NT reference to **Children of divorced parents,** but it does start a series that leads to it. Specifically, **Divorce** provides an RT reference to **Divorced people;** this heading, in turn, provides an NT reference to **Divorced parents;** and this heading, in turn, provides NT references to both **Adult children of divorced parents** and **Children of divorced parents.** (The latter term then provides a further RT reference to **Children of single parents,** which may be of comparative interest.)

Knowledge of the narrower/broader nature of the cross-reference structure can help you to refine or expand your search, sometimes through an extended scale of headings, such as the following:

*Descending order*
**Chordata**
    NT Vertebrates
**Vertebrates**
    NT Mammals
**Mammals**
    NT Primates
**Primates**
    NT Monkeys
**Monkeys**
    NT Baboons
**Baboons**
    NT Hamadryas baboon

*Ascending order*
**Hamadryas baboon**
    BT Baboons

**Baboons**
    BT Monkeys
**Monkeys**
    BT Primates
**Primates**
    BT Mammals
**Mammals**
    BT Vertebrates
**Vertebrates**
    BT Chordata

Broader and narrower labels are always relative to other terms. For example, while **Dreams**, on the face of it, is a rather general term (certainly in relation to **Children's dreams**), it is nevertheless a narrower term itself in relation to **Subconsciousness** or **Visions**. BT and NT designations are thus not absolute labels. A heading that is BT, or broader in relation to narrower terms below it, can simultaneously be NT, or narrower in relation to broader headings above it. No matter where you enter the sequence, however, just remember to move in the direction of the tightest-fit headings for whatever topic you ultimately have in mind.

To sum up, the first way to find the right subject headings is to look in the red books and use the cross-reference codes, paying particular attention to the NT (narrower term) references.

**2.   Look for narrower terms that are alphabetically adjacent to your starting-point term in the *LCSH* list.**   Not all narrower headings in the red books receive explicit NT cross-references pointing to them. In Figure 2, for example, note that the NT references under the general term **African Americans** do not include any other headings that start with the phrase "African American(s)"; and yet there are over a dozen pages of narrower terms that are alphabetically adjacent to the general heading.

Thus, preceding "African Americans" are entries such as the following:

**African American actors**
**African American book collectors**
**African American capitalists and financiers**
**African American law teachers**

**African American women travelers**
(May Subd Geog)
    UF  Afro-American women travelers
        [Former heading]
        Women travelers, African American
    BT  Women travelers—United States
**African American wood-carving**
(May Subd Geog)
    UF  Afro-American wood-carving
        [Former heading]
        Wood-carving, African American
    BT  African American decorative arts
        Wood-carving—United States
**African American wrestlers**
(May Subd Geog)
    UF  Wrestlers, African American
    BT  Wrestlers—United States
**African American young adults**
(May Subd Geog)
    UF  Afro-American young adults
        [Former heading]
        Young adults, African American
    BT  Young adults—United States
**African American young men**
(May Subd Geog)
    UF  Afro-American young men
        [Former heading]
        Young men, African American
    BT  Young men—United States
**African American youth**   (May Subd Geog)
    UF  Afro-American youth
        [Former heading]
        Negro youth
        [Former heading]
        Youth, African American
    BT  Youth—United States
    NT  Church work with African American
        youth
**African American yuppies**   (May Subd Geog)
    UF  Afro-American yuppies
        [Former heading]
        Buppies
        Yuppies, African American
    BT  Yuppies—United States
**African American yuppies in motion pictures**
    UF  Afro-American yuppies in motion
        pictures
        [Former heading]
    BT  Motion pictures
**African Americans**   (May Subd Geog)
    [E184.5-E185.98]
    Here are entered works on citizens of the United
States of black African descent. Works on blacks who
temporarily reside in the United States, such as aliens,
students from abroad, etc., are entered under Blacks—
United States. Works' on blacks outside the United
States are entered under Blacks—place.
    UF  African Americans—United States
        Afro-Americans
        [Former heading]
        Black Americans
        Colored people (United States)
        Negroes
        [Former heading]
    BT  Africans—United States
        Blacks—United States
        Ethnology—United States
    SA  subdivision African Americans under
        individual wars, e.g. World War,
        1939-1945—African Americans; and
        headings beginning with African
        American
    NT  Africa—Civilization—African
        American influences
        Asia—Civilization—African American
        influences
        Associations, institutions, etc.—African
        American membership
        Church work with African Americans
        Music—African American influences

*Fig. 2*

**African American men in popular culture**
**African American quiltmakers**
**African American teenage girls**
**African American whalers**
**African American women surgeons**

Similarly, other alphabetically adjacent narrower terms follow the general heading, among them:

**African Americans and mass media**
**African Americans in advertising**
**African Americans in literature**
**African Americans in motion pictures**
**African Americans in the motion picture industry**
**African Americans on postage stamps**
**African Americans with disabilities**

As with the formal NT cross-references, none of these alphabetically adjacent narrower terms is "included" in the general heading **African Americans**; in the library catalog, each must be searched directly. In the current edition of *Library of Congress Subject Headings* there are sixteen pages of phrases starting with **African American(s)**.

Narrower-term entries do not receive formal NT linkages when they are already adjacent to the terms to which they would otherwise be NT-linked. As a practical matter for researchers, this means you have *two* places to look for the more specific terms; the cross-reference structure alone is insufficient to alert you to all of them.

Another practical tip: many computer-catalog browse displays have software that enables you to scroll *down* from your starting-point term, but not *up*. In this case, such displays would enable you to scan downwards, after **African Americans**, to see subsequent terms such as **African Americans in mass media** and so on. But the same software may not allow you to scan upwards, to see **African American actors** or **African American women surgeons**. The fact that the same terms can appear in both the *LCSH* list and the computer catalog does not mean that you can *spot* them equally readily in both. The paper copy format of the subject heading list will often enable you to see important terms that are hidden by software limitations in the computer catalog.

**3.   Within the library catalog itself, look for subject tracings on relevant records that are retrieved by other means.**   Sometimes a good starting point can be secured in a catalog simply by finding one good title. To return to a previous example, a researcher looking for information on the Cockney dialect started by doing a simple keyword search for "Cockney"; this led to a list of titles that included *Cockney Dialect & Slang*, amid many other irrelevant (mainly fictional) hits. (See Figure 3.)

In looking at the catalog record for the one relevant *title* he'd found, he could then discover on it the *subject headings* that the catalogers had added; in this case, again, the best heading was **English language—Dialects—England—London**. Typing in the proper category term then led him to dozens of other relevant titles, most of which lacked the keyword "Cockney."

This, then, is the third way to find the right subject heading: find any good record at all, by keyword or author searching, and then look at what is called the "subject tracing" field on it. These are the terms to use for similar books. The crucial point is that you must understand the difference between keyword (or title) searching and subject searching; in library catalogs they are distinct.

One advantage of using tracings is that they will often provide you, in effect, with cross-references among terms that are not captured by the formal BT, RT, and NT designations, and which also escape "alphabetical adjacency" searches. For example, a book with the title *Crime and the Occult: How ESP and Parapsychology Help Detection* has two subject tracings:

**Parapsychology in criminal investigation**
**Occultism and criminal investigation**

These headings are not linked to each other in the red books; but their appearance together on the same catalog record effectively alerts researcher to the existence of both.

There is also a disadvantage here. Keep in mind that using subject tracings *alone* to find the best headings is not a good habit, although many academics fall into this rut. The problem is that headings listed as subject tracings do not provide any of the formal cross-references to narrower or

| | |
|---|---|
| **LC Control Number:** | 81165873 |
| **Type of Material:** | Text (Book, Microform, Electronic, etc.) |
| **Personal Name:** | Wright, Peter, 1923- |
| **Main Title:** | Cockney dialect and slang / Peter Wright. |
| **Published/Created:** | London : Batsford, 1981. |
| **Related Titles:** | Cockney dialect & slang. |
| **Description:** | 184 p. : ill. ; 23 cm. |
| **ISBN:** | 0713422424 : |
| **Notes:** | Spine title: Cockney dialect & slang. Includes index. Bibliography: p. 174-175. |
| **Subjects:** | English language–Dialects–England–London. English language–Slang. London (England)–Social life and customs. |
| **LC Classification:** | PE1961 .W7 |
| **Dewey Class No.:** | 427/.1 19 |
| **National Bib. No.:** | GB81-15959 |
| **Geog. Area Code:** | e-uk-en |
| **CALL NUMBER:** | PE1961 .W7 Copy 1 |
| **– Request in:** | Jefferson or Adams Bldg General or Area Studies Reading Rms |
| **– Status:** | Not Charged |
| **DATABASE NAME:** | Library of Congress Online Catalog |

*Fig. 3*

related terms, nor do they provide browse displays of alphabetically adjacent subdivisions or other narrower headings. Tracings by themselves are cut off from several important *displays of relationships* that may be important to the ultimate success of your research. There are thus real trade-offs—both advantages and *disadvantages*—in using tracings alone, without the other mechanisms of the *LCSH* system. If, for example, a student interested in the effects of divorce on children simply types in the keyword "divorce," then the tracings on all of the retrieved records will themselves be at the wrong level of generality. They will all be valid *LCSH* terms—but they will also be the wrong terms for desired topic. It is thus bad advice to rely *exclusively* on subject tracings to find the right headings—if the keywords with which you start your search aren't accurate enough, the tracings they lead to will also be skewed.

**4.  Within the library catalog, browse through *all* of the subdivisions of any relevant subject heading you find.**   The fourth way to find the right subject term(s) for your topic is to look through the arrays of *subdivisions* that show up under appropriate headings in the catalog.

For example, one researcher interested in the history of Yugoslavia asked for help at the reference desk because, on his own, he'd simply done a Boolean combination of the keywords "Yugoslavia" and "history," and had been overwhelmed with too many irrelevant records. The solution to this problem was the use of the online catalog's *browse displays*. When doing a subject (not keyword) search under **Yugoslavia**, a browse display of many screens' length was automatically generated; it included headings such as these:

**Yugoslavia—Antiquities**
**Yugoslavia—Antiquities—Bibliography**
**Yugoslavia—Antiquities—Maps**
**Yugoslavia—Armed Forces—History**
**Yugoslavia—Bibliography**
**Yugoslavia—Biography**
**Yugoslavia—Biography—Dictionaries**
**Yugoslavia—Boundaries**
**Yugoslavia—Civilization**
**Yugoslavia—Civilization—Bibliography**
**Yugoslavia—Commerce—History**
**Yugoslavia—Commerce—Pakistan**
**Yugoslavia—Commercial treaties**
**Yugoslavia—Constitutional history**
**Yugoslavia—Description and travel**
**Yugoslavia—Economic conditions**
**Yugoslavia—Encyclopedias**
**Yugoslavia—Ethnic relations**
**Yugoslavia—Foreign economic relations**
**Yugoslavia—Foreign relations—Great Britain**
**Yugoslavia—Foreign relations—Soviet Union**

Yugoslavia—Foreign relations—United States
Yugoslavia—Geography—Bibliography
Yugoslavia—History—1992–2003
   [NT cross-reference to **Yugoslav War, 1991–1995**]
Yugoslavia—History—Bibliography
Yugoslavia—History—Chronology
Yugoslavia—History—Dictionaries
Yugoslavia—History, Military
Yugoslavia—History—Soviet occupation, 1979–1989
Yugoslavia—Kings and rulers—Biography
Yugoslavia—Maps
Yugoslavia—Pictorial works
Yugoslavia—Politics and government [with period subdivisions]
Yugoslavia—Relations—India—Bibliography
Yugoslavia—Relations—Pakistan—Chronology
Yugoslavia—Road maps
Yugoslavia—Social conditions
Yugoslavia—Social life and customs
Yugoslavia—Statistics
Yugoslavia—Strategic aspects
Yugoslavia—Yearbooks

These are only a sample of the full list. The researcher, in this case, was delighted: he could immediately see that he had many more options for his topic than he had realized. He was particularly excited by the —**Antiquities** subdivisions, which his keyword search under "history" had missed entirely.

All of this material would have been missed if the searcher had simply typed "Yugoslavia" and "history" into a blank search box in a massive full-text database such as the newly proposed Google Print project, which plans to digitize millions of books. The Google software cannot display browse menus of subjects with subdivisions and cross-references, which would allow researchers to simply recognize options that they cannot specify in advance. Library catalogs provide much more efficient and systematic overviews of the *range* of books relevant to any topic. Searching for all relevant book texts via a simple Internet-type search box would be like trying to get an overview of a whole country while looking at it only through a bombsight. While the Google project may enhance *information seeking*, it will greatly curtail *scholarship*—which requires connections, linkages, and overviews—if it is regarded as a replacement for real libraries and traditional cataloging. (See Chapter 3 for more on Google Print.)

I cannot recommend this too strongly: use your library catalog's browse displays. When there are multiple screens of subdivisions, *take the time to look through all of them.* You will *usually* be able to spot important aspects of your topic that you would never have otherwise noticed. This technique is almost tailor-made to solve the frequent problem of getting too much junk via keyword searches.

The larger a library's catalog, the more researchers must rely on *menu listings* that enable them to simply *recognize* relevant options that they could not specify in advance. There are three such menus you need to look for: the cross-reference lists of NT and RT terms, the alphabetically adjacent narrower terms in the red books, and—especially—the rosters of subdivisions that automatically appear in online-catalog subject searches. A great deal of intellectual time and effort by catalogers goes into the creation of these menus; without them, you simply have to guess which terms to use; and, as in this **Yugoslavia** example, no one will be able to think up beforehand all of the relevant topics that could readily be of use in researching the country's history. Online browse displays of subject subdivisions are the kinds of things researchers would kill to have in Internet searches—but Net search engines simply cannot produce them. This radical advantage is available to researchers only in library catalogs.

Note a further important point: most of the subdivisions that you see listed in online browse displays in the library's catalog (e.g., —**Bibliography**, — **Description and travel**, —**Social life and customs**, etc.) will not be recorded in the red books set of *LCSH* terms. Most subdivisions are "free floating," which means that, within certain rule restrictions, catalogers can attach them wherever needed without recording the attachment in the *LCSH* list. (If every subdivision of every heading were indeed recorded, the set would be too expensive to print.) Since one of the functions of subdivisions is to give narrower focus to general terms, you will therefore find many of the narrow terms you need *only in the catalog itself—not in the red books.*

## Precoordination and Postcoordination

Naive students of library science will sometimes say, "Libraries could save a lot of money if we simplify cataloging by eliminating multi-element strings and simply record each element separately, because the computer software can combine the separate elements into the same results." While it is true that the computer can indeed combine **Yugoslavia** and **Antiquities** as separate terms, or **Yugoslavia** and **Bibliography**, the real problem lies with the researchers themselves—the human beings who use the computers. *They* cannot combine the two elements when they are separate (rather than linked in a string of terms that shows up automatically in a browse display) unless it occurs to them in advance that **Antiquities** and **Bibliography** are indeed viable options. Real people cannot do this without the help of menu displays. When catalogers have taken the trouble to create linked strings it is known as "precoordination" of terms; when the terms appear only as separate elements on the catalog record (and in the thesaurus), and have to be combined afterwards by computer manipulations, it is known as "postcoordination." (Thus **Philosophy—History** is a precoordinated string; **Philosophy** AND **History** would be a postcoordinate combination.) The important point is that precoordinated strings of subdivisions under a heading offer a major advantage that cannot be matched in a postcoordinate system: a precoordinate system enables you to *recognize*, in browse displays, multiple important aspects of a topic that you could never think up beforehand.

This is why it is so important to look systematically at any and all subdivisions that appear in the library catalog. Even if there are many screens of them, *skim through them all*. (This insight is something that took years to crystallize for me. It is not immediately obvious that you should look at the whole roster, and so most researchers just don't do it. But I've found through experience that doing this works so well, and in such surprising ways, and in so many instances, that the technique should be used consciously and deliberately.)

Some of the many subdivisions that are possible—and that, as a reference librarian, I've found most useful to look out for—are these:

    **[LC Subject Heading]—Bibliography**
               **—Bio-bibliography**
               **—Case studies**
               **—Civilization**
               **—Collections**
               **—Commerce**

—**Correspondence**
—**Costume**
—**Criticism and interpretation**
—**Description and travel**
—**Diaries**
—**Dictionaries**
—**Directories**
—**Economic conditions**
—**Encyclopedias**
—**Foreign economic relations**
—**Foreign relations**
—**Great Britain** [or other country
       subdivisions]
—**Guidebooks**
—**Handbooks, manuals, etc.**
—**History**
—**History—Bibliography**
—**History—Sources**
—**Illustrations**
—**Interviews**
—**Law and legislation**
—**Management**
—**Maps**
—**Military relations**
—**Personal narratives**
—**Pictorial works**
—**Quotations**
—**Rating of**
—**Relations**
—**Social life and customs**
—**Sources**
—**Statistics**
—**Study and teaching**
—**United States**
—**United States—Bibliography**
—**United States—History**
—**Views on** [topic]

Obviously not all of these subdivisions will appear under any one heading; but these are among the most important ones you should be on the lookout for. Recognizing options is fine; consciously searching for them is even more effective. Success in using subdivisions depends on your "getting the feel" of which ones you can expect to find. They are frequently overlooked in library catalogs because readers aren't taught their importance and because there are so many of them to look through.

Many subject headings can be subdivided geographically as well as topically; thus, for example, you would have an advantage if you suspected in advance that **Mass media—United States** or **Mass media—Canada** might be better headings than **Mass media** alone. The best works on the topic you have in mind may well appear with the geographic qualification; but you may miss the form unless you are deliberately looking for it. The *LCSH* list provides a major clue in that it adds a parenthetical note *"(May Subd Geog)"* after all headings capable of geographic subdivision; but the best way to avoid any problems is, again, to browse quickly through *all* subdivisions of your topic in the catalog.

## Miscellaneous Tips on Subject Headings

A problem that students often have at the beginning of their projects is that of narrowing down their topic to a manageable size. It should now be apparent that are several formal mechanisms in the cataloging system that enable you to do precisely this, and in a systematic manner. They are precisely the same four ways that lead you to the proper specific (rather than general) subject headings for your topic.

A kind of "fifth way" to find the right headings is through computer combinations of two or more subject elements—that is, sometimes there isn't a single term that expresses the subject you want, but you can still hit the nail on the head, at a specific level, by combining separate headings (e.g., **Mexican Americans** AND **Education, bilingual**). Such Boolean combinations will be discussed in Chapter 10.

Here are a few miscellaneous additional tips about using *Library of Congress Subject Headings*:

- The *LCSH* list usually does not list *proper names*, but they can still appear as valid subject headings within the catalog itself.

- If you are looking for foreign-language books on a subject, you still have to use the *English-language subject headings* to find them. For example, I once helped a professor who wanted only Italian books on the city of Venice. He had made the mistake of searching under "Venezia." The proper heading is **Venice (Italy)**; in the Library of Congress catalog, it rounds up books in all languages. The retrieved set could then be limited to only those in Italian. A large number of the Italian books do not themselves use the word "Venezia" in their titles; for example:

  *Il campiello sommerso*
  *Veneto: itinerari ebraici*
  *La chiesa del Tintoretto*
  *Le sculture esterne di San Marco*
  *Santi e contadini: lunario della tradizione orale veneta*

- The *LCSH* list includes a Table of Pattern Headings in its Introduction. As noted above, not all subdivisions of topics are listed under every heading; but the full range of subdivisions appropriate to certain categories of subjects are indeed listed under "type specimen" headings. Thus, for example, all of the subdivisions that could be appended to any example of "Plants or crops" are spelled out under *one* of them: **Corn**. The subdivisions listed *only* here are then useable under any other such plant or crop. There are a couple dozen such categories listed, with their corresponding headings. These pattern headings are mainly useful to catalogers, but I've had researchers, too, tell me they were useful to browse through.

The subject heading—or controlled vocabulary—searches discussed in this chapter are only one of several methods of gaining access to information. For the sake of providing a large overview, let me anticipate points to be discussed in subsequent chapters, and mention here that eight alternative methods of searching can be used when no subject heading exists or when you wish to turn up sources in addition to those found via subject headings:

- General and focused browsing (see Chapter 3)
- Keyword searching (see Chapters 4 and 5)

- Citation searching (see Chapter 6)
- Related record searching (see Chapter 7)
- Boolean combination searching (see Chapter 10)
- Using people sources (see Chapter 12)
- Type of literature searching (see Chapter 15)

Each of these approaches—like that of searching with controlled vocabulary terms—has its advantages and disadvantages. Collectively viewed, each has a strength that compensates for a weakness in the others. An awareness of this basic structure of relationships, among only these few distinct methods of searching, can have a profound effect in increasing the efficiency of your research.

## Note

1. "Fewer added entries are required and no more than one or two subject headings need be added to the core record." (Willy Cromwell, "The Core Record: A New Bibliographic Standard," *Library Resources & Technical Services*, 38 [October, 1994], p. 422.)

# 3

## *General Browsing, Focused Browsing, and Use of Classified Bookstacks*

The fact that books in libraries are shelved by subject, rather than by accession numbers or by the height of the volumes, gives researchers a major advantage in gaining subject access to their contents—one that, in many cases, cannot be matched by any computer searches. This advantage, however, is nowadays in jeopardy from many library administrators who often assume that the shelving of books by subject is no longer necessary in a "digital age." Part of this view stems from the library profession's difficulty in distinguishing the real from the imaginary capabilities of computers, and especially in a willful blindness to the difficulty researchers have in trying to actually read book-length texts in electronic formats. Another part springs from inexperienced theorists who believe that all books relevant to a topic can be identified through the prior specification of uncontrolled keywords, in the complete absence of alternative search mechanisms that enable scholars to simply recognize important texts that they cannot specify in advance. Yet another part of the problem springs from academics in the library field who assert that "all formats of information records are equal." Their conclusion is that, since audiocassettes and DVDs are never sensibly stored in subject arrangements, books, too, do not merit costly preferential treatment in shelving.

It is indeed possible to shelve books in arrangements other than by the traditional subject categorizations of the Dewey Decimal or the Library of Congress Classification systems. A library could, for example, simply arrange its volumes in the order of their acquisition. In this case, catalogers would then have only to assign sequential whole numbers to the books (1, 2, 3, . . . ). Such a system would be capable of storing an infinite number of items; and, as long as the number that appears on the computer record corresponds to the number on the book, readers who find the catalog entry would then be able to locate its corresponding volume on the shelves. The library would save thousands of dollars every year if this scheme were used, since it would require professional catalogers only for describing the books and devising subject headings for the catalog records, and not for also creating systematic call numbers with intricate relationships to each other. It would especially save money, too, in preventing the need for the redistribution of already-shelved books caused by unanticipated bulges of growth in particular subject classes. In a whole number or "dummy number" system, the only area that needs room for growth is the very end of the sequence. No empty spaces need be left on any shelf but the last one, because no new books would ever be interfiled with those already in place—all incoming books would be shelved *only* at the end of the sequence, simply in the order in which they happen to arrive.

Another possibility is that the library could shelve books strictly according to their height—all six-inch-tall books together, all twelve-inch books together, and so on. In this scenario, the vertical distance between bookshelves could be adjusted precisely so that there would be no wasted space above the volumes cause by height differentials. Given that there are miles of books in any large library, this expedient would enable shelving to be much more space-efficient, which would save money and create room for larger collections. Just such a system, in fact, is used by the Center for Research Libraries in Chicago, which stores hundreds of thousands of little-used volumes that are available to other libraries through interlibrary loan.

A third alternative would be to store books in tubs in large warehouses, on shelves dozens of yards higher than any that could be reached by human researchers. As long as the number on the computer catalog record for the book is coded to link to the number on the book itself, and then to the tub in which it rests, the actual retrieval of the tub can be accomplished by a robotic mechanism. Such systems are becoming common for research libraries' "remote storage" areas—those that hold the book volumes deemed to be of lesser importance, or the runs of bound journals replaced by electronic full-text services such as *JSTOR* (see Chapter 5).

All of these shelving schemes would be much less expensive to hard-pressed library budgets than the traditional practice of maintaining books in a subject-classed arrangement. So why is the latter still desirable when cheaper alternatives are available? Why shouldn't remote-storage techniques be used not just in offsite warehouses, but within the main library buildings themselves? Alternatively, why couldn't massive digitization projects such as Google Print replace rather than merely supplement onsite book collections shelved in classified order? What difference does the method of shelving make to the researchers who have to *use* the books?

There are two problems with the cheap alternatives: they diminish the possibility of discovering relevant books by simple recognition (as opposed to prior specification); and they entirely rule out the possibility of in-depth, focused subject browsing.

The first disadvantage in a non-classified shelving operation, in other words, is that if someone wants books on any subject, he or she must be able to determine which books are relevant solely from the brief catalog records that *represent* the books within the computer catalog—or the researcher must be able to specify the right keywords in a full-text database in such a way that its ranking algorithms will bring relevant materials to the top of a list of hundreds of thousands of hits, and do so in a way that does not bury equally relevant sources among thousands of records having the right words in the wrong contexts.

Remember, when you search the library catalog, you are not searching the full texts of the actual books; you are searching only catalog records *of* the books. There is no possibility of efficiently or systematically browsing the actual volumes themselves when their subjects are irrelevant to their shelf arrangement. In a height system, if one book on anthropology is six inches tall and another is ten inches, they may be shelved on entirely different floors; or, in a sequential system, if one book came into the library a year after the other, they may be separated by hundreds of feet of cookbooks, car-repair manuals, and Gothic novels.

Remember, too, that when you are searching a full-text database with Internet software, you are not retrieving books *categorized by subject*; rather, you are getting texts arranged by *keyword ranking* mechanisms. The latter display results not by conceptual relationships, but by weighted counts of the frequency of word appearances and by the number of links to the texts. Ranking keywords is not the same as categorizing by subject headings or classification-number groupings that collocate like materials regardless of the keywords (whether English or foreign) that they use.

One of the major advantages of a classified arrangement of materials, in contrast, is that it enables you to simply recognize relevant works that you could not specify in advance. The segregation of books into defined categories also enables you to see whatever words you spot within the boundaries of the given subject concept. Such shelving allows for—indeed, positively encourages and enables—*discovery by serendipity* or *recognition.* The value of such discovery may be incalculable for any given search. One historian of prison labor, for example, found through stacks browsing the only known image of prisoners on a treadmill in the United States. "Neither the book title, nor the call number, nor the author led me to this report," he commented. "Only a hands-on shelf check did it."[1] In a similar manner, I once found an illustration of a slave coffle—a line of shackled slaves being marched under guard—very different from another one that is widely reproduced, in a book I noticed next to another volume that I was actually looking for. This illustration proved to be very welcome to an historian writing a book on slavery. The presence of this particular illustration is not indicated by the book's catalog record in the computer; nor does the word "coffle" appear as a searchable keyword in the illustration's caption.

Having said this, I must also point out that much research that used to be carried out simply on the basis of browsing in the bookstacks is indeed much better accomplished today by *not* going directly to the shelves and "just looking around." There are multiple purposes, not one, for direct inspection of subject-shelved book groups: not just *general* browsing but *focused* browsing and *recognition* searching. The former is the primary method used by some researchers to try to discover "what's available" on their topic; *this* goal, however, is nowadays much better accomplished by search techniques other than direct browsing of bookshelves. (These alternative techniques are the topics of other chapters in this book.) To put it bluntly, if you still regard shelf-browsing as the *primary* means of orienting yourself to the literature of the topic that interests you, then you are making a big mistake. You will be missing much more material than you find, and you will not be able to achieve an overview of the range of relevant materials that actually exists beyond the small areas in which you browse. You will miss all journal articles, essays in anthologies, dissertations, government documents and reports, all nonbook formats—and also the many other *books* treating different aspects of the same subject (which will be shelved in other class areas). When library administrators, trying to save money through cheaper shelving methods, point out that browsing is no longer necessary for *this* purpose of "gaining a systematic overview of relevant literature," they are right. General browsing will not reveal most of the relevant literature of most topics; computer catalogs and other databases (as well as other resources such as published bibliographies) are usually much better in showing the *range* of books and articles relevant to any topic.

But two very different purposes for direct examination of classified bookstacks are not rendered unnecessary or unimportant by the proliferation of computer databases. The first is that direct access is still necessary for *focused examination* of contiguous, subject-related *full texts*. There are times when *depth* of searching is the goal, not *range* of searching. The main problem with nonclassified shelf arrangements is that all subject access to their books is at only a very superficial level, via surrogate records within the library's catalog. You cannot search down to the page and paragraph level within the books themselves in subject categories, in other words; you can search only catalog records in subject groups. And the *content* of catalog records is necessarily much more superficial than that of the actual books they point to.

The second purpose of browsing classified stacks is that it enables scholars to simply *recognize* relevant texts whose keywords they cannot specify in advance. This important function cannot be accomplished by full-text databases dependent on the prior specification of all relevant keywords.

Let me give a few examples:

I once had to answer a letter from an historian seeking information on traveling libraries that circulated among lighthouse keepers at the turn of the twentieth century; these were wooden bookcases, each with a different selection of books, that were rotated among the lighthouse tenders in order to relieve the boredom and monotony of their isolated lives. I first tried searching the computer catalog of the books at the Library of Congress—with no luck. Even after searching other databases on the mainframe system and several commercial indexes to journals and dissertations (including the largest commercial index to American history journals) I still found nothing—only, occasionally, the right words ([lighthouse? OR light(w)house?] AND [book? OR librar?]) in the wrong contexts.

So I decided to look directly at the books on lighthouses in the library's bookstacks. The major grouping for this topic is at VK1000–1025 ("Lighthouse service"); this area had, by a quick count, 438 volumes on 12 shelves.

I rapidly scanned all of this material—literally paging through, quickly, all of the volumes.

I found 15 books that had directly relevant sections—a paragraph here, a half page there, a column elsewhere—containing descriptions of the book collections, reminiscences about them, official reports, anecdotes, and so on. I also found another seven sources of tangential interest—on reading or studying done in lighthouses, but without mentioning the traveling libraries —and photocopied these, too, for the letter writer. The primary 15 contained a total of about 2,100 words on the traveling libraries, including a partial list of titles.

Particularly noteworthy is the fact that, of the 15 prime sources, not one mentioned the libraries in its table of contents; and nine of them (60%) did not mention the libraries in their index, either—or did not even have an index to begin with. Equally noteworthy is the fact that thirteen of the sources were twentieth century publications—nine of them published after 1970— and thus still probably under copyright protection (a barrier to Google Print type republication [see below]). In other words, this information could not have been found *even if the books' tables of contents and indexes had been entered into a database*. This depth of research in book collections can be achieved *only* by focused browsing: inspecting the actual full texts in a systematic fashion—not by looking at *any* surrogate catalog records, no matter how detailed.

With the classification scheme's arrangement of books, however, the needed information could indeed be found both systematically and easily. Retrieving, via call slips, 438 books scattered by random accession numbers would be so time-consuming and difficult as to be effectively impossible in the real world. And determining in advance which 15 had the right information from the catalog would also be impossible—the surrogate catalog records just do not contain that *depth* of information. A reader who had to *guess* in advance which 15 of the 438 volumes had the right information would necessarily miss most of what the library actually had to offer— information that is readily retrievable as long as we remember that *there are other ways to do full-text searches besides using computers, and that some of these ways simply cannot be fitted into computers.*

Note in this case that searching by class numbers *in the catalog* is not the equivalent of searching by class area *in the actual bookstacks*. Even if the former allowed for the construction of a list of the same 438 books, it would still not be possible to determine from that list which 15 books contained the needed information. The use of subject-classified arrangements of full texts—printed *books* arranged in subject groupings on bookshelves in libraries with walls—thus provides a *depth* of subject access that *cannot be matched by any computer searches of mere surrogate catalog records.* (Nor can shelf-browsing be replaced by searching digitized full texts accessible only by a keyword search mechanism—a point to which I shall return, below.)

Another example: a researcher writing a book on the Third Crusade needed to find the definition of an obscure medical term, *arnaldia*; this disease, whatever it was, affected both Richard the Lionheart and his troops. The *Oxford English Dictionary* does not record the word, so I tried various specialized medical dictionaries in the reference rooms of the Library of Congress, with no luck. I also tried every database I could think might be relevant, and the entire open Internet. Again, no luck. I finally had to go back into the bookstacks to the call number areas for our retrospective collection of medical dictionaries, nomenclatures, and encyclopedias; in the LC system, this is the range of R121 through R125. At the Library of Congress, at the time, we had 2,148 volumes on 121 shelves in this area. I quickly searched through the entire range, looking especially for fat volumes in old bindings. In short order I found two old dictionaries that defined the term (it is an illness characterized by loss of hair).

While I was looking in the "*arn*" sections of the alphabets of these works, however, I also found a lengthy article nearby on "*Army* Medical Statistics" in an eight-volume encyclopedia from 1923. Its comparative tables of causes of death of military personnel in various countries over many years, going back into the nineteenth century, caught my eye and struck me as possibly useful to another regular researcher at the Library. This other researcher was a government contractor working on a long-term study of the effects of drug and alcohol abuse in military forces around the world; she was delighted to have the article brought to her attention, and she photocopied the whole thing.

This instance exemplifies both of the benefits of shelving by subject: *depth* of access and *serendipity*—i.e., discovery by *recognition*. Even though the Library's computer catalog allows for searching by call number, a computerized list of 2,148 catalog records with class numbers R121–125 on a screen would still not have told me *which two* referred to books containing the specific word *arnaldia*. Nor, from the catalog records alone, would I have been able to notice the contents of one article within a multi-volume encyclopedia, when the online record alerted me only to the existence of the set as a whole.

Let me offer one more example of the need for focused browsing of contiguous full texts. A scholar from France, working on a study of the writer Paul Valery and his times, needed to pin down an important bit of information regarding Valery's connection to the famous Dreyfus case, in which a French military officer of Jewish descent was convicted of treason, and, only years later, acquitted. The woman had hearsay information from Valery's children and daughter-in-law that he had signed his name to a "petition" or "liste" on the issue at the time, but had no specifics of place or date. The large online *Tresor de la langue francaise* database of full-text sources did not solve the problem, nor did biographies of Valery, nor did the *Historical Abstracts* or *FRANCIS* databases (the latter having an emphasis on French studies), nor did two massive published bibliographies on Valery (each over 600 pages). I finally had to go back into the bookstacks, where, at the Library of Congress, we have 186 volumes on 6 shelves in the classes DC354–354.9 ("Dreyfus case"). As a shortcut, I was particularly looking for a volume that a browse display in the computer catalog had alerted me to, with the subject heading **Dreyfus, Alfred, 1859–1935—Trials, litigation, etc.—Sources**. (The **—Sources** subdivision indicates a published compilation of primary sources concerning the actual event.) This volume, shelved at DC354.8.Z65 1994, however, did not reprint or identify the particular newspaper petition with Valery's signature. On the shelf above it, however, I noticed another book which, it turned out, did indeed have the necessary information. As an extra serendipitous bonus, the same volume turned out to contain additional information about one of Valery's close friends—information that solved another problem for the researcher, that she hadn't specifically asked about.

Once again, a search of the computer catalog—even by call number— could not identify *which one* of the 186 volumes had the exact information that was needed. If all of these volumes had been scattered by acquisition number, or shelved according to their many different heights, it would not have been possible to find the right book without making separate requests and waiting for 186 individual deliveries. (The volumes could not even be delivered *en masse* if they were not shelved next to each other in the first place.) In the real world, the prospect of that degree of "hassle" effectively precludes the necessary scholarship from being accomplished.[2] Libraries that do not take into account the Principle of Least Effort in information-seeking behavior are simply not functional, no matter how much money they may save; the purpose of a research library is to facilitate scholarship, not to save funds.

I emphasize the point because many library administrators these days do indeed think that "remote storage" techniques can be used within central library buildings themselves. This is something academics need to watch out for: if your library committees do not take active steps to prevent this erosion of shelving by subject, you will wind up with book collections that cannot be browsed or focus-examined down to the level of individual pages or paragraphs. In that case, you will no longer have systematic access to the "depth" parts of the books not contained on their catalog records: not just tables of contents and indexes, but maps, charts, tables, illustrations, diagrams, running heads, highlighted sidebars, binding information, typographical variations for emphasis, bulleted or numbered lists, footnotes, and bibliographies. All such material is readily searchable by focused browsing of subject-classified book collections.

One looming possibility is that the browsing search mechanism that presently allows you to recognize relevant books, or individual pages and paragraphs within them, may be replaced by blank search boxes on computer screens that require you to specify in advance, in detail, every word or phrase that may possibly be related to your topic. The aforementioned Google Print project aims to digitize the full texts of fifteen million books, from a variety of research libraries, and make them freely available for keyword searching on the Internet. It is not yet clear exactly how the project will segregate works still under copyright protection (life of author plus 70 years) from those in the public domain; but in any event the announcement of the operation has caused some observers to assert that local, onsite book collections will no longer be necessary if every text is keyword-searchable on the Internet.

There are, however, real problems with that assumption. Those who hold it are apparently innocent of experience in the ways real scholars must actually work. Let me return to the above examples. (Google Print would likely index about 4.5 billion pages of keywords. Since that pool is not yet searchable, I will use the regular Google Web engine, indexing over 6 billion Web sites, for a comparison.)

If I wish to research the question on "lighthouse libraries" on the Web, I can type in a combination of the keywords "library" and "lighthouse" or "lighthouses" in Google's advanced search page. The problem is that this search produces *173,000* hits. Even in a Google Print database confined exclusively to book texts, a search of billions of pages would undoubtedly produces similar chaos. (Searches of existing full-text databases such as *LexisNexis* produce large retrievals of irrelevant results on the organization "Lighthouse for the Blind," which publishes reading materials for sight-impaired readers.) The actual result would thus be directly contrary to the naive expectations of digital-library proponents: efficient retrieval of books—and efficient depth-searching of their contents—would not be *enhanced*; it would in fact become effectively *impossible*. Keywords retrieved in full texts without controlled subject headings and classification numbers could not be efficiently segregated by mere ranking mechanisms from hundreds of thousands of hits on the right words in the wrong contexts.

In the *arnaldia* example, a Google Print source would indeed be a god-send. Such an unusually distinctive keyword is not likely to be retrieved within large swamps of irrelevant contexts. Note, however, the very impor-tant loss of *recognition* scholarship that would result: if I had simply typed *arnaldia* into a blank search box, I could never have noticed the alphabeti-cally adjacent article on "Army Medical Statistics" in one of the old ency-clopedias, because I had not thought to specify those keywords in advance.

Similarly, with the Paul Valery example, the researcher told me that she could not have found the necessary information even in a huge full-text database like Google Print. One problem is that Google may not be able to mount copyrighted texts, which would include the French book that pro-vided the information in this case. The other, more serious problem is that the researcher did not know in advance the right keywords to type in. Again, the Valery family members simply said the writer had, at some point, signed a "petition" or a "liste." It turns out that it was actually a subscription fund to provide money for the widow of one of the individuals involved in the scandal; and the text in question, *L'Affaire Dreyfus et la Presse* (Armond Colin, 1960), reports that the names were published in the journal *La Libre Parole* in 1898. The researcher, however, did not know the name of this journal in advance; nor does the French text use the words "petition" or "liste" to describe the roster—it uses the words "souscription" and "souscripteurs" instead. In other words, the scholar would not have been able to type in the right keywords to find the information even if the copyrighted text were fully searchable online.

A search in the Google Web engine on "Paul Valery" and "Dreyfus" already produces over 3,500 hits. Keyword searching in a Google Print file is likely to produce similar mounds of chaff—especially since the single instance of Valery's name in the entirety of the *L'Affaire Dreyfus et la presse* (272 pages) would not have ranked this text at the top of any retrieval set derived from all of the words on 4.5 billion pages, or from the frequency of links to this one very obscure book. Focused browsing in classified bookstacks, enabling scholars to simply recognize what they cannot specify in advance, remains crucial to advanced scholarship.

It is especially noteworthy that any proposed use of Google Print to replace classified bookstacks would entirely segregate foreign language materials into multiple electronic "zones" that could not be searched simultaneously by the specification of English keywords. With classified bookstacks, on the other hand, books in all languages are grouped together by subject in the same locales; and oftentimes researchers can simply notice relevant foreign books on a topic simply by their illustrations or other visual cues. Google Print enthusiasts would unwittingly re-create in reality the disastrous consequences mythologized in the Tower of Babel story.

Google Print will be a wonderful supplement to classified bookstacks in real research libraries, but a terrible substitute. The overriding reason is that mere relevance-ranking algorithms cannot solve the massive problem of out-of-context keyword retrievals in full-text databases.[3] Any large digitization project without the filtering, structuring, segregating, and channeling elements provided by traditional library categorizations would do much more actual harm than good—assuming, as the digital paradigm does, that digitized book collections would replace rather than supplement onsite print collections—because the efficient *categorizing of books by subject* is not a problem that technology can solve through any *ranking* algorithms of keywords. *Information seeking* at the level of finding discrete data would improve, but *scholarship* (being dependent on contexts, connections, and webs of relationships) would be made much more difficult under the "replacement" scenario. Any attempt at a structured overview of resources would be precluded right from the start by inadequate filtering, segregating, linking, and display mechanisms.

Faculty Library Committees need to be aware that most library administrators fail to note the distinction between (a) general browsing to see what's available, versus (b) focused searching for definite, and very specific, information likely to be found within a limited range of full texts, *recognizable* within that range even when its keywords cannot be specified in advance. If this difference is blurred, then all of the (valid) objections against general browsing as the primary way to do systematic research come into play, and none of the arguments for recognition-access to the depth contents of contiguous full texts are noticed. Although all historians, anthropologists, linguists, and others have experienced the advantages of direct access to classified bookshelves, almost no one bothers to write down the numbers of contiguous volumes examined, as in the above examples. It just takes too much time, and most academics have never perceived a need to do so. Nor do they articulate clearly the crucial need, in many research situations, for recognition access rather than prior-specification search techniques. (It is the dismissal by library administrators of any concern for recognition mechanisms that is especially galling to working academics, as it is usually done with the patronizing air that advocacy of anything other than computerized keyword retrieval is merely "sentimental" rather than rational.) Until recently, scholars could simply assume that no research library administrator would even think of undermining the practice of shelving books by subject. Unfortunately, that assumption is no longer a safe one—the abandonment is being actively promoted by bean counters who overlook the operation of the overall system in which the beans are situated.

## The Complementary Relationship of the Library Catalog and the Classified Bookstacks

I mentioned that "general browsing," while still valuable for its facilitation of serendipity, is no longer the best way to do research systematically—i.e., to gain a systematic overview of "what's available" within book collections on a topic. To understand why this is so requires a grasp of the relationship of the classified bookstacks to the library's catalog. The advantages and disadvantages of searching one source rather than the other—the trade-offs —are rather neatly complementary.

One disadvantage of an online catalog is that it will usually tell you only the subject of a book as a whole, not the contents of individual sections, paragraphs, or sentences. (Nor will it give you the book's maps, tables, il-lustration, bibliography, etc.) You cannot search it down to the level of indi-vidual pages or paragraphs, because this level of information is not digitized on catalog records. The problem of superficiality of access in the catalog, however, is corrected by the classified bookstacks—any book you find on the shelves will immediately present its full contents for your inspection. You will have not just a title and a few subject headings to look at, but the table of contents, index, preface, introduction, full text, and footnotes to examine—and all of this information will be perceptible *in relation to* other full text information on the same subject, immediately adjacent in the same area.

One disadvantage of the shelf scheme is that any book within it can be shelved at only one call number, even though it may cover many subjects. A book such as *Women, Philosophy, and Sport: A Collection of Critical Es-says* (Scarecrow Press, 1983), for example, could conceivable be assigned by a cataloger to either women's studies (HQ), philosophy (B), or sports (GV) classification areas—which are nowhere near each other on the shelves. In any such case, the cataloger simply must make a choice—which means that the book will be classed in only one of the three possible areas. And this means, in turn, that browsers who are looking for a book on this subject in the other two classes will not see it. This problem (that a book can be as-signed to only *one* class area on the shelves) is remedied by the catalog, which provides multiple points of access for each record (i.e., author, title, class number, and usually at least two or three subject headings). The trade-off here is between the depth of access to a particular work and the number of points of access to it.

Conversely, a single subject may have many different aspects: philo-sophical, ethical, religious, biographical, historical, social, sociological, economic, political, legal, educational, musical, artistic, dramatic, fictional, medical, scientific, statistical, technical, military, bibliographical, and so on. In such cases the in-depth access that you need may be impeded by the many relevant books being scattered throughout the classification scheme. For example, in the Library of Congress system the range of class numbers

E51–59 contains a wealth of material on the history and culture of **Indians of North America**. However, books on Indian languages are in PS505 and PS5891; the history of Colonel William Crawford's Indian campaign is in E328; amateur Indian plays are in PN6120.16; Indian laws are in KF8201–8228; works on hospitals for Indians are in RA981.A35; and bibliographies on Indians are in Z1209.[4]

Similarly, while materials under the heading **Drinking and traffic accidents** have a home base at HE5620.D7, such materials also appear in nine different K and KF legal classes; in seven different RC medical classes; in seven different HV social pathology classes; and in several other areas, including AS36, J905.I3, QC100, TL152.3, and Z7164.T81—for a total of *over thirty different browsing sections*. Anyone who simply looks in the HE5620.D7 area may miss at least as much important information as he or she finds. The situation with **Drug abuse** is similar: even if one found the bulk of material contained in several different classes within the HV5800s, one would still be likely to overlook dozens of other areas, including AS36 (societies), BV4470 (pastoral theology), several H classes (social sciences) other than HV, several KF classes (U.S. law), LB1044 (teaching), a number of P (fiction) and R (medicine) areas, QP37 (human physiology), TX943 (food service) and two different Z classes (bibliographies).

It is the likelihood of such scattering within any topic of a certain magnitude that makes *general* browsing of the bookstacks inefficient when it is done as either the *first* or the *only* search technique. *Focused* browsing, in contrast, will always retain its value for both *depth* and *recognition* searching within limited contexts; but it is not a good technique for gaining an overview of the *range* of available sources.

If your topic is indeed scattered among many class areas, how do you determine which areas to search? Here again the complementary nature of the library catalog comes to the rescue. Works that are scattered among many different classes in the bookstacks are grouped together under uniform subject headings in the catalog, enabling you to find which classes you should then browse. (In the above examples, the grouping function is achieved by the three subject headings that appear in boldface type.) The catalog, via its subject headings, thus serves as the functional index to the classification scheme in the bookstacks—that is, a single subject heading in the catalog may bring up records that steer you to several different areas of the class scheme. Usually in such situations the records retrieved under any one heading, if they do indeed have different class numbers, will tend to fall into different clusters. If you look through all of the records retrieved by any heading, you will usually notice that some class numbers appear much more often than others; those indicate the bookstack areas in which you may wish to concentrate your focused browsing efforts. The trade-off here is between the depth of subject access to particular aspects of a broad subject (created by contiguous full texts on the shelves) and the range or extent of access to all of them (brought about the by the subject headings in the catalog, especially those with browse displays collocating a variety of subdivision aspects).

A related problem is that bookstacks provide no cross-references to other areas of the stacks that may contain related books. Works on the subject **Children's dreams**, for example, tend to be classed in BF1099 (Dreams), whereas works on the related subject **Children—Sleep** tend to be classed in RJ (Pediatrics). Neither area of the bookshelves will alert you to the existence of the other. The subject heading system in the catalog (or in the red books), however, does provide the necessary cross-reference linkage between the two headings, under which you will *then* find the different call numbers recorded.

Here then are the trade-offs and remedies:

- The library catalog corrects the weaknesses of the classified stacks by providing multiple points of access to works that can have only one position in the classified shelves. It does this by grouping together under one subject heading records that are scattered among many classes, and by providing both cross-references and browse-menu–display linkages to other, related topics in different classes.
- The shelf-browsing system—the arrangement of the actual books in subject groupings—in turn corrects the shortcomings of the catalog by providing in-depth "recognition" access to full texts, down to the page and paragraph level, in a way that is systematic and yet free of the constraints and filters of an artificial vocabulary of subject headings arranged alphabetically rather than logically.

This complementary relationship is underscored by the policy of the Library of Congress in assigning subject headings to topical or documentary films. Since it is impossible to browse a film collection for subject content (i.e., you cannot just pick up a film and flip through it as you can with a book), and since users must therefore rely almost entirely on catalog records for retrieval, LC provides such materials with extra subject headings.[5] Note the underlying assumption held by the librarians that this exception points out: in normal circumstances readers will not rely entirely on the catalog records for subject access, but will supplement its approach with shelf-browsing.

If you don't use both approaches, in other words, you are not using the library as it is designed to be used. The most efficient way to do library research is to match your retrieval technique to the library's storage technique, for in this way you will be exploiting the *internal structure* of the system.

I emphasize the point for three reasons. The first, already covered, is that ignorance of the overall structure of trade-offs and balances is nowadays leading some library administrators to think that shelving books by subject is no longer necessary. Such a view disregards the superficial level of subject access to book collections provided by computer catalogs alone—which level is simply not adequate to answer the kinds of questions that focused browsing of full texts accomplishes. It also entirely overlooks the need that scholars have for recognition access to the contents of relevant materials, grouped in such a way as to be segregated from other books that might share the same keywords in irrelevant contexts.

The second reason is that there seems to be a kind of "threshold of awareness" that many readers have to cross regarding the value of browsing in bookstacks. While most researchers have had, at one time or another, experiences of serendipitous discovery in a library, many of them regard such experiences as more due to luck than to system. But it actually *is* the system that is working in such cases—and if you are aware of this, you can exploit that system *consciously* and *deliberately* rather than haphazardly. You can make your "luck" improve in a *systematic* way. (By contrast, it would indeed have been *real* "luck" at work—rather than *system*—if I had been able to discover which one book, of the 186 on Dreyfus, contained the reference to Paul Valery, if the books had been shelved non-contiguously by height, by accession number, or by random bar coding.) The word "serendipity" is misleading, because in its normal sense it does not imply the existence of the highly structured categorization of materials that lies behind its use in a library context.

Third, the importance of focused browsing makes it essential that books actually be on the shelves where they should be so that people can discover them. In this light, it is very detrimental to researchers that some college professors check out large numbers of books and keep them for whole semesters, even years, in their offices. Subject access to these volumes is significantly diminished, for the information in them cannot be completely identified or recognized through the library's catalog *or* through prior keyword specifications in a Google Print type database. It is all the more serious a problem because the books removed from the system in this way are often the very best works on their subjects. Ironically, these same professors would be up in arms over any plan by their libraries to stop shelving books by subject; and yet the professors' own removal of books from the shelves effectively puts those same volumes in "remote storage" areas for all other researchers. Professors should remember to return *all* books they are not currently using. To say "I'll return it if someone asks for it" is to display a fundamental disregard of the way researchers have to work.

## Browsing in Other Contexts

The larger principles of browsing for information have applications beyond the use of library bookstacks. Another situation, for example, is that of using primary sources in archives or manuscript collections. Primary records are those generated by a particular event, by those who participated in it, or by those who directly witnessed it; and they are often unpublished. Thus, a researcher interested in World War II propaganda would be interested in such primary sources as copies of leaflets dropped from airplanes, typescript accounts of the flights written by those who planned or flew them, and firsthand accounts of civilians on the ground who found the leaflets. Secondary sources are the later analyses and reports written by nonparticipants, usually in published literature—although a published source can itself be primary if it is written by a participant or a witness or if it directly quotes one. Many collections of primary manuscripts exist on an incredible array of subjects and can be identified through the sources identified in Chapters 13 and 14 of this book. However, such collections are more often than not poorly indexed, or not indexed at all, and are not arranged by subject. In such cases, researchers must simply browse through the material to see what's there.

Similarly, "focused browsing" might be the term applicable to direct inspection of particular sites or physical areas. For example, genealogists may wish to know where, exactly, a certain ancestor lies buried in a cemetery; but existing maps of the area may not be detailed or complete enough to show this level of information. In such cases, direct examination of the relevant site is necessary. The principle is the same, however: *If you don't know exactly where the needed information exists, put yourself in a situation or a physical area where it is* likely *to exist, and then look around so that you can recognize valuable clues or indicators when you see them.* Some of the major themes of the present book are that a variety of techniques can be used to find information, that each of them always has both advantages and disadvantages, and that no one of them can be counted on to do the entire job of in-depth research. What is required is usually a mixture of approaches so that the various trade-offs can balance and compensate for each other. My observation, however, is that in this age of proliferating Internet resources, the research techniques of general and focused browsing of printed books on library shelves, for both depth penetration and recognition access, tends to be overlooked by researchers who do not understand the limitations of the Web—in both content and search mechanism capabilities—or of computer databases in general. The fact remains, however, that the vast bulk of humanity's memory contained in books does not exist in digitized form, and probably never will (for copyright and preservation reasons); and that Internet-search mechanisms, which require prior specification of keywords and then merely rank rather than categorize the results, cannot provide adequate overviews or conceptual groupings of all material relevant to a topic. Researchers who neglect the direct inspection of the full texts of books arranged in subject groupings on library bookshelves are missing a vast store of information that cannot be efficiently retrieved through any other search techniques.

## Notes

1. David H. Shayt, quoted in the *Washington Post*, July 5, 1992, p. C8. A copy of the illustration Shayt found appears with his remarks.

2. Thomas Mann, "The Principle of Least Effort" and "Bibliography" in *Library Research Models* (Oxford University Press, 1993). The same book provides numerous other examples of information that can be found only by direct examination of subject-categorized books; see pp.17–18.

3. See, for example, the recent remarks of the CEO of Northern Light, as reported by Shirley Duglin Kenney, "Computers in Libraries 2004," *Information Today* 21 (May, 2004): 1, 33:

> "David Seuss, CEO of Northern Light Group, LLC, gave the second day's keynote speech, 'Ten Years into the Web: The Search Problem is Nowhere Near Solved.' . . . 'Web search results decline in quality with the size of the database,' Seuss said. He questioned the wisdom of attempting to include everything, a la Google, which has 6 billion pages indexed. One unintended consequence: 'A multimillion dollar industry has grown up around spamming the Google results list.' / And, he pointed out, *since the focus of the search engine industry in on advertisers rather than end users, the industry cannot be relied on to organize the Web in a way that would be more useful to searchers*" [emphasis added]. The same article quotes Stephen Abram, president-elect of the Canadian Library Association regarding "massive archives" online: "The information professional needs to step in here in order to filter information for users 'so they can drink a glass of water, not drown.'"

4. This example is taken from a useful booklet, *The Library of Congress Shelflist*, edited by Linda K. Hamilton (University Microfilms International, 1979).

5. See Lois Mai Chan, *Library of Congress Subject Headings: Principles and Applications*, 3d ed. (Littleton, Colo: Libraries Unlimited, 1995), p. 230.

# 4

# Subject Headings and Indexes to Journal Articles

A library's online catalog will be useful for identifying books relevant to your topic; it may also cover a few selected Web sites, but it will not index journal, magazine, or newspaper articles. The reason is that the best databases indexing these serial publications are commercially produced, and cannot be merged seamlessly into online catalogs because of copyright and site-license restrictions. (Many libraries make their online catalogs freely searchable on the Internet; they could not do this if the same catalogs included proprietary subscription information.) As a rule, then, you will have to do your searches for journal articles in files other than those that catalog books. The book catalogs may indeed list journal titles and their call numbers; but they will not index their individual articles.

While all databases that index journals can be searched by keywords, some of them can also be searched by subject headings or "descriptors"—the latter being another designation for controlled-vocabulary terms, although descriptors are usually single words or short phrases and do not have the more elaborate phrase structures of *Library of Congress Subject Headings* with subdivisions. Nonetheless, the purpose of descriptors is like that of subject headings: within a given database, they serve as standardized collocation mechanisms. In *Historical Abstracts*, for example, the descriptor **Normandy Landing** serves to round up articles whose titles and abstracts use many different keywords: "D-Day," "Overlord," "Omaha Beach," "The Longest Day," and so on. If you find the right descriptors for your topic, your results will be much better than if you simply type in keywords. Descriptors, like subject headings, solve the problem of variant synonyms for the same concept.

Many databases use no descriptors at all; in those, you do need to think up as many relevant keyword terms and phrases as you can, and you'll essentially use the same keyword "guesses" in all of the uncontrolled files you search. When you search files using descriptors as subject terms, however, you usually have to tailor your searches individually within each database, because it is not a safe assumption that the descriptors are standardized across multiple databases. (In contrast, it generally *is* safe to assume that *book* catalogs will use the same list of *Library of Congress Subject Headings* for their category terms.) There are some exceptions, however: *Historical Abstracts* and *America: History and Life*, the two largest indexes to history journals, use the same descriptors; and many of the family of files known as the Wilson indexes (all produced by the H. W. Wilson Company) tend to use *Library of Congress Subject Headings*, although with more individual variations than would be allowed in book catalogs. The latter indexes include *Readers' Guide to Periodical Literature, Social Sciences Index, Humanities Index, Applied Science and Technology Index,* and many others. The variation exists because journal articles tend to reflect new topics more quickly than books do, and the people who create the indexes for them cannot wait for terms to become standardized in the *LCSH* list, which, being geared to book catalogs, is rather slow to change.

Many databases have individual thesauri, which are lists of approved subject descriptors for use in their own file, for example:

- *Thesaurus of ERIC Descriptors* (Oryx Press, revised irregularly) is the list of terms for the largest index to journal articles and research reports in the field of education.
- *Thesaurus of Psychological Index Terms* (American Psychological Association, revised irregularly) is used for the *Psychological Abstracts, PsycINFO,* and *ClinPSYC* files.
- *Art & Architecture Thesaurus* (Oxford U. Press, irregular) is used by the *Avery Index to Architectural Periodicals* and the *Bibliography of the History of Art.*
- *Thesaurus of Sociological Indexing Terms* (Sociological Abstracts, irregular) is used by *Sociological Abstracts.*
- *Religion Indexes: Thesaurus* (American Theological Library Association, irregular) is used by the *ATLA Religion Database.*

It is worthwhile to inspect each of these lists in its paper copy format, since, as with the *LCSH* red books, you can often spot relevant terms that are alphabetically adjacent to other terms of interest, which are not formally linked by cross-references. Additionally, many of these thesauri have "rotated" lists of terms that will bring to your attention words occupying medial positions within phrases that you might not otherwise think of—for example, in the *ERIC* list, the term **Job Simplification** is filed under "J", but is also rotated to file in the "S" part of the alphabet, so that it will be brought to your attention there, too.

The online display of the descriptor terms within any particular database that uses them may be problematic, however. The reason is that the lists of proper subject words will not be as easily browsable online as they are in their book formats. And, in most cases, searchers using controlled-vocabulary files will not have a printed list of its descriptors handily nearby. Researchers in such situations will generally have to rely on the display mechanisms of the databases themselves. There are interesting variations here: all controlled databases will allow inspection of "descriptor fields," but some files will also have software capable of showing either browse displays (with subdivisions) or "Related Subjects" (which are ranked lists of descriptors culled from records retrieved via keyword searches).

Descriptor fields in online records for journal articles are analogous to the subject tracings that show up on catalog records for books. They show the controlled terms that the indexers have added to the merely transcribed keywords of the article citation itself. Thus, in a standard library catalog, the book with the title *Chechnya: Tombstone of Russian Power* is cataloged with the subject tracing **Chechnia (Russia)—History—Civil War, 1994–**. In the *Historical Abstracts* database covering journal articles, however, an article with the title "Russo-Chechen Conflict, 1800-2000: A Deadly Embrace" is indexed with three different single-word descriptors: **Russia, Chechnya,** and **War**. Note that this important descriptor/subject field does not show up in the database's default "Short Entry Display" of retrieved hits; to see it you must take the extra step of looking individually at the retrieved citations by clicking on the "Display Full Entry" bar at the top of the record (see Figures 4 and 5).

*In other words, just as with subject tracings on book records, you must resist the temptation to simply look at your retrieved records only in the default short-form display in which they initially appear; if you want to use*

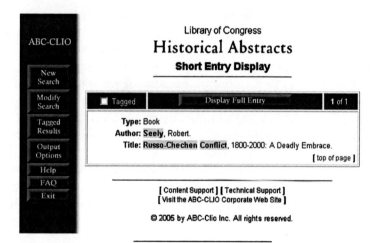

*Fig. 4*

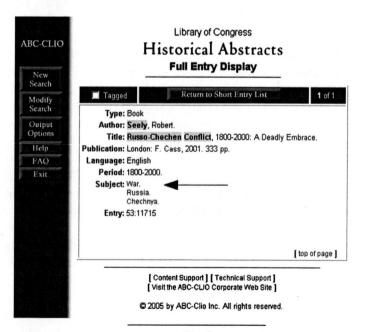

*Fig. 5*

*the journal database efficiently, you have to look at the "full" format of display.* Only the latter will show you the controlled terms that the indexers have assigned, which are the subject words you will need to use for the most systematic retrieval.

Access to descriptor terms via this technique will always be possible, even when you do not have a copy of the database's printed thesaurus at hand. (Be aware of the trade-offs, however: without the printed list, your access to the cross-reference network will be correspondingly diminished, as will your ability to see alphabetically-adjacent relevant terms.)

Note, too, that databases using descriptors as indexing terms often use very broad categories (e.g., **War**). The assumption is that specificity will be achieved by Boolean "AND" combinations of several terms, each serving to limit the scope of the others when all are specified simultaneously. (See the discussion of precoordination vs. postcoordination in Chapter 2.)

## Eureka Databases

The databases available in what is known as the Eureka system provide an additional avenue of tracking descriptors in the absence of a printed thesaurus (that is, beyond the mechanism of displaying them in the "full" record format), through unusually good browse displays. The Eureka system is a subscription service produced by the Research Libraries Group, a nonprofit organization of over 160 universities, national libraries, archives, and historical societies. It includes about two dozen databases in scholarly subject areas; libraries that subscribe to the service can pick and choose which files they wish to pay for, so different libraries will offer different aggregates. None of the Eureka files are freely available on the open Internet.[1] University libraries, however, may make remote access possible to accredited faculty and students with approved I.D. cards. Before discussing the search features of this overall system, let me first list a few of its databases to which libraries often subscribe:

- *RLG Union Catalog.* This is the combined catalog of the 160+ member institutions of the Research Libraries Group, which consists of most of the largest research libraries in the United States, and several foreign national libraries (Great Britain, France, Canada, and

Germany among them). It includes over 130 million records for books, journals, maps, manuscripts, photographs, posters, musical scores, films, sound recordings, and computer files. Each item is linked to a list of the libraries that own it.

- *Anthropology Plus* is an index to over 3,600 journals in anthropology since the late nineteenth century.
- *Avery Index to Architectural Periodicals* indexes over 2,800 periodicals, mainly since the 1930s, but selectively back to the 1860s.
- *Bibliography of the History of Art* indexes over 4,300 periodicals from 1973 forward.
- *Chicano Database* covers about 130 titles from the 1960s forward.
- *English Short Title Catalog* is a listing of all books in the English language from the beginning of printing through the year 1800; it covers almost 470,000 titles. (Many research libraries own a corresponding microfilm set of the books themselves.)
- *FRANCIS* is an index created in France to journals published internationally in the humanities and social sciences. It covers over 4,300 periodicals in a variety of languages from 1984 forward.
- *Handbook of Latin American Studies* is an index to over 2,900 journals since 1990. (Another version of this same index exists as a free Web site, however, covering back to 1936; it can be found at http://memory.loc.gov/hlas.)
- *Index to 19th-Century American Art Periodicals* covers 42 titles published in the 1800s.
- *Inside Information Plus* is an index to current journals, covering 20,000 titles from 1996 forward.

As of this writing, these databases (and several more specialized files not listed here) cannot be searched simultaneously; they have to be used one at a time. They all share a common search software, however.

One of the best features of the Eureka software is that it is capable of showing unusually good browse displays of subject headings with subdivisions, for those files (such as the *RLG Union Catalog*) that use precoordinated strings of terms. Thus, for example, in the *RLG* file, which combines over 160 library catalogs, if you simply type in the subject term "Photography," you will automatically be presented with a menu of its many subject subdivisions, as in Figure 6.

◯ Title  ◯ Author  ◉ Subject  ◯ Keyword  |  ◯ Command Line  |  Advanced Search

`photography`  Search  Clear  Search Tips

**Other Eureka Databases > Home > Subjects**

**Browse** for **Subject photography**
Display records for one Subject by clicking on the Subject or for selected Subjects
by checking the Subjects you want and choosing List, Brief, or Full.

Display records as: List  Brief  Full

≤ ≥

| | | Count | Subjects |
|---|---|---|---|
| 1 | ☐ | 1 | Photographu Artistic - Exhibitions |
| 2 | ☐ | 1 | Photographuy Artistic - Exhibitions |
| 3 | ☐ | 4000+ | **Photography** |
| 4 | ☐ | 3 | Photography - Abstracting And Indexing |
| 5 | ☐ | 19 | Photography - Abstracts |
| 6 | ☐ | 1 | Photography - Abstracts - Indexes |
| 7 | ☐ | 15 | Photography - Abstracts - Periodicals |
| 8 | ☐ | 1 | Photography - Addresses Essays And Lectures |
| 9 | ☐ | 94 | Photography - Addresses Essays Lectures |
| 10 | ☐ | 1 | Photography - Advertisement - History |
| 11 | ☐ | 3 | Photography - Advertising |
| 12 | ☐ | 15 | Photography - Aerial |
| 13 | ☐ | 26 | Photography - Aesthetics |
| 14 | ☐ | 2 | Photography - Aesthetics - Addresses Essays Lectures |
| 15 | ☐ | 2 | Photography - Aesthetics - Congresses |
| 16 | ☐ | 1 | Photography - Aesthetics - Essay - Women |
| 17 | ☐ | 1 | Photography - Aesthetics - Exhibitions |
| 18 | ☐ | 2 | Photography - Aesthetics - 19th20th Centuries |
| 19 | ☐ | 3 | Photography - Aesthetics - 20th Century |
| 20 | ☐ | 1 | Photography - Afghanistan |
| 21 | ☐ | 28 | Photography - Africa |
| 22 | ☐ | 2 | Photography - Africa - Bibliography |
| 23 | ☐ | 1 | Photography - Africa - Catalogs |
| 24 | ☐ | 1 | Photography - Africa - Computer File |
| 25 | ☐ | 22 | Photography - Africa - Exhibitions |
| | | Count | Subjects |

≤ ≥

Display records as: List  Brief  Full

Back to the Top

*Fig. 6*

This is the kind of thing you would see in a well-constructed catalog of an individual library. To have the same capability in searching *scores* of research library catalogs simultaneously is a major advantage: the arrays of subdivisions provide contextual information allowing you to recognize options within your topic that, oftentimes, you would not be able to specify in advance. In this case, as an added bonus, you will be inspecting at the same time the holdings of major libraries around the world, not just those of your local institution. (The *WorldCat* database and the other files in the OCLC system, discussed below, do not have this browse capability of showing subject subdivisions; this is a major difference between the two systems.) The same browse software works not just for subject searches, but for authors and titles, too: all you need to do is type in the first word, and the software will automatically display all of the multi-word strings or phrases (authors' names or titles) starting with that single term. Thus, the system enables you to recognize variant phrasings that would not otherwise have occurred to you. This same display capability can be exploited in all of the Eureka databases. All in all, Eureka offers much more efficient searching than is possible with Web-type engines such as Google or Teoma.

## FirstSearch Databases and WilsonWeb Counterparts

Another, even larger aggregate of commercial databases is provided by the OCLC FirstSearch system. Whereas the Eureka files are more likely to be accessible only in larger libraries, the FirstSearch databases are likely to appear in almost any library, academic or public. This system consists of more than 70 files; individual libraries' subscriptions may vary widely regarding which portions they select. Variant versions of some databases are available: the least expensive simply provide index information to citations; more expensive versions provide abstracts of articles; and some files, at the costliest level, also provide full texts.

The H. W. Wilson Company is the supplier of many files; it is progressively converting its printed index backfiles to online formats, and adding abstracts and full texts to more recent years of coverage. Some variants of some Wilson databases are available from FirstSearch; others are accessible via subscription directly from the Wilson Company, in its WilsonWeb site. The matter of which files are available from which source is subject to change.

Among the more important and more commonly available FirstSearch databases[2] that cover journal articles (and, when available, their WilsonWeb counterparts) are the following:

*WorldCat* combines into one database the catalogs of over 45,000 libraries in eighty-seven countries; it has over 52,000,000 records in 400 languages for all formats of material: books, journals, computer programs, maps, manuscripts, musical scores, newspapers, sound recordings, videotapes, and so on. Like the *RLG Union Catalog* in the Eureka system, it lists library locations for every one of its items. (This file is now freely searchable in Google and Yahoo, and may soon be available through other search engines. The Web search software, however, is not nearly as good as that on the subscription file.)

*Applied Science and Technology Index* covers over 600 journals from 1983 to the present; *Applied Science and Technology Abstracts (ASTA)* adds abstracts since 1994. (*Applied Science & Technology Full Text*, available on WilsonWeb, adds texts starting in 1997.)

The print version of this index shares its earlier years with *Business Periodicals Index/Wilson Business Abstracts* under the title *Industrial Arts Index* (1913–57), which then divided into *Business Periodicals Index* and *Applied Science and Technology Index* (1958– ). It covers aeronautics and space science, artificial intelligence and machine learning, chemistry, computer technology and applications, construction industry, data processing, electricity, energy resources and research, engineering (civil, electrical, mechanical), engineering materials, environmental sciences and waste management, fire and fire prevention, food and food industry, geology, industrial and mechanical arts, machinery, marine technology and oceanography, mathematics, metallurgy, meteorology, petroleum and gas, physics, plastics, product reviews, robotics, telecommunications, textile industry and fabrics, and transportation.

*Art Abstracts* covers over 400 U.S. and foreign art–related journals and museum bulletins, including some in foreign languages, from 1984; it adds abstracts of articles starting in 1994. (*Art Full Text* provides texts from 1997; it is available on WilsonWeb, as is an online backfile, *Art Index Retrospective* covering 1929–1984.)

The print version, *Art Index*, began in 1929. It covers art, antiques, archaeology, architecture and architectural history, art history, city planning, computer graphics, computers in art and architecture, crafts, fine arts, folk art, glassware, graphic arts, industrial design, interior design, jewelry, landscape design, motion pictures, museology, painting, photography, pottery, sculpture, television, textiles, video, and woodwork. Even if your library does not own the retrospective decades of coverage in database form, it will very likely own the print volumes.

*ArticleFirst* covers over 15,000 journals from 1990 to the present.

There is no print counterpart to this database. It indexes a mixture of both popular magazines and scholarly journals in business, humanities, medicine, popular culture, science, social science, and technology.

*ATLA Religion* indexes over 600 periodicals from 1949 to the present, as well as articles appearing in over 15,300 multi-author books; some indexing of journals extends back into the 19thcentury. It is produced by the American Theological Libraries Association.

This database includes the entire run of the corresponding print index; it covers not just religion, theology, and philosophy, but other subjects from the perspective of religion: anthropology, business, history, law, medicine, psychology, and sociology.

*Biography Index* is a Wilson database covering biographical articles from over 2,700 periodicals and over 1,800 books from 1984 forward.

The print version, *Biography Index*, extends back to 1946. This source indexes autobiographies, bibliographies, biographies, book reviews, critical studies, diaries, drama, fiction (biographical novels), interviews, journals, juvenile literature, letters, memoirs, obituaries, pictorial works, and poetry. It provides access by names of individuals and by occupations and subject categories (e.g., Architects, Economists, Handicapped, Murder victims).

*Biological and Agricultural Index* covers over 335 journals from 1983 to the present. (*Biological and Agricultural Index Plus*, the WilsonWeb version, adds full texts starting in 1997.)

The print version of this index started out under the title *Agricultural Index* (1916–63); it assumed its current title in 1964. Coverage includes agricultural chemicals, agricultural economics, agricultural engineering, agronomy, animal husbandry, bacteriology, biochemistry, biology, biotechnology, botany, conservation, cytology, dairying, ecology, entomology, environmental sciences, fishery sciences, food sciences, forestry, genetics, horticulture, limnology, livestock, marine biology, microbiology, mycology, nutrition, pesticides, physiology, plant pathology, poultry, soil science, veterinary medicine, virology, wildlife, and zoology.

***Book Review Digest***, another Wilson index, provides abstracts of reviews from more than 117 journals since 1983.

The print version, under the same title, extends back to 1905. It provides access through controlled subject headings, as well as by authors' names and titles of books. The virtue of this source lies in its providing not just citations to book reviews, but abstracts or short full texts of them.

***Education Index*** covers over 655 sources from 1983 forward; ***Education Abstracts*** adds abstracts starting in 1994. (***Education Full Text***, in Wilson-Web, adds texts from 1996 forward.)

The print version of *Education Index* extends back to 1929. It covers administration and supervision, adult education, athletics, classroom computers, comparative and international education, competency-based education, counseling, educational technology, English-language arts, government funding, health and physical education, higher education, language and linguistics, library and information science, literacy standards, multicultural/ethnic education, personnel service, physical education, prayer in public schools, preschool and elementary education, psychology and mental health, religious education, science and mathematics, secondary education, social sciences, special education, teacher education and evaluation, teacher/parent relations, teaching methods and curriculum, and vocational education.

***ERIC*** indexes more than 2,000 journals, as well as tens of thousands of research reports available on microfiche from 1966 forward.

The database version covers everything in the printed indexes *Resources in Education* and *Current Index to Journals in Education*, both of which started in 1966. Subjects covered are similar to those in *Education Index*. (As of this writing there are plans to include full texts of educational research reports [the ones with "ED" numbers, not the journal articles with "EJ" numbers] online in the near future.)

***Essay and General Literature Index***, a Wilson file, covers essays appearing in book anthologies; it indexes more than 300 volumes and 20 annual or serial publications since 1985.

The print version extends back to 1900. Subjects covered include archaeology, architecture, art, children's literature, classical studies, drama, economics, fiction, film, folklore, history, linguistics, music, poetry, political science, religion, and women's studies.

***General Science Abstracts*** covers over 160 American and British journals and popular magazines from 1984 to the present; it adds abstracts since 1993. (***General Science Full Text*** in WilsonWeb adds article texts starting in 1995.)

The print version of this index began in 1978. Subjects covered include anthropology, astronomy, atmospheric sciences, biological sciences, botany, chemistry, computers, earth sciences, environment and conservation, food and nutrition, genetics, mathematics, medicine and health, microbiology, oceanography, physics, physiology, psychology, pollution biology, and zoology.

***Humanities Abstracts*** covers over 465 scholarly journals from 1984 to the present; it adds abstracts since 1994. (***Humanities & Social Sciences Index Retrospective***, covering the full backfile of the paper copy version from 1907–1984, is available in WilsonWeb, as is ***Humanities Full Text***, 1995 forward.)

The print version of this index started out with the title *International Index* (1907–65), then became *Social Sciences and Humanities Index* (1965–74), after which it split into *Social Sciences Index* (1974– ) and *Humanities Index* (1974– ). It covers archaeology, area studies, art, classical studies, dance, drama, film, folklore, history, journalism and communications, language and literature, literary and political criticism, music, performing arts, philosophy, religion, and theology. (Note that history is covered more in this index than in *Social Sciences Index*.)

***Index to Legal Periodicals and Books*** covers over 925 journals and 1,400 monographs from 1981 to the present. (***Index to Legal Periodicals Full***

*Text*, 1994– , is available in WilsonWeb, as is *Index to Legal Periodicals Retrospective: 1918–1981.*)

The print version *Index to Legal Periodicals* extends back to 1908. It indexes law reviews, bar association journals, yearbooks, and government publications originating in the United States, Puerto Rico, Canada, Great Britain, Ireland, Australia, and New Zealand. Subjects covered include banking, constitutional law, corporate law, court decisions, criminal law, environmental protection, labor law, landlord/tenant decisions, malpractice suits, multinational corporations, public law and politics, real estate law, securities and antitrust legislation, and tax law and estate planning.

*Library Literature* covers over 360 journals, and books and other sources, from 1984 to the present. (*Library Literature & Information Science Full Text* in WilsonWeb adds full texts starting in 1994.)

The print index *Library Literature* extends back to 1921. Coverage includes automation, cataloging, CD-ROMs, censorship, children's literature, circulation procedures, classification, copyright, education in librarianship, employment, government aid, information brokers, Internet software, library associations and conferences, library equipment and supplies, library schools, personnel administration, preservation of materials, public relations, publishing, online searching, and Web sites.

*Medline* indexes over 9,500 journals since 1965.

The print version, *Index Medicus*, started in 1879. Subjects include clinical medicine, dentistry, education, experimental medicine, health services administration, nursing, nutrition, pathology, psychiatry, toxicology, and veterinary medicine.

*MLA International Bibliography*, from the Modern Language Association, indexes over 4,400 journals from 1963 forward.

The print version extends back to 1921. Coverage includes folklore, language, linguistics, and literature.

*PAIS International*, from Public Affairs Information Service, indexes over 3,600 journals since 1972. (*PAIS Archive*, a separate file, covers 1915–1976.)

The print version, *Public Affairs Information Service Bulletin,* covers from 1915 forward; it has a separate fifteen-volume cumulative subject index covering 1915–1974. Coverage includes all public policy issues and all levels of government: administration of justice, agricultural and forestry policy, banking and public and private finance, business and service sectors, culture and religion, demographics, economic conditions and policy, education and education policy, environment and environmental policy, government, health conditions and policy, human rights, international relations, labor conditions and policy, law and ethics, manufacturing and heavy industry, media and information policy, military and defense policy, politics, population groups and policy, science and technology policy, social conditions and policy, telecommunications policy, trade and trade policy, and transportation and transportation policy.

*PsycINFO* covers nearly 2,000 journals from 1872 to the present. *PsychFIRST* covers the most recent four years of 1,300 periodicals.

Coverage includes psychology and psychological aspects of related disciplines: anthropology, business, education, law, linguistics, medicine, nursing, pharmacology, physiology, psychiatry, and sociology.

*Readers' Guide Abstracts* is an index to over 300 general newsstand-type magazines, and many scholarly journals, published in the United States from 1983 forward, with abstracts of articles since 1984. (*Readers' Guide Retrospective* in WilsonWeb covers the years 1890 through 1982; *Readers' Guide Full Text* starts in 1994.)

The printed set of *Readers' Guide to Periodical Literature* (1900– ) and *Nineteenth Century Readers' Guide* (covering the 1890s) will usually be available in libraries that do not have their online counterparts. Subjects covered include aeronautics, African-Americans, aging, antiques, archaeology, arts, business, computers, crafts, current events and news, dance, drama, education, entertainment, fashion, fiction, film and television, fine arts, food and cooking, gardening, health and medicine, history, literature, music, nutrition, photography, politics, popular culture, religion, science, sports, and travel.

*Social Sciences Abstracts* covers over 550 scholarly journals from 1983 to the present; it adds abstracts from 1994. (*Humanities & Social Sciences Index Retrospective* covering the full backfile of the paper copy version from 1907–1984 is available in WilsonWeb; *Social Sciences Full Text* starts in 1995.)

The paper version of this index, like *Humanities Index*, extends back to 1907 under different titles, *International Index* (1907–65), *Social Sciences and Humanities Index* (1964–74), and *Social Sciences Index* (1974– ). It covers anthropology, area studies, community health and medical care, consumer affaires, economics, environmental studies, geography, gerontology, human ecology, international relations, law and criminology, minority studies, nursing, pharmacology, political science, psychiatry, psychology and psychological tests, public administration, public health, social work, sociology, and urban studies.

*Wilson Business Abstracts* covers over 600 journals from 1986 to the present, with abstracts since 1990. (*Wilson Business Full Text*, starting in 1995, is available in WilsonWeb.)

The print version of this index started out as *Industrial Arts Index* (1913–57), then split into *Business Periodicals Index* (1958– ) and *Applied Science and Technology Index* (1958– ), both of which are still published. The *Business* file covers accounting, acquisitions and mergers, advertising and marketing, automation, banking, building and construction, communications, computers, economics, electronics, engineering, finance and investment, government regulations, industrial relations, insurance, international business, investments, labor, management, marketing, occupational safety and health, oil and gas, personnel, public relations, publishing, real estate, retail trade, small business, specific businesses, specific industries, specific trades, and taxation.

*Wilson Select Plus* is a merged file of multiple databases from the Wilson Company. It indexes over 1,600 periodicals from 1994 forward. (The *Wilson OmniFile* in WilsonWeb indexes over 3,000 periodicals from 1982, with full texts from over 1,600 from 1997 forward.)

Subject coverage includes indexing from the *Applied Science & Technology*, *Art*, *Biological & Agricultural*, *Education*, *General Science*, *Humanities*, *Index to Legal Periodicals*, *Library Literature*, *Readers' Guide*, *Social Sciences*, and *Wilson Business* databases.

The software of the FirstSearch databases is basically uniform from one file to the next; but since the files come from several different suppliers, there are variations in which fields are searchable and how they are labeled.

As of this writing, it is possible to search up to three FirstSearch databases —any three of your choosing—simultaneously. While this can be a time-saving feature, it also entails an important drawback. The problem is that any such cross-file searching eliminates one of the most useful features available in FirstSearch; it is the "Related Subjects" display capability of the software.

The Related Subjects feature is not available in all of the FirstSearch files, but it does appear in all of the basic indexes supplied by the Wilson Company, and in some others, too—*provided that you search them one at a time, not in combination*. This search option provides a very helpful bridge to get you from the keywords that you might think of on your own to the best subject headings available within the given database; but it disappears entirely when you search more than one file at a time.

For example, in *General Science Abstracts*, if you type in the keywords "space aliens," (see Figure 7) you will get dozens of hits. At the point of their display, however (Figure 8) , an icon for Related Subjects will appear above the list of citations; if you click on this, you will get a ranked list of the subject headings or descriptors that appear most often attached to the keyword records you have retrieved (Figure 9). In this case, the display steers you to controlled subject headings such as the following:

**Aliens (Visitors from space)**
**Flying saucers**
**Interstellar communication**
**Life on other planets**

If you do the same keyword search in *ReadersGuideAbs*, you will again get a ranked list of subject headings, among them:

**Aliens (Visitors from space)**
**UFOs**
**Roswell (N.M.)**
**SETI (Search for Extraterrestrial Intelligence)**

The same keyword search in *Social Sciences Abstracts* will produce a different list of Related Subjects headings:

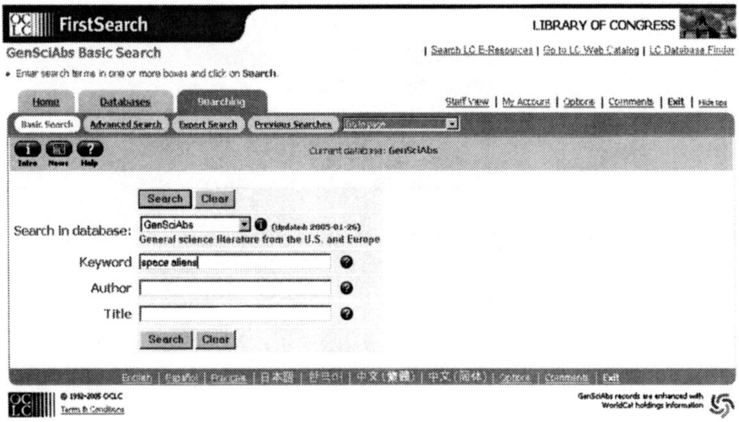

*Fig. 7*

**Autobiographical memory**
**Alien abduction**
**Unidentified flying objects**

A repetition of the search in *Wilson Business Abstracts* produces a list including the following:

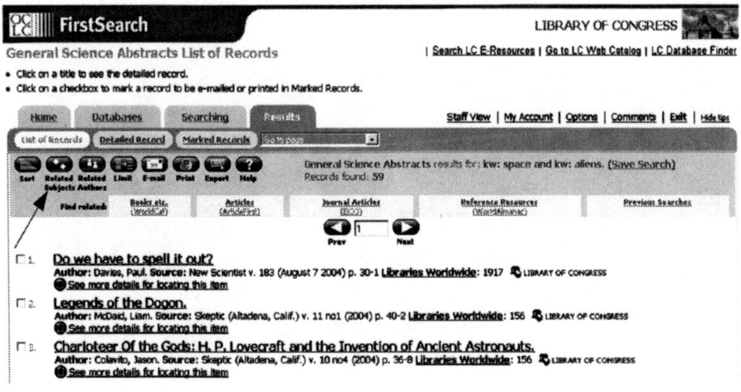

*Fig. 8*

## Find Subject Search Terms

- This screen helps you find the best search terms for subje
- Up to the first 50 records in your results have been examir
- Click on a subject to search for it.
- Select multiple subjects to search for any of those selected

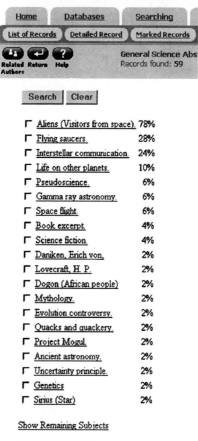

| Home | Databases | Searching |

**List of Records** | **Detailed Record** | **Marked Records**

General Science Abs
Records found: 59

Related Return Help
Authors

Search | Clear

| | | |
|---|---|---|
| ☐ | Aliens (Visitors from space). | 78% |
| ☐ | Flying saucers. | 28% |
| ☐ | Interstellar communication. | 24% |
| ☐ | Life on other planets. | 10% |
| ☐ | Pseudoscience. | 6% |
| ☐ | Gamma ray astronomy. | 6% |
| ☐ | Space flight. | 6% |
| ☐ | Book excerpt. | 4% |
| ☐ | Science fiction. | 4% |
| ☐ | Daniken, Erich von. | 2% |
| ☐ | Lovecraft, H. P. | 2% |
| ☐ | Dogon (African people) | 2% |
| ☐ | Mythology. | 2% |
| ☐ | Evolution controversy. | 2% |
| ☐ | Quacks and quackery. | 2% |
| ☐ | Project Mogul. | 2% |
| ☐ | Ancient astronomy. | 2% |
| ☐ | Uncertainty principle. | 2% |
| ☐ | Genetics | 2% |
| ☐ | Sirius (Star) | 2% |

Show Remaining Subjects

Search | Clear

*Fig. 9*

**Aliens (Extraterrestrials)**
**Aliens (Extraterrestrials) in advertising**
**SETI Institute**

Note the crucial point: the subject headings used in any given database may be significantly different from those used in other files—e.g., **Flying saucers, UFOs, Unidentified flying objects**—even when they come from the same publisher. *Controlled vocabulary subject heading searches must always be tailored to the particular list of subject headings being used by the given database. Cross-file searching blurs distinctions that may be very important for the most effective retrieval.* (The same point can be made, with even greater emphasis, regarding "federated searching" of *any* group of disparate databases at the same time.) Many of the Wilson files tend to use *Library of Congress Subject Headings* where possible, and these phrases often provide good starting points; but you still need to watch for variations of terminology from one database to the next.

The Related Subject indexing capability, in essence, gives you a quick way to look at the subject tracing (or descriptor) fields in all of your retrieved records—in ranked order—without your having to laboriously look at each one individually. It is a very useful aid to systematic subject searching.

Note, however, that FirstSearch databases do not provide subject *browse displays* such as those you can call up in the Eureka system—or in WilsonWeb. A search software allowing you to call up menus of related headings, with displayed subdivisions, can be enormously helpful in enabling you to get a structured overview of research that has already been done on your topic. For example, in *Readers' Guide Retrospective* (in the WilsonWeb system), you can simply type in "Afghanistan" as a heading and immediately see a whole roster of subdivisions, among them the following:

**Afghanistan / Antiquities**
**Afghanistan / Boundaries**
**Afghanistan / Description and travel**
**Afghanistan / Economic Conditions**
**Afghanistan / Economic relations**
**Afghanistan / Foreign relations**
**Afghanistan / Foreign relations / Pakistan**
**Afghanistan / History**

**Afghanistan / History / Soviet invasion, 1979–1989 / Economic aspects**
**Afghanistan / Indigenous peoples**
**Afghanistan / Industries**
**Afghanistan / Maps**
**Afghanistan / Social conditions**
**Afghanistan / Social life and customs**

Again, such menus enable you to recognize aspects of your subject that you may not be able to specify in advance. The presence of this browse capability in WilsonWeb makes searching very efficient; the absence of such browse capability in FirstSearch is noteworthy. On the other hand, FirstSearch has the Related Subject capability lacking in WilsonWeb. Once again, if you are aware of the important trade-offs you can approach the same topic via different search methods, and obtain different results.

Remember that you can *always* use the technique of doing keyword searches initially, then calling up subject heading/descriptor fields to find proper controlled terms (in any database that uses controlled headings to begin with). Beyond this basic procedure, however, be sure to make use of the additional techniques of using *browse displays in Eureka and WilsonWeb databases* and *Related Subjects displays in FirstSearch databases* to be even more efficient.

## EBSCO Host Research Databases

Another set of subscription online files is provided by EBSCO Publishing. The full-text databases from this source, among them *Academic Search Premier* and *MasterFile Premier*, will be discussed in Chapter 5. EBSCO offers a number of individual databases as well, many of which (e.g., *ATLA Religion, MLA International Bibliography, PsycINFO, Art Index Retrospective*) are available via other services, such as FirstSearch or WilsonWeb.

Several features of EBSCO stand out. One is that a subscription to this service can be configured in such a way as to allow an inquirer to search *all* of the subscribed files simultaneously. This is called "federated searching"; it is very useful for quick-and-dirty searches if you have unusually distinctive keywords to start with. However, as illustrated by the "space aliens" example in the FirstSearch system, such crossfile searching can be problematic. *The advice here is simple: be careful not to rely on superficial "seamless" searches of multiple databases simultaneously. You will probably get much better results if you go back and search the most appropriate databases individually, using the "full display" formats to look at the different descriptor terms used by each file.*

Another very important feature is that the default search mode in EBSCO databases is by keyword. My experience in helping students with these files is that they seldom notice that controlled subject terms are also available. At the top of any EBSCO screen is a option bar that is too often overlooked (Figure 10). Note that "Indexes" appears to the right of the "Keyword" radio button. For example, if (in the *Academic Search Premier* database) you click here and then select, from the resultant drop-down menu, "Subject Terms," and type in the controlled term **Monasteries**, you will get, essentially, a *browse display* of subject subdivisions and alphabetically adjacent headings, including the following:

**Monasteries**
**Monasteries & State**
**Monasteries—Bulgaria**
**Monasteries—Guest Accommodations**
**Monasteries, Buddhist**
**Monasteries, Dominican**
**Monastery Gardens**
**Monastic & Religious Life**
**Monastic Libraries**
**Monasticism & Religious Orders**
**Monasticism & Religious Orders—Dietary Rules**
**Monasticism & Religious Orders—Habit**
**Monasticism & Religious Orders for Women**
**Monasticism & Religious Orders, Buddhist**
**Monasticism & Religious Orders, Islamic**

Such menus of related terms are always very useful when you are trying to orient yourself within the literature of any topic.

Within the same area showing the radio buttons for the "Keyword" and "Indexes" (again, Figure 10) there are still other options to look for deliberately;

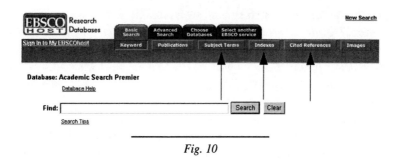

*Fig. 10*

these include "Images" (which will lead to a file of photos and other illustrations and "Cited References" (for searching footnote citations; see Chapter 6).

## Dialog and DataStar Databases

The Dialog company and its sister-service DataStar offer a total of about 1,200 commercial databases. The DataStar collection overlaps with the Dialog files, but does not contain all of them; however, it offers several scores of files not in Dialog, primarily in biomedical and pharmaceutical subject areas. The large number of files makes it impossible to provide a brief overview, but further information can be found at the main Web site (www.dialog.com); click on the "Dialog Bluesheets" or "DataStar Datasheets" links. In general, it can be said that Dialog and DataStar provide especially good coverage of scientific and business information. Databases in social sciences and humanities within the Dialog system include many of the same titles discussed in the FirstSearch and WilsonWeb sections above. A particularly useful feature of the Dialog system is its File 411 *Dialindex* database; typing keywords into this file will give you a ranked listing of the other databases in the system that contain the most hits on those search terms.

## ProQuest Databases

ProQuest is another vendor offering a roster of very useful files, some of which offer access via controlled descriptors, some of which are strictly keyword files. These will be discussed in the section on full-text databases in Chapter 5. To do controlled vocabulary searches in ProQuest databases, look for the "Topic Guide" option near the top of the search screens. Note that those databases within this system having subject descriptors will alert you to their existence via something called the "Smart Search" feature. This is an automatic display that shows up whenever you do a keyword search; in addition to retrieving the articles themselves that have hits on your key-words, you will also see boxes designated "Suggested Topics" which list the controlled vocabulary terms that have been assigned to those articles. These are analogous to the subject tracings that you would find on catalog records for books; they are also comparable to the Related Subjects displays that can be called up in some of the FirstSearch databases. For example, if you type in the keywords "space aliens" (Figure 11) you will get a results screen with a SmartSearch box showing "Suggested Topics" (Figure 12)—these are the controlled descriptors that this database uses in place of "space aliens."

Yet another way to get from the keywords that you think of to the proper headings, within ProQuest databases, is through the search tab "Topic Guide" (Figures 11 and 12) ; if you click here and then type in search terms, the program will lead you directly to the controlled vocabulary descriptors that best correspond to the keywords you've entered.

## Miscellaneous Databases with Controlled Descriptors

Not all subscription databases are "aggregated" by services such as Eureka, FirstSearch, WilsonWeb, or EBSCO; your library may have many individual subscriptions to other files not under these umbrellas. Among the more use-ful of these—and this list is only a sample—are the following:

*America: History and Life.* This database, published by ABC-CLIO, is the best single index for articles on United States and Canadian history, from prehistoric times to the present. It covers over 1,700 journals internation-ally. A corresponding database, *Historical Abstracts*, scans the same 1,700 journals for articles on the history of every other country or region *except* the U.S. and Canada; the period covered here is from Byzantine times to the present. The indexing for both is for articles published from the late 1950s to the present.

ProQuest®

Basic Search | Advanced Search | Topic Guide | Publication Search | Marked List : 0 documents  My Research Summary

Databases selected: Multiple databases...

## Basic Search

Tools: Search Tips   Browse Topics

space aliens                                      [Search] [Clear]

Database:        Multiple databases...            ▼  Select multiple databases
Date range:      All dates                        ▼
Limit results to:  ☐ Full text documents only 📄
                   ☐ Scholarly journals, including peer-reviewed 👆 About

More Search Options

*Fig. 11*

---

ProQuest®

Library of Congress Databases & E-Resources | Help

Basic Search | Advanced Search | Topic Guide | Publication Search | Marked List : 0 documents  My Research Summary

Interface language:
English ▼
New scholarly features & content!

Databases selected: Multiple databases..

**Results** – powered by ProQuest® Smart Search

12204 documents found for: space aliens  [Set up Alert]  About

All sources | 👆 Scholarly Journals | Magazines | Trade Publications | Newspapers | Reference/Reports

☐ Mark / Clear all on page  |  View marked documents            📄 Show only full text           Sort results by: Most recent first ▼

☐ 1. DO'S A DON'TS OF DATING DUMB . THERE'S A CUTOFF . ISN'T THERE?
       Michael Kane. **New York Post**. New York, N.Y.: Jan 23, 2005. p. 095
       📄 Full text                      📄 Abstract

☐ 2. Area sports
       **Bismarck Tribune**. Bismarck, ND: Jan 21, 2005. p. 2
       📄 Full text                      📄 Abstract

☐ 3. A Dogg's Life: [Final Edition]
       Doug Elfman. **Las Vegas Review - Journal**. Las Vegas, Nev: Jan 21, 2005. p. 28.J
       📄 Full text                      📄 Abstract

* * * * * * * * * * * *

☐ 10. Gay-sex bomb? Maybe it wasn't a great idea : Researcher's memo pondered use of strange weapons
       Timothy R. Gaffney. tgaffney@DaytonDailyNews.com. **Dayton Daily News**. Dayton, Ohio: Jan 15, 2005. p. A1
       📄 Full text                      📄 Abstract

1-10 of 12204                                              ‹ First | ‹ Previous  1 2 3 4 5 6 7 8 9 10  Next ›

Want an alert for new results sent by email?  [Set up Alert]  About                          Results per page: 10 ▼
Did you find what you're looking for? If not, revise your search below or try these suggestions:

| Suggested Topics  About          ‹ Previous | Next › | Browse Suggested Publications  About   ‹ Previous | Next › |
|---|---|
| Extraterrestrial life | New Scientist. London |
| Extraterrestrial life AND Space exploration | Astronomy. Milwaukee |
| Extraterrestrial life AND Mars | The Skeptical Inquirer. Buffalo |
| Extraterrestrial life AND Astronomy | Scientific American. New York |

*Fig. 12*

*L'Année Philologique.* Published by the Société Internationale de Bibliographie Classique, this is the best database for Classical Studies; it covers 1,500 periodicals from 1969 forward. (The print version of this index extends back to 1928).

*Iter: Gateway to the Renaissance and Middle Ages.* This file, published by Iter, covers literature dealing with the Middle Ages and Renaissance (400–700); it indexes 730 scholarly journals published since 1842. It also indexes books and collections of essays.

*CPI.Q (Canadidan Periodicals).* Available from the Gale Group, this database indexes over 415 Canadian journals from 1980 forward, many of which are full text searchable.

*IBZ Online: International Bibliography of Periodical Literature.* This is the Web version of the printed index *Internationale Bibliographie der Zeitschriftenliteratur*; the database is available from K. G. Saur Verlag. While the print version began in 1886, the online version (as of this writing) starts in 1983. It indexes 12,000 journals internationally, although with a German emphasis (much as the *FRANCIS* database in Eureka has a French emphasis). It focuses mainly on subjects in the humanities and social sciences. Subject headings are in both German and English.

*Bibliography of Asian Studies.* Published by the Association for Asian Studies, this is the best index to Western-language journals on this area of the world; it indexes over a half-million articles from 1971 forward. (The print version extends back to 1941).

The best printed directory for identifying which subscription databases exist in all subject areas is the annual *Gale Directory of Databases* (Thomson/Gale); it lists both online sources and CD-ROMs (and other formats). Since these files are not freely available on the Web, however, your best bet is to check with the reference librarians of your own library to find out which subscriptions you have access to. When you talk to the librarians, however, do not just ask for particular databases; be sure to tell them the subject or the information that you are ultimately trying to find, and ask them for recommendations on which files to search.

## Cross-Disciplinary Searching

One of most important concepts to remember in doing any kind of subject searching is that any database covers not just the subject indicated in its title but also *other subjects from the perspective of that discipline.* (The same point applies to specialized encyclopedias, discussed in Chapter 1.) For example, articles on **Indians of North America** appear not just in *Humanities Abstracts* and *Social Sciences Abstracts*. The same topic is covered—confining ourselves just to the Wilson databases—in *all* of the following:

*Applied Science & Technology Index/Abstracts*
*Art Index/Abstracts*
*Biological and Agricultural Index*
*Education Index/Abstracts*
*Essay and General Literature Index*
*General Science Index/Abstracts*
*Index to Legal Periodicals and Books*
*Readers' Guide*
*Wilson Business Abstracts*

To press the inquiry into other databases (both controlled and keyword), you could also find material on the same subject (although expressed in different words) in *America: History & Life, Anthropology Plus, Bibliographic Index, Dissertation Abstracts, Fiction Catalog, GPO [Government Printing Office], MLA Bibliography, NewsAbs [Newspaper Abstracts], Nineteenth Century Masterfile, PAIS, Periodicals Contents Index, Short Story Index* (in WilsonWeb), and *Subject Collections* (a printed guide to libraries with special holdings in various subject areas).

You could also use a comparable range of sources on many other subjects (e.g., art, African Americans, communications, computers, developing countries, management, religion, shipwrecks, tea, women, et al.). The point is that virtually no subject is limited to a single index; rather, all the indexes may cover any subject, but from differing perspectives.

Sometimes the cross-disciplinary potential of the various indexes (both online and printed) is surprising, as is shown in the following examples.

- *Business Periodicals Index* picks up an article titled "Case Study of a Decision Analysis: Hamlet's Soliloquy" from the journal *Interface*.
- *Index to Legal Periodicals* cites a law review article "Hamlet and the Law of Homicide," and others such as "Shakespeare and the Law," "The Lady Doth Protest Too Much Methinks: The Use of Figurative Language from Shakespeare's Hamlet in American Case Law," and "Examples Gross as Earth: Hamlet's Inaction and the Problem of Stare Decisis."
- *General Science Index* locates an article "Was Shakespeare a Playwright?" from *Science Digest*.
- *Art Index* picks up such things as an article in an architectural journal on the reconstruction of the Globe Theatre in London, and an *Art News* report on the discovery of a long-lost portrait of the Bard.
- *Biological and Agricultural Index*, too, occasionally covers an article on the Shakespeare Gardens in Central Park in New York; in 1987 it also picked up an essay on the use of a medicinal term in one of the Shakespeare plays.
- A printed issue of *Applied Science & Technology Index* has cross-references under **Art** to **Architecture, Ceramic art,** and **Photography and sculpture**; under **Art and science** there is an article titled "Robots Take the Lead in Ballet." Similarly, a volume of the printed version of *General Science Index* has references under **Art** to the following:

> **Animals in art**
> **Biological illustrations**
> **Birds in art**
> **Computers–Art uses**
> **Fish in art**
> **Paintings**
> **Plants in art**

There are also articles or references under alphabetically adjacent terms:

> **Art, Prehistoric**
> **Art and mathematics**

**Art and mental illness**
**Art and science**

Of course, in most cases a researcher will not need to use the full range of perspectives available on her topic (e.g., even though *Applied Science & Technology Index* does cover **Indians of North America**, the reader may be quite satisfied with what she finds in only *Social Sciences Index* or *Humanities Index*). Nevertheless, it is important for researchers to realize that many indexes outside their own discipline may cover articles within their area of interest. Given that you must "draw the line" somewhere in bringing an inquiry to a close, it is preferable to be able to choose a stopping point while knowing what the options are for continuing, rather than to have to stop simply because you have run out of alternatives.

I would emphasize in particular the complementary nature of literary, historical, and social-sciences databases. For example, if you want information on French writers at the turn of the last century, don't use just the *MLA International Bibliography*—try *Historical Abstracts, FRANCIS, Dissertation Abstracts, Periodicals Contents Index* (covering 1770 to 1995), *IBZ*, and the *Web of Science* (covering journals in all subject areas, not just science). If you are searching in anthropology, don't use just *Anthropology Plus*—try the *MLA Bibliography, Historical Abstracts, Social Sciences Index, Humanities Index, ATLA Religion Index,* and the others just mentioned. The rule is this: *don't confine yourself to only those databases that have your subject words in the title of the database.* Most indexes are much more cross-disciplinary in their subject coverage than their titles indicate.

## Finding Where Journals Are Indexed and Which Journals are Available Electronically

A question that often comes up regarding periodicals is that of finding where a particular journal is indexed—that is, which databases will provide subject (or other) access to the one journal in which you are interested. A related question concerns which titles are available electronically (for keyword searching), and from which online services they are accessible. A number of sources, both online and printed, are useful in supplying this information:

- Three subscription databases will tell you which journals are available in electronic form (and keyword searchable) from your home library's terminals. (Undoubtedly there will be further competition in this area.) The problem here is that many individual vendors or files (e.g. Proquest, *InfoTrac, JSTOR*) now provide overlapping full-text electronic access to some journals; oftentimes, however, different services offer the same journals with different years of coverage. If you want to know which electronic serials are accessible from your library's terminals, check *Serials Solutions, TDNet,* or *EZB: Electronic Journals Library*. Each of them identifies which electronic journals are available through all of your library's *other* database subscriptions, with notes on how many years of coverage are available for each journal within each subscription. Live links to the online journals are provided. Each of these subscription files—if your library offers it at all—will always be tailored to list only the electronic holdings of your own library.
- The FirstSearch system, with its 70+ databases, indexes thousands of journals. A free Web site will tell you which journals are indexed by which databases. It can be found at (www.oclc.org/home/) under Librarian's Toolbox, at "FirstSearch periodical titles." The direct URL, as of this writing, is (www2.oclc.org/oclc/fs/fstitle/).
- The Eureka system, with its 20+ databases, also indexes thousands of journals. As of this writing, it does not have a single, comprehensive list of which journals are covered by which databases (as FirstSearch does); but, if you suspect in advance that a particular journal may be covered by one of its files, you can call up a listing of all titles indexed by any given database. In other words, you have to start with the particular database, and then go to a list of journals indexed in it to see if your desired title is there, rather than (as in FirstSearch) start with a particular journal title and then find out which database covers it. The listings of which Eureka databases index which titles may be found at (www.rlg.org/citadel.html).
- Within the Dialog system, File 414 *Journal Name Finder* tells you which titles are indexed by which databases; the *JOUR* file in DataStar is comparable. These files are not freely available on the Web; however, there is a way to find out which journals are indexed in any of the Dialog databases from an open URL: go to (www.dialog.com),

click on Dialog Bluesheets, and then on Dialog Journal Name. At present, there is no comparable free listing of journals indexed in DataStar.

- *Fulltext Sources Online* (Information Today, semiannual) is a printed directory that lists nearly 20,000 periodicals, newspapers, newsletters, newswires, and TV/radio transcripts that are commercially available online; it also tell which aggregator services provide which years of coverage.

- *Ulrich's Periodicals Directory* (Bowker, annual) is another printed directory (an online subscription version is available); it is the largest roster of which journals and periodicals are currently being published, worldwide. It lists over 170,000 titles (including 30,000 journals available electronically), and for each one it will tell you which indexes or databases, if any, cover that periodical. The same listings provide bibliographic information on the journals, and their publishers' addresses and subscription costs. The titles are categorized in broad subject groupings.

- *Magazines for Libraries*, by Cheryl LaGuardia with Bill Katz and Linda Sternberg Katz (Bowker, revised irregularly), is a selective, annotated guide to the most important journals in all subject areas—the titles to which libraries will try to subscribe. Over 6,950 serials (arranged by broad subject areas) are described; selective indexing information is included.

- *Indexed Periodicals: A Guide to 170 Years of Coverage in 33 Indexing Services* by Joseph Marconi (Pierian Press, 1976) is useful for finding index coverage of old periodicals.

- *Chicorel Index to Abstracting and Indexing Services* (Chicorel Index Series, vols. 11 and 11A; 2d ed., 1978) also provide information on where older periodicals are indexed.

Most journals are not available electronically, and many thousands are simply not indexed anywhere. Nevertheless, you may wish to be aware of the existence of unindexed serials in your field of interest, since the information in them (especially for current awareness purposes) may be of great value. To identify all of the journals being published in any subject area, use *Ulrich's* in combination with *The Standard Periodical Directory* (Oxbridge Communications, annual). The former is the largest list worldwide; the lat-

ter is the largest list of U.S. and Canadian periodicals, also arranged in subject categories. (It no longer provides information on where titles are indexed, however.) Another source, the *Gale Directory of Publications and
Broadcast Media* (Gale, annual) provides an excellent listing of U.S. and
Canadian newspapers, general-circulation magazines, and journals—
arranged, however, by State or Province and city of publication rather than
by subject (although it has a subject index). It also lists radio and television
stations and cable systems.

## Identifying the Best Journals

To find out which periodicals are considered the best or the most important
in their subject fields, use *Magazines for Libraries*. If your library subscribes
to it, the *Journal Citation Reports* database from the Institute for Scientific
Information (ISI) provides ranked listings of which journals in the sciences
and social sciences are most heavily cited by other journals—a good indication of their importance. (As of this writing, humanities journals are not
similarly covered.) The print versions of the ISI's *Science Citation Index,
Social Sciences Citation Index*, and *Arts & Humanities Citation Index* also
provide lists of which journals are indexed by each source, in broad subject
categories. These lists are another way of determining the most important
titles within each category, because those that are selected for indexing, to
begin with, are the journals that are most heavily cited.

## Problems with Abbreviations of Journal Titles

One frustrating problem that researchers often have with older serials is one
that can usually be prevented with a bit of foresight; it concerns abbreviations
of journal titles. Online indexes, as a rule, provide citations with full journal-
title information rather than abbreviations; but many of the older printed
indexes—which are still valuable for years of coverage not available online—
often give citations that do abbreviate the journal titles. Each printed index
will *also* have a separate listing, at the front of the volume, that spells out the
abbreviations into the full wordings of the complete titles—and it is very
important to write down these *full titles rather than abbreviations*. If all you

have is the latter, you may have considerable trouble in trying to look up the title in your library's catalog (e.g., "Educ" can stand for "Education" or "Educational"; "Ann" can be "Annual" or "Annals"; "Com" can be "Community" or "Commerce"; "Res" can be "Resources" or "Research"; "Soc" can be "Society" or "Social"; and so on).[3] The articles or prepositions that are left out can also cause problems. One researcher looking for *Bull. Hist. Med.* assumed that it meant *Bulletin of Historical Medicine.* It doesn't— it's *Bulletin of the History of Medicine.* Minor variations like these greatly complicate computer keyword searches. And these abbreviated forms show up not just in old, printed indexes to journals, but in many a current footnote in contemporary articles.

A wise researcher then, in copying or creating a journal citation, will *never abbreviate the title of a journal. Never.* The few extra seconds it takes to look up the full title (from the list at the front of the index volume) may save you hours of frustration at a later date—especially if you are looking for an article in a library other than the one in which you wrote down the citation.

There are, however, reference sources that will provide full titles of most journal abbreviations; and while they can solve many such problems, they won't solve all of them, so it's better to avoid creating the problem in the first place. The best sources for expanding abbreviated or incomplete journal title references are these:

- *Periodical Title Abbreviations* (Gale, revised irregularly) lists nearly 200,000 abbreviations and their spelled-out forms.
- *Acronyms, Initialisms & Abbreviations Dictionary* (Gale, annual) is a multi-volume set not limited to journal abbreviations, but it does have some that are not in *Periodical Title Abbreviations.*
- *World List of Scientific Periodicals* (Butterworth, 1963 & supplements). This venerable set is still very useful for spelling out the full titles of old scientific journals from around the world published from 1900 to the 1970s.

## The Change in Cataloging Rules for Serials

Another problem with serials is that there was a change in library cataloging rules as of 1981. In current practice, a journal such as *Journal of the*

*American Medical Association* would be entered under just this title. Under the old rules, however, it would appear as *American Medical Association. Journal.* The old rule was the *if the name of the society or organization appears in the title*, then catalog the journal under the first word of the *society name* and not under the first word (e.g., *Journal, Annals, Bulletin, Proceedings,* etc.) of the title. Note the important distinction, however: the old rule applied only if the name of an *organization* appeared in the title; thus a form such as *Journal of Medicine* would file "as is," but a form such as *Journal of the Medicine Society* would file as *Medicine Society. Journal.*

This distinction obviously caused—and continues to cause—much confusion in the search for old periodical titles, especially those that both began and ceased publication during the period before 1981, for it leads many researchers who look under the wrong entry form to conclude that a library does not own a particular serial when it actually is available. Compounding the problem is the fact that many journals that began publication prior to 1981 are still coming in—but if they were cataloged at the time of their initial appearance, the library's record for that title may still be under the old form. This means that you may have to look under the old form of entry (under the organization's name rather than under *Journal* or *Proceedings*) in order to find the call number for *current* years of the journal. The important point is that you need to be aware of the potential problem with this kind of journal title.

Let me take this opportunity to emphasize a more general rule: *if you fail to find any title that your are looking for, under any circumstances, be sure to talk to the reference librarians.* There are many tricks and exceptions to cataloging rules that are not obvious to non-librarians, so always talk to the reference staff whenever you have *any* problem in locating any item you've identified.

## Notes

1. One exception may be the *RedLightGreen* database at www.redlightgreen.org that corresponds to the *RLG Union Catalog*, discussed immediately below. As of this writing, a final business plan for this file has not been determined, which will govern whether it is offered freely or not, and how much of the file will be included.

2. The lists of subjects covered by the various databases are taken directly from promotional literature and Web sites of both the FirstSearch system, at www.oclc.org/firstsearch/datbases/menu.htm, and the H. W. Wilson Company at www.hwwilson.com.

3. A study by John Martin and Alan Gilchrist, *An Evaluation of British Scientific Journals* (ASLIB, 1968), once found that in the *Science Citation Index* citing authors abbreviated *Proceedings of the Institute for Electrical Engineers* twenty-four different ways.

# 5

# *Keyword Searches*

Many of the Eureka, FirstSearch, WilsonWeb, EBSCO Host, and other commercially available databases discussed in the previous chapter, like the library's book catalog, are of the subject-heading or controlled vocabulary type. The advantage of such an encoding method is that it solves the problems of synonym variations (e.g., "death penalty," "capital punishment"), of foreign-language terms ("peine de mort," "pena capitale"), and of relationship connections to other topics (through BT, RT, and NT cross-references, thesaurus menus, online-browse displays, and linkages of headings to classification numbers). The collocation function of controlled vocabularies saves researchers the considerable trouble of having to look under a wide variety of terms for material on one subject, and the associative function provides formal pathways to multiple related topics.

But there are corresponding disadvantages to any controlled vocabulary system. First, the grouping function is sometimes achieved at the expense of blurring fine distinctions between or among subjects. Several years ago, for example, a reader was interested in the idea of "patients actively participating in the therapeutic process"; at the time, this was a new field of interest in the medical profession. The only subject heading available was **Patient compliance**, which is not the same thing as active participation; nonetheless, this term was used to include the latter idea until enough of a literature grew up that a new heading, **Patient participation**, was created to deal with it. Similarly, I once helped a reader who wanted books on "subfractional horsepower electric motors." I showed her the *LCSH* heading **Electric motors, Fractional horsepower**, but she insisted that she wanted only *sub*fractional and not fractional. When we looked at the entries under the **Fractional** heading, however, we saw that it included works on subfractional motors. Evidently the cataloger, seeing no separate heading in the list for "Subfractional," simply chose the closest heading that did exist. This often happens—especially if the cataloger has not noticed any new works being written on the narrower topic. *Distinctions that are important to subject specialists may not be perceived as important by library catalogers, especially at their first appearance. If you wish to retrieve library materials efficiently you must use the terms chosen by the catalogers.* LCSH headings thus often include subject areas that are not precisely indicated by the terminology of the heading. (If there is any doubt about what a heading means or includes, simply call up the list of records cataloged under it; the retrieved titles and note fields will clarify the scope of coverage.)

Second, a controlled vocabulary system cannot get too specific within one subject without losing its categorization function. This is particularly true of a book catalog, which seeks to summarize the contents of works as a whole (rather than indexing individual parts, sections, chapter, or paragraphs). Thus the researcher who was looking for material on the dental identification of Hitler's deputy Martin Bormann could find a general heading on **Bormann, Martin, 1900–1945** but not a precise one on "Bormann, Martin, 1900–1945—Dental identification." Similarly a researcher looking for "effects of wing design on reducing heat stress at supersonic speeds in military aircraft" will not find a controlled vocabulary term that is nearly as precise as he would wish.

Note, however, that many headings sometimes referred to as "orphans"— those that are applied to only one book—are in fact parts of larger categories, in spite of apparently retrieving only one item. For example, the headings **Church work with cowgirls** and **Church work with employed women** (as of this writing) both point to only one book apiece. And yet the collocation function is still served by the appearance of both headings within a larger browse display of alphabetically adjacent related terms:

**Church work with abused women**
**Church work with alcoholics**
**Church work with cowgirls**
**Church work with disaster victims**
**Church work with divorced people**
**Church work with employed women**

**Church work with families**
**Church work with immigrants**
**Church work with people with disabilities**
**Church work with tourists**
**Church work with women**
**Church work with youth**

The full menu of related terms extends to hundreds of such phrases (many with further subdivisions). *LCSH* terms that are "orphans" in terms of their individual coverage are seldom orphans in terms of their relationships.

A third difficulty with controlled vocabularies is that, by nature, they are relatively slow to change. The reason for this is that a cataloger cannot simply insert a new term into the *LCSH* list without integrating it with the existing terms through a web of cross-references that must extend from the new word to others, and to the new word from the others, with BT, RT, or NT relationships defined in both directions. A new term may also have to be linked to particular classification numbers. This intellectual work takes considerable time and effort, so catalogers are cautious about acting too quickly—they find it is often advisable to wait until a new subject has achieved a recognizable "critical mass" in standardizing its own vocabulary. If your topic is in a new field, then, or is of recent development—or if it was a kind of "flash in the pan" academic fad—its terms may not appear in the system. For example, you will find an established heading for **Behaviorism (Psychology)** but not for "neobehavorism" or "behavior*a*lism".

Fourth, the formal cross-references of a controlled vocabulary system may not be adequate to get you from the terms you know to the heading that is acceptable. In *Psychological Abstracts*, for instance, articles on the psychological problems of hostages were indexed for many years under the term **Crime victims**. A cross-reference from "Hostages" to this heading was introduced only in 1982; and **Hostages** did not become a descriptor in its own right until 1988.

In spite of such disadvantages, however, researchers must also keep clearly in mind the fundamental advantages of controlled vocabulary sources. Just to stay with online catalogs using the *Library of Congress Subject Headings* system for a moment, keep in mind the following:

First, *LCSH* terms round up not just unpredictable keyword-variant titles in English (see the **Capital punishment** and **Cockney** examples in Chapter 2);

the same headings retrieve all of the library's foreign-language book records. Lack of English-language subject control of foreign works would decimate the research potential of most major research libraries and deny to English-speaking (as well as other) scholars the knowledge that the non-English works exist; the same lack would remove from researchers' ken any awareness of foreign books' bibliographies (which may cite English works) or illustrations. (This will be a major disadvantage of Google Print.)

Second, the *LCSH* headings in the catalog do much more than just round up title keywords that are alphabetically scattered or variant; they also round up, in the catalog, *classification numbers* for works on the same topic that are widely scattered in the bookstacks. (See the examples on **Indians of North America**, **Drinking and traffic accidents**, and **Drug abuse** in Chapter 3.) The use of the classification scheme in the stacks requires an index that tells researchers which areas to browse or scan; and the subject headings in the catalog serve as this index.

Third, a catalog structured by *LCSH* brings to researchers' attention a wide variety of *types* or *genres* of reference sources that they would never think to specify in advance. (See Chapter 15.)

The aggregate of such features produces the characteristic of *plenitude* in a controlled catalog: an ability to show users, in a systematic manner, many more relevant options for researching their topics than they are capable of articulating beforehand. Plenitude is entirely lost in a keyword system, which will retrieve only the terms that are precisely specified.

When all is said and done, keyword searching necessarily entails the problem of the *unpredictability* of the many variant ways the same subject can be expressed, both within a single language ("capital punishment," "death penalty) and across multiple languages ("peine de mort," "pena capitale"). And no software algorithm will solve this problem when it is confined to dealing with only the actual words that it can retrieve from within the given documents (or citations or abstracts) themselves. (Remember that controlled terms, unlike keywords, are not merely *transcribed from* existing documents; they are *added to* them by thinking human catalogers or indexers, to create retrievable points of commonality that would otherwise not be present.)

Nonetheless, just as with controlled headings, there are positive advantages to keyword searching as well as drawbacks. The major advantage shows up precisely in the area where subject headings don't work well. The fact is, there will always be many topics that simply fall between the cracks of any subject heading or descriptor system. No thesaurus has a term for "managing sociotechnical change," for example; but a keyword search of the exact word "sociotechnical" combined with "manag\*" or "plan\*" (the asterisk being a truncation symbol) will turn up multiple hits, in several databases, that are directly relevant. The basic trade-off is between *precision* on the one hand, and *predictability, categorization,* and *plenitude* on the other.

There are now many thousands of online databases (and CD-ROMs) that enable researchers to do keyword inquiries. All of the Eureka, FirstSearch, and WilsonWeb files discussed in the previous chapter allow it (oftentimes in addition to controlled searching). There are a number of important subscription databases, however, that are *only* keyword searchable, having no controlled terms at all. We will consider, first, databases that provide indexing information (some of it extending to the level of abstracts), followed by full-text databases.

## Index/Abstract-Level Keyword Databases and Printed Sources

Among the more important of these are the following:

*Web of Science.* This file, available from the Institute for Scientific Information (ISI) in Philadelphia (a part of Thomson ISI), indexes over 8,500 journals internationally in all fields of the hard sciences, the social sciences, and the arts and humanities. (See Chapters 6 and 7 for a more extensive discussion of this database.) Journals selected for indexing are chosen on the basis of how frequently they are cited by articles appearing in other journals, and so this one source covers "the cream of the crop" of academic journals in all fields remarkably well. Libraries that subscribe to it have many options in how they may configure their access: some subscribers choose only the *Science* or *Social Science* portions; some chose only recent years of coverage rather than the full backfiles. (Be sure to check the extent of your own library's coverage before you search.) The indexing extends to citations and abstracts, not full texts. A particularly useful feature is that the titles of indexed journal articles written in foreign languages are translated into English for keyword searching (although the original language of the article will always be clearly specified). In other words, you can do your searches *only* with English-language terms, although your results may then include citations to articles in languages other than English. This same database allows you to determine which journal articles cite, in their footnotes, any source that you've already identified. Note an important limitation: since the criterion of importance for coverage is determined by the numbers (and weightings) of footnote citations, this index focuses only on journals that *have* footnotes to begin with—it does not "see" important news or commentary magazines and journals whose articles lack this scholarly apparatus. Many of the more popular and influential newsstand-type publications are of this "non-footnote" type, and so are not indexed here. Boolean combinations, set nesting with parentheses, and word truncation are possible.

*Periodicals Contents Index (PCI).*    This database, available from Chadwyck-Healey Products (a ProQuest subsidiary), indexes citations to articles in over 4,500 journals from 1770 to 1995. Coverage is international in English, French, German, Spanish, Italian, and most other Western languages. Unlike the *Web of Science*, the *PCI* does not translate foreign-language article titles; as a practical matter, this means that you have to think up keyword synonyms and phrase variations in all of the languages in which you want retrieval. Searches can be limited by language, by years of publication, and by broad subject categories of journals. Boolean combinations and word truncations are allowed. Coverage is weak in scientific areas but strong in social sciences and humanities. (One historian of slavery, for example, found here an article with specific data on the cost of transporting a slave from Baltimore to New Orleans; she hadn't found such information elsewhere because the article appeared in an obscure economics journal rather than in a history journal. But *PCI* covers both fields simultaneously.) Most databases cover only recent decades of publication; the fact that *PCI* covers so many journals internationally over a span of more than two centuries makes it an extremely valuable resource.

*19th Century Masterfile (NCM).*    This database, from Paratext, includes a complete computerized version of a venerable printed source, *Poole's Index to Periodical Literature* (1802–1906), which covers nearly 500 American and English periodicals, as well as several other indexes to 19th century magazines, newspapers, and government publications (both American and British). Among these are *A.L.A. Index to General Literature* (an index to book contents), *A.L.A. Portrait* Index (listing citations to 40,000 portraits of individuals before 1906), *Congressional Record 1789–1925* (including *Annals of Congress, Register of Debates,* and *Congressional Globe*), *Jones and Chapman's Index to Legal Periodical Literature* (1786–1922), *The Psychological Index* (1894–1905 and 1906–1935), *New York Times Index* (1863–1905), *New York Daily Tribune Index* (1875–1906), *Palmer's Index to the Times (London)* (1880–1890), *Harper's Magazine Index* (1850–1892), *Library Journal Index* (1876–1897), and Benjamin Perley Poore's *Descriptive Catalogue of the Government Publications of the United States* (1774–1881). The publisher of the database keeps looking to add other sources. One can, in effect, do Boolean and word truncation searches through a menu of search qualifiers ("singular and plural forms," "word variants," "exact phrase," "all of the words," "any of the words").

**Index to Pre-1900 English Language Canadian Cultural and Literary Magazines.** As of this writing, this database is available only as a CD-ROM, from Dataware Technologies in Canada, and not in a Web version. It covers 190 early Canadian periodicals.

**Dissertation Abstracts Online or Digital Dissertations.** Available from ProQuest in the FirstSearch system (and elsewhere), these databases provide the best access to American doctoral dissertations. *Dissertation Abstracts* covers over 1,560,000 of them from 1861 to the present. From 1980 forward, abstracts can be searched; prior to that, only titles are searchable for subject content. Master's theses are abstracted from 1988 forward. Dissertations are a true gold mine of information in all subject areas—as with the *Web of Science* and *Periodicals Contents Index*, give this file a try no matter what topic you are researching. There are controlled headings at *very* broad levels (e.g., **Law; History; United States; Education, Higher; Sociology, General; Literature, Modern; Literature, American; Women's Studies**; and so on), but these are useful only in combination with uncontrolled keywords. Remember that you must play around with synonyms in this database, without the help of any cross-references (e.g., "cattle industry" in addition to "beef industry"). Boolean combination and word truncation are possible. *Digital Dissertations* adds full texts of dissertations, *but only from 1997 forward.* (Note that the Library of Congress, alone of all libraries in the world, owns a full set of American doctoral dissertations—

but not master's theses—on microfilm and microfiche. Foreign doctoral dissertations are systematically collected, and made available via interlibrary loan, by the Center for Research Libraries in Chicago. Some Canadian theses are available full text online at www.collectionscanada.ca/thesescanada.)

Three printed keyword indexes for which there are no online equivalents are occasionally useful for searching older journals; all were published by the now-defunct Carollton Press, Inc. They are:

- *Combined Retrospective Index to Journals in History 1838–1974* (11 vols.)
- *Combined Retrospective Index to Journals in Political Science 1866–1874* (8 vols.)
- *Combined Retrospective Index to Journals in Sociology 1895–1978* (6 vols.)

Two good sources for identifying printed indexes to older journals, for which there are no database equivalents, are these:

- Bonnie R. Nelson's *A Guide to Published Library Catalogs* (Scarecrow Press, 1982). Many research libraries over the years have specialized in collecting resources in particular subject areas; oftentimes these libraries published printed catalogs of their holdings, and sometimes these old catalogs included entries not just for books, but for individual journal articles within the subject areas of the catalog. For example, before the appearance of the H. W. Wilson Company's *Art Index* (covering articles from 1929 forward), the Metropolitan Museum of Art in New York did extensive indexing of art periodicals, which can be found in its published *Library Catalog of the Metropolitan Museum of Art* (48 vols., 2nd ed.; G. K. Hall, 1980). Nelson's book identifies dozens of such catalogs in all subject areas.
- Robert Balay's *Early Periodical Indexes: Bibliographies and Indexes of Literature Published in Periodicals before 1900* (Scarecrow, 2000). This is an annotated list of about 400 indexes to old journal articles, categorized by broad subject areas with a more detailed index by specific topics.

These guides to old indexes are often useful when sources like *Readers' Guide to Periodical Literature, Periodicals Contents Index,* or *19th Century Masterfile* don't turn up the information you need.

## Full-Text Databases

The number of databases offering full-text search capability of journals, newspapers, and books is growing rapidly. Nonetheless, it is important to remember that the vast majority of books and journals in any research library is not digitized at all, and that significant barriers of costs, copyright restrictions, and preservation problems will continue to prevent "everything" from being freely available online. Format difficulties are also noteworthy: most readers simply do not wish to read lengthy texts on computer screens. As a result, e-book databases are having a much harder time competing in the marketplace than are those files offering shorter, article-length texts. Your best access—not just physical, but cognitive as well—to large collections of significant *books* will always be within the walls of research libraries.

The best full-text databases allow you to search keywords anywhere in their actual articles (not just in citations or abstracts). While the default setting of most such sources—ProQuest, EBSCO, *InfoTrac,* etc.—is for keyword rather than controlled-vocabulary searching, it is important to note that most of these online files *also* enable you to search by controlled terms. My experience in helping readers, however, is that most people do not even notice this option; they simply accept the default setting to keyword searching and then try to deal with whatever jumble of results they wind up with. Of course there are times when you will want to find exact words or phrases within the actual texts of journal or newspaper articles, and for this purpose— let's call it **Purpose A**—the many keyword full-text databases are wonderful. But many researchers who use these databases actually have something different in mind, although they do not make the distinction consciously or articulately: they actually wish to find as many relevant articles as they can identify on their topic—whether or not the articles use only the exact keywords the searchers can think of—and then read (or print/download) the articles immediately, online. For *this* purpose—which we'll call **Purpose B**—the keyword text-search capability is actually of secondary importance; when the goal is that of getting an overview of all relevant articles, rather than finding a specific phrase, researchers really ought to *start* with the controlled vocabulary search option, and *then* try keyword searching if the controlled inquiries do not provide good results. In other words, most of the searchers who use these full-text databases are not using them efficiently; they are, in effect, doing keyword searching and completely ignoring searches via controlled descriptor fields. I strongly advise readers to clearly understand the difference—it will change the way you search and eliminate a great deal of clutter in your retrieval results.

There is an additional danger for quality research lurking in full-text databases: unless you are careful, the convenience factor of having instant access to something—even *anything*—can outweigh the fact that better quality resources may well be available only in printed formats. As only one of many examples I could cite, I once helped a graduate student who wanted a history of the Royal Geographical Society, based in London—and who insisted on trying to find the information in ProQuest, which he chose simply because it was the largest full-text database he knew about. When he ignored my suggestions for alternatives of higher quality and relevance—simply because they were not online—I quickly searched, first, the *Reference Universe* database, which indexed an article on the Society in a printed encyclopedia immediately available in the library's reference collection; I then searched the online catalog under the Society's name as a subject. This produced the catalog record for Ian Cameron's *To the Farthest Ends of the Earth: 150 Years of World Exploration by the Royal Geographical Society* (Dutton, 1980), a 288-page history of the organization. Only when I put the encyclopedia article itself under the researcher's nose, and the citation and call number information for the printed history, did he finally realize he would be better off with sources other than the convenient, but very limited, full-text database of journal articles that he was using.

There is an important line here that separates the professionals from the amateurs among researchers: when you've reached the point of internalizing the lessons of this book, and know *yourself* when (and where and how) to look beyond the simple convenience of online resources—without the nagging of a reference librarian!—then you've started to catch on to the value of real libraries. Crossing this line involves changing the way you initially formulate your questions. Rather than ask, "What can I get immediately online?," you'll find yourself asking, "What path(s) will lead me most efficiently to the best information, whether online or not?" My experience is that researchers who opt immediately for an online "quick fix" actually waste more time plowing through masses of superficial and irrelevant keyword-retrieval results than those who use the more formal avenues of access to printed library resources. (The trick is to be as aware of what you are not getting, as well as what you are getting, from online resources; and that requires a larger overview of your options, which I hope this book will provide.)

That said, there are times when the use of full-text databases is indeed the best way to proceed. It goes without saying that the database-vendor marketplace is subject to constant change. (This fact, in itself, makes commercial sources unreliable for long-term preservation of digitized offerings; but this concern is, at present, more relevant for library administrators than for users of libraries. It will become more of a concern for the latter group as previously available resources start to vanish.) As of this writing, several full-text services are very useful, among them the following:

## ProQuest Databases

This company offers an aggregation of many different databases, most of which provide full texts of journal articles, fully keyword searchable. The configurations of what is covered by a particular library's subscription can vary from institution to institution, because several subfiles may or may not be selected locally. In other words, it doesn't mean much to say, simply, that you "have access to ProQuest"—the real question is "which of the many *components* of ProQuest are included in your local subscription?" Among the database options in ProQuest are the following:

- *ABI/INFORM Global* is an index to about 1,800 business publications internationally with coverage from 1971 forward. Full-text articles from over 700 periodicals are accessible.
- *American Periodicals Series* is a collection of full texts of 1,100 American periodicals published between 1740 and 1900.
- *Health & Medical Complete* indexes over 380 source publications on thousands of medical topics, with full-text articles from more than 300 of them. Coverage is from 1987 forward.

- *ProQuest Education Journals* provides full texts of over 400 titles, dating from either 1988, 1991, or 1992, depending on the particular journals. Coverage includes material on primary, secondary, and higher education and specialized topics.
- *ProQuest Medical Library* combines *Medline* indexing with full images of over 200 important medical journals.
- *ProQuest Newspapers* provides full-text coverage of over 300 U.S. and international newspapers. A separate subscription, *ProQuest Historical Newspapers*, contains complete runs of *The New York Times* (back to 1851), *The Wall Street Journal* (back to 1889), and *The Washington Post* (back to 1877); as of this writing full backfiles of the *Los Angeles Times*, *The Christian Science Monitor*, and *The Chicago Tribune* are now also being digitized.
- *ProQuest Religion* provides full-text coverage of over 90 religion publications from 1986 or the early 1990s.
- *ProQuest Science Journals* provides full-text coverage of over 260 titles from roughly the mid- or late 1990s forward. (Some titles go back to the late 1980s.)
- *ProQuest Research Library* combines coverage of all of the subfiles into one database.

ProQuest also offers some of the H. W. Wilson Company databases, *Wilson Applied Science & Technology Abstracts Plus Text* and *Wilson Education Abstracts Plus Text* among them. (Note, again, that the same databases can be offered by different vendors. Since it is impossible for any book to tell you which ones are available from which sources in your own local library, be sure to talk to the local reference librarians.)

## EBSCO Host Research Databases

We saw in Chapter 4 that EBSCO offers some databases providing bibliographic citations without full texts; it also offers some large text files:

- *Academic Search Premier.* This is one of the largest scholarly, multidisciplinary full-text databases. It indexes over 8,000 academic journals, with full texts of 4,600 of them keyword searchable. Indexing extends, for some titles, as far back as 1965. The online description of this file says it offers "information in nearly every area of academic study including: social sciences, humanities, education, computer sciences, engineering, physics, chemistry, language & linguistics, arts & literature, medical sciences, ethnic studies, and many more."

- *MasterFILE Premier.* This database is designed for public libraries; it indexes over 2,700 periodicals and provides full texts of over 2,000. Its online descriptions says that "This database features: 5,000 full text *Magill Book Reviews*, 316 reference and travel books including *World Almanac & Book of Facts* . . .; full text [of] 88,000 biographies, 83,500 full text primary source documents, *American Heritage Dictionary, 4th Edition* and an image collection of 107,000 photos, maps and flags."

- *Military & Government Collection.* According to its online description, this database indexes about 500 periodicals and provides full texts of about 400 of them.

Coverage of all of these resources will increase in the future. As noted in Chapter 4, EBSCO offers the possibility of searching all of its files and subfiles simultaneously—with the qualification, again, that different libraries will have differently configured subscriptions. In spite of the apparent convenience of this crossfile or federated search capability, however, remember that it is more prudent to search the individual components separately, using the "Subjects" option for controlled terms within each, if you have **Purpose B** rather than **Purpose A** in mind.

## *InfoTrac* Databases

There are many of these, all available from Thomson/Gale. The two most important ones for full-text searching, as of this writing, are:

- *InfoTrac OneFile.* This is a huge database indexing 8,000 academic journals, general magazines, newspapers, and newswires from 1980 to the present, with more than 4,200 of the titles available in full text. It does not cover nearly as many newspapers as ProQuest, however; nor does it provide full texts of newspapers—only indexing information for *The New York Times, The Wall Street Journal, The Washington Post,* the *Los Angeles Times,* and *Christian Science Monitor.* It does, however, cover about 90 wire services not available in ProQuest. It covers topics across the board: agriculture, anthropology, arts, business and industry, communications, economics, engineering, health care, history, law, literature, political science, psychology, religion, sciences, technology, and others.

- *Expanded Academic ASAP* is an InfoTrac database focusing on academic journals; it indexes 3,500 of them and provides full texts of 1,900 from 1980 to the present.

As with the other full-text sources discussed above, these databases offer a "Subject Guide" option that will enable you to get beyond keywords into controlled vocabulary searching.

## *JSTOR*

This file (pronounced "jay-store," short for "journal storage") is an online collection of full backfiles of over 350 academic journals; hundreds more titles will be added in the future. In each case, the vendor goes back to Volume 1, Number 1 of each title and digitizes the entire run of the journal, up to about the mid-1990s. In other words, the virtue of this database is its retrospective coverage: some of the full-text journals here go all the way back to the 1870s and 1880s. There are a number of potentially separate "core" collections to which libraries can subscribe, including Business, Ecology & Botany, General Science, Language & Literature, Mathematics & Statistics, and Music; again, check with your local reference librarians to see what are the configurations of your own library's subscription.

## *Project Muse*

This is a file of about 250 relatively current high quality academic journals, from 40 publishers, generally from the mid- or late 1990s, or early 2000s, forward.

## *LexisNexis*

This huge database started began by offering full texts of legal documents, statutes, court decisions, and so on, and has greatly expanded into general research areas, although retaining particular strengths in the subject areas of law, current events, and public policy. The fullest version of this file provides full texts of over 36,000 sources, including about 3,000 newspapers and 8,700 journals from (roughly) 1975 forward, including newspapers, magazines, newsletters, transcripts of news broadcasts, and wire services. Various subfile sections are available for libraries that wish to tailor their subscriptions; the following descriptions are taken largely from the Web site's own explanatory matter:

- *LexisNexis Academic Service* is a much smaller subfile of the larger system; it is frequently accessible at low cost through academic libraries—and it is, frankly, a way in which the company "hooks" students into using the product. It can be configured to include both portions of *Lexis* (full texts of federal and state case law, legislation, law reviews, *Shepard's Citations* for all U. S. Supreme Court cases back to 1789, and specialty areas of law) and *Nexis* (non-legal sources including full texts of over 7,000 newspapers, newsletters, business magazines, trade journals, wire services, and other sources. *Nexis* includes many sub-sections in particular subject areas, such as Accounting, Company Information, Energy, Entertainment, Marketing and Advertising, Medical, and People (biographical sources), each covering an extensive array of full-text material. The major point to remember, however, is that *LexisNexis Academic* provides only about one-fourth of the materials available in a full *LexisNexis* subscription.
- *LexisNexis Country Analysis* provides economic, business, and political risk information on 190 countries; over 300,000 full-text documents are searchable.
- *LexisNexis Company and Financial* provides extensive current data on twenty million U.S. and 15 million foreign companies.
- *LexisNexis Congressional* includes the *CIS Congressional Index* (1970– ) and *CIS Legislative Histories* (1984– ), as well as full texts of bills, committee reports and prints, many hearings, the *Federal*

*Register* (1980– ), and information on floor votes and campaign contributions.

- **LexisNexis Environmental** searches full texts of journals, conference papers, federal and state government reports, major newspapers, consumer and trade magazines, newsletters, law reviews, environmental codes, case law, and regulatory agency decisions.
- **LexisNexis Government Periodicals Index** indexes over 200 U.S. federal government magazines and periodicals from a wide variety of agencies and departments.
- **LexisNexis Primary Sources in African American History** is a full-text collection of manuscripts, court cases, statutes, speeches, autobiographies, photographs and images, and government documents; it also includes over 1,100 scholarly articles.
- **LexisNexis Primary Sources in U.S. Presidential History** is a full-text collection of manuscripts, speeches, government documents, photographs and images, and over 500 biographical reference articles.
- **LexisNexis Primary Sources in American Women's History** is a full-text collection of manuscripts, statutes, court cases, autobiographies, government documents, photographs and images, and hundreds of scholarly articles.
- **LexisNexis Statistical** is an online cumulation of three printed indexes to statistical publications, *American Statistics Index* (covering U.S. federal publications), *Statistical Reference Index* (covering non-federal U.S. publications from State, local, business, nonprofit, and pollster organizations), and *Index to International Statistics* (covering U.N. and other intergovernmental agencies' publications).

Searches in this system read multi-word terms as phrases, by default; but you can also use quotation marks to define phrase strings. The asterisk (*) is used for single-letter replacement; the exclamation point (!) is used for general truncation. You can also use parentheses in combining terms, and proximity operators. (A search on "life w/3 insurance" would find the two words either adjacent, or within three words of each other, in any order.)

Due to the complexity of the *LexisNexis* universe of sources, and the possibility of different libraries subscribing to different segments of it, it is particularly important either to ask librarians for help, or to attend free training sessions offered by the company's own staff.

## Web Sites on the Open Internet

The purpose of the present book is to increase your understanding and use of important research resources that are not freely available on the Web—i.e., sources which cannot be freely tapped into from anywhere, at anytime, by anybody, but which are indeed freely available within the walls of research libraries. It is the *where* restriction—limitation of access to users in a particular place—that enables online publishers and vendors to make a profit from their databases while simultaneously enabling libraries to make expensive copyrighted resources freely available to anyone who comes in the door. As mentioned in this book's Preface, it is precisely this imposition of the *where* restriction on access that allows research libraries to circumvent the *what* and *who* barriers of cyberspace. Libraries need not limit *what* they can make freely viewable, within their walls, to only copyright-free resources; nor must libraries limit *who* can freely view copyrighted resources within their reading rooms. (Those libraries that make proprietary databases searchable by remote users, in loosening the *where* restriction, necessarily impose a *who* restriction instead, confining the offsite access only to taxpayers in the libraries' own regions, or to students paying local tuition fees. Such payments cannot be covered by taxes at the national level.[1])

Although the primary focus of this book, then, is not on the open Internet, it remains true that the Net itself is one of the important resources that research libraries offer to scholars—even though, of course, such access is not confined to terminals within library walls. Some general thoughts about the open Internet—those segments that can indeed be freely tapped into from anywhere, at anytime, by anybody—are therefore appropriate here.

It is useful to think of the Net as having a three-part structure, consisting of: 1) search engines, 2) subject directories, and 3) invisible Web sites.

**Search engines** are the mechanisms by which resources on the Net can be found via keyword searches. Among the more popular, and useful, engines are Google, Teoma, AllTheWeb, and AltaVista. Some of them, particularly Google and Teoma, have elaborate algorithms for ranking the keywords that are retrieved, to lessen the jumble of results in an attempt to display the most "relevant" items first. These ranking mechanisms can be very clever: words can be weighted in proportion to their frequency within texts, or according to their appearance in initial paragraphs or topic sentences within documents, or according to their italicization or use in titles or subdivision designations, or according to the number pages linking to an initial page on which the words appear—with further weights assigned according to the quality of the linking pages themselves—and so on. The crucial point to remember about Web keyword searching, however—a point that also applies to some library catalog keyword capabilities—is that *ranking* is not at all the same thing as *categorizing*. The latter function involves the creation of subject groupings that transcend the actual keywords used by any particular item within the category; and categories of conceptually related sources are usually much more informative than mere ranked lists of items that simply have certain keywords in common.

The properties of the various search engines are subject to continual modification; for this reason it is highly advisable to examine—and re-examine a few times every year—any of several excellent comparative charts of their different capabilities:

- "Search Engine Watch" (www.searchenginewatch.com); search within the site for its "Search Features Chart".
- "Search Engine Showdown" at www.notess.com/search/features/
- "How to Choose a Search Engine or Directory" at http://library. albany.edu/internet/choose.html

The URL addresses of these sites are themselves changeable; if you search their title phrases (in quotation marks above), however, in Google they should still appear.

One tip in particular to keep in mind is that AltaVista.com and AllTheWeb.com allow not just conventional Boolean searches with AND, OR, and NOT, but also word proximity searches with the operator NEAR; both also allow nested searches using parentheses. AltaVista allows word truncation (with the * symbol), which most of the other engines do not. (These features are often useful in trying to pin down a quotation whose exact phrasing is not clearly remembered.)

It is also advisable to check any engine's "advanced search" option instead of its default-screen simple search. Advanced options often include the possibility of limiting by date or file type (for example, ".gov" or ".edu"—which often serve as rough filters against much of the garbage of ".com").

Other tips: use different engines for the same search (they will produce different results), and change the word order of your inquiries (this can change the way they are weighted).

**Subject directories** are human-compiled listings of Web or Net resources. Yahoo, About.com, and Google ("Directory" tab on home page) are examples. These sites provided *categories* of resources that cannot be assembled by raw keyword inquiries in search engines. For example, if you want a listing of Great Books freely available online, the first screen of Yahoo will provide a menu of categories, among them "Arts & Humanities"; clicking on this option will provide successively narrower options:

Arts & Humanities
  Humanities
    Literature
      Electronic Literature
        Web Directories
          Great Books and Classics
          Great Books Index
          On-Line Books Page
          Texts and Books Online
          Western European Literature

Many of the resultant sites would be missed by a simple keyword search on "great books" in any of the search engines.

Most of these directories have an internal search box that allows you to bypass the hierarchical browsing steps, to find keywords directly within the category level you've chosen.

A useful tip here is that three subject directories are particularly useful to reference librarians:

- "Librarians' Index to the Internet": www.lii.org
- "Refdesk.com": www.refdesk.com; scroll down to "Refdesk Subject Categories"
- "Library Spot" http://libraryspot.com

Students who routinely search Google, and nothing else, may find themselves pleasantly surprised at the greater search efficiency that is often possible—depending on the nature of the inquiry—from subject directories.

**Invisible Web sites** are freely accessible pages, the contents of which are not efficiently indexed—or indexed at all—by conventional search engines. As of this writing, both public records repositories and online library catalogs are examples of such sites; Web search engines may get you to them (at the home page level), but not into their full contents. The Library of Congress page, for example (www.loc.gov), contains links to many further resources, among them the Library's online book catalog and a separate catalog for prints and photographs, both of which are fully searchable from those links—but the contents of these catalogs are not directly searchable by Google, Teoma, or AllTheWeb. In such situations, the best that the conventional engines can do is get you to a "top" screen which then provides its own internal search boxes, with which you can then mine the otherwise-hidden internal contents of the site. There are many thousands of rich resources whose contents fall into this "invisible" category. The subject directories listed above are particularly useful in turning them up. Other entries into the invisible Web are provided by the following:

- GeniusFind: www.geniusfind.com
- Invisible-Web.net: www.invisible-web.net
- Resource Discovery Network: www.rdn.ac.uk
- Search.Com: www.search.com/subjects/
- Complete Planet: the deep Web directory: http://aip.completeplanet.com/

The **Google Print** project is, as of this writing, a new entry on the open Internet. This is planned as a separate file within Google—i.e., not merged with the regular Web page—containing the full texts of up to fifteen million books, digitized from several large research libraries. As noted in Chapter 3, it is too early to say exactly how it will deal with the bulk of the books published in the 20th century, which are still under copyright protection. One likely problem, however, is that Google's keyword-ranking search software, now in use for the Web portion of its searching, will also be offered as the search tool for entry into this pool of what may be 4.5 billion book pages. Although this will be a real boon for searching very distinctive terms, it will likely produce the same jumble of results in the book file that it already produces in the Web segment. Again, ranking keywords is not the same thing as categorizing them within sets defined by controlled-subject headings; nor will it enable researchers to simply recognize relevant texts whose keywords they cannot specify beforehand. (See the examples given in Chapter 3.) Moreover, access to book texts simply via blank search boxes requiring prior specification of keywords—rather than via controlled vocabulary category terms, browse menus of subdivisions, and cross-references—will also effectively separate from each other all works on the same subject written in different languages. Exact keywords within each language would have to be specified in advance, rather than simply recognized within conceptual categories.

## Summary

To sum up keyword searching—whether in bibliographic citation, full-text, or Web sources—it is advisable to remember first and foremost that this search technique is only *one* avenue of approach to *some*—not *all*—knowledge records. It is equally important to grasp the distinction between keyword vs. controlled vocabulary searching before even touching a keyboard, because without this prior understanding, most readers unconsciously, and unrealistically, expect the former technique to provide the more inclusive overview results of the latter. Keyword searching is at the same time both very powerful in what it can turn up, and very weak in its tendency to miss as much relevant material as it finds. It has both strengths and weaknesses in comparison to either controlled vocabulary searching or browsing—and also in comparison to several other distinct search techniques, to which we shall now turn.

## Note

1. For a fuller discussion of these points see Thomas Mann, "The Importance of Books, Free Access, and Libraries as Places–and the Dangerous Inadequacy of the Information Science Paradigm," *Journal of Academic Librarianship*, 27, 4 (July, 2001), 268–281.

# 6

# *Citation Searches*

We have seen so far that the techniques of controlled vocabulary searching, general browsing and focused browsing in classified bookstacks, and keyword searching each have advantages and disadvantages. There are still other means of gaining subject access to written records; one of the most important is citation searching. This approach, like the others, is potentially applicable in any subject area; and it, too, has both strengths and limitations.

In citation searching you must start with a known source that is relevant to your topic. It may be a book, a journal article, a conference paper, a dissertation, a technical report, an unpublished manuscript—it can be any kind of knowledge record. Further, the date of the starting-point source is irrelevant: it can be something published last year or centuries ago. What a citation search will tell you is whether someone has written a subsequent scholarly journal article that cites your source in a footnote, as a follow-up discussion of it, or at least reference to it. The assumption is that a later work which cites an earlier one is probably talking about the same subject. This is sometimes not true—a work can be cited in a context irrelevant to your interests—but the connection works often enough that you will want to make use of it.

Three basic indexes enable you to do citation searches in all subject areas; a merged Web version of all three called *Web of Science* is also available. All are published by the Institute for Scientific Information (ISI), a subsidiary of Thomson ISI in Philadelphia. The configurations of library subscriptions to these resources are variable—some years of coverage may be accessible in print form, others in CD-ROM, and others via the Web. You will have to check with your local librarians. The three indexes are these:

***Science Citation Index Expanded***, or ***SCI*** (print, 1945– ; CD-ROM,
1981– ; Web, 1945– ). This source currently indexes nearly 5,800 journals
internationally, including over 150 book series and "annual review" type
publications in all science and technical fields.[1] (For the earlier decades of
coverage, fewer titles are indexed.) Abstracts of most articles are searchable
from 1991 forward in the electronic formats. A separate subscription, ***Century of Science***, extends the ***SCI*** all the way back to 1900. Journals in all of
the following areas are covered:

Acoustics, Agricultural Economics & Policy, Agricultural Engineering,
Agriculture (Dairy & Animal Science), Agriculture (Multidisciplinary),
Agriculture (Soil Science), Agronomy, Allergy, Anatomy & Morphology,
Andrology, Anesthesiology, Astronomy & Astrophysics, Automation &
Control Systems, Behavioral Sciences, Biochemical Research Methods, Bio-
chemistry & Molecular Biology, Biodiversity Conservation, Biology, Biol-
ogy (Miscellaneous), Biophysics, Biotechnology & Applied Microbiology,
Cardiac & Cardiovascular Systems, Cell Biology, Chemistry (Analytical),
Chemistry (Applied), Chemistry (Inorganic & Nuclear), Chemistry (Medici-
nal), Chemistry (Multidisciplinary), Chemistry (Organic), Chemistry (Physical), Clinical Neurology, Computer Science (Artificial Intelligence),
Computer Science (Hardware & Architecture), Computer Science (Information Systems), Computer Science (Interdisciplinary Applications), Computer
Science (Software Engineering), Computer Science (Theory & Methods),
Construction & Building Technology, Critical Care Medicine, Crystallogra-
phy, Dentistry (Oral Surgery & Medicine), Dermatology & Venereal Diseases, Developmental Biology, Ecology, Education (Scientific Disciplines),
Electrochemistry, Emergency Medicine, Endocrinology & Metabolism, En-
ergy & Fuels, Engineering (Aerospace), Engineering (Biomedical), Engineering (Chemical), Engineering (Civil), Engineering (Electrical &
Electronic), Engineering (Environmental), Engineering (Geological), Engineering (Industrial), Engineering (Manufacturing), Engineering (Marine),
Engineering (Mechanical), Engineering (Multidisciplinary), Engineering
(Ocean), Engineering (Petroleum), Entomology, Environmental Sciences,
Evolutionary Biology, Fisheries, Food Science & Technology, Forestry, Gas-
troenterology & Hepatology, Genetics & Heredity, Geochemistry & Geo-
physics, Geography (Physical), Geology, Geosciences (Multidisciplinary),
Geriatrics & Gerontology, Health Care Sciences & Services, Hematology,
History & Philosophy of Science, Horticulture, Imaging Science & Photo-
graphic Technology, Immunology, Infectious Diseases, Information Science
& Library Science, Instruments & Instrumentation, Integrative & Complementary Medicine, Limnology, Marine & Freshwater Biology, Materials
Science (Biomaterials), Materials Science (Ceramics), Materials Science

(Characterization & Testing), Materials Science (Coatings & Films), Materials Science (Composites), Materials Science (Multidisciplinary), Materials Science (Paper & Wood), Materials Science (Textiles), Mathematics, Mathematics (Applied), Mathematics (Interdisciplinary Applications), Mechanics, Medical Ethics, Medical Informatics, Medical Laboratory Technology, Medicine (General & Internal), Medicine (Legal), Medicine (Research & Experimental), Metallurgy & Metallurgical Engineering, Meteorology & Atmospheric Sciences, Microbiology, Microscopy, Mineralogy, Mining & Mineral Processing, Multidisciplinary Sciences, Mycology, Neuroimaging, Neurosciences, Nuclear Science & Technology, Nursing, Nutrition & Dietetics, Obstetrics & Gynecology, Oceanography, Oncology, Operations Research & Management Science, Ophthalmology, Optics, Ornithology, Orthopedics, Otorhinolaryngology, Paleontology, Parasitology, Pathology, Pediatrics, Peripheral Vascular Disease, Pharmacology & Pharmacy, Physics (Applied), Physics (Atomic, Molecular & Chemical), Physics (Condensed Matter), Physics (Fluids & Plasmas), Physics (Mathematical), Physics (Multidisciplinary), Physics (Nuclear), Physics (Particles & Fields), Physiology, Plant Sciences, Polymer Science, Psychiatry, Psychology, Public & Environmental & Occupational Health, Radiology & Nuclear Medicine & Medical Imaging, Rehabilitation, Remote Sensing, Reproductive Biology, Respiratory System, Rheumatism, Robotics, Spectroscopy, Sport Sciences, Statistics & Probability, Substance Abuse, Surgery, Telecommunications, Thermodynamics, Toxicology, Transplantation, Transportation Science & Technology, Tropical Medicine, Urology & Nephrology, Veterinary Sciences, Virology, Water Resources, Zoology.

***Social Sciences Citation Index***, or *SSCI* (print, 1956– ; CD-ROM, 1981– ; Web, 1956– ). This multidisciplinary index covers more than 1,700 scholarly journals published worldwide. It also picks up, selectively, social science articles within approximately 3,300 science and technology journals. (Fewer titles are covered in the early decades.) Abstracts of most articles are searchable from 1992 forward in the electronic formats. Journals are indexed in all of these disciplines:

Anthropology, Applied Linguistics, Area Studies, Business, Business (Finance), Communication, Criminology & Penology, Demography, Economics, Education & Educational Research, Education (Special), Environmental Studies, Ergonomics, Ethics, Ethnic Studies, Family Studies, Geography, Gerontology, Health Policy & Services, History, History & Philosophy of Science, History of Social Sciences, Industrial Relations & Labor, Information Science & Library Science, International Relations, Law, Management, Nursing, Planning & Development, Political Science, Psychiatry, Psychology,

Psychology (Applied), Psychology (Biological), Psychology (Clinical), Psychology (Developmental), Psychology (Educational), Psychology (Experimental), Psychology (Mathematical), Psychology (Multidisciplinary), Psychology (Psychoanalysis), Psychology (Social), Public Administration, Public & Environmental & Occupational Health, Rehabilitation, Social Issues, Social Sciences (Biomedical), Social Sciences (Interdisciplinary), Social Sciences (Mathematical Methods), Social Work, Sociology, Substance Abuse, Transportation, Urban Studies, Women's Studies.

*Arts & Humanities Citation Index*, or *A&HCI* (print, 1975– ; CD-ROM, 1975– ; Web, 1975– ). This source indexes approximately 1,130 journals internationally. It also picks up, selectively, humanities related articles appearing in about 7,000 science and social sciences fields. (For example, an article on the medical problems of ballet dancers' feet, appearing in a medical journal, is indexed here.) Abstracts of most articles are searchable from 2000 forward in the electronic formats. Journals are indexed in all of the following disciplines:

Archaeology, Architecture, Art, Asian Studies, Classics, Dance, Film & Radio & Television, Folklore, History, History & Philosophy of Science, Humanities (Multidisciplinary), Language & Linguistics Theory, Literary Reviews, Literary Theory & Criticism, Literature, Literature (African, Australian, Canadian), Literature (American), Literature (British Isles), Literature (German, Dutch, Scandinavian), Literature (Romance), Literature (Slavic), Music, Philosophy, Poetry, Religion, Theater.

The Web version of these indexes, *Web of Science*, is available in various configurations. At its most extensive, it merges all of the years of coverage of all three indexes. Individual libraries, however, may opt for subscriptions to one or two of the files, rather than all three; and they may select which years of coverage they wish to purchase. In any event, the important point is this: *Do not be misled by the word "Science" in the title of the Web version; your library's subscription may well include full coverage of social sciences and humanities journals as well.*

The overall value of these indexes is that they provide *three* different ways of doing subject searches for journal articles in any subject area: by keywords, by footnote citations, and by related records (see Chapter 7 for the latter). Each of these search methods compensates for weaknesses in controlled-vocabulary indexes; two of them (citation and related record) compensate for weaknesses in keyword searching, too—that is, they enable you find articles that lie in "blind spots" to the alternative indexing methods.

The citation search method is particularly valuable because it circumvents vocabulary problems entirely. When you do this kind of search, you do not have to worry about finding correct controlled headings, nor do you have to think up unpredictable synonyms or variant phrases for your topic. All you need is the author and title/source of a good starting point book or article (or other record); from that information alone, these indexes will generate lists of scholarly journal articles that have made subsequent use of your initial source. (Note that books or monographs can be cited sources but not citing. The citing sources that you end with will always be journal articles.)

An example is provided by the reader who was interested in the Norse colonization of America before Columbus. He had already found one good scholarly article discussing the evidence; but on running it through the SSCI he found a subsequent article by another scholar who disagreed with the conclusions of the first. And this was followed by a rebuttal by the original writer. The combination of perspectives developed by this dialog brought up considerable information that did not appear in the first article by itself.

There are, of course, limitations to this technique: you must already have a good source to start with; and there is no guarantee that the best sources are linked by footnote citations. It is quite possible that good works were produced entirely independently of each other. Sometimes, too, a source will be cited by another in a context that is irrelevant to your interest. And the citation indexes cover articles written only from, mainly, the late 20th century forward (compared to the much greater retrospective coverage of many subject heading and keyword catalogs and indexes). Again, no one method of searching will find everything. Each is very likely to find something the others miss; a combination of methods is needed for thoroughness.

The cross-disciplinary reach of the ISI indexes deserves particular emphasis. Of course the Web version merges all three files so that they can be searched simultaneously; but even the print and CD-ROM versions of the SSCI and the A&HCI are remarkable by themselves. Again, the SSCI picks out social sciences articles not just from the 1,700 journals it indexes cover-to-cover, but also those that appear within the nearly 3,300 science and technology journals that are covered by the Science Citation Index. Similarly, the *A&HCI* finds articles on humanities topics not only in the 1,130 journals it indexes cover-to-cover, but also insofar as they appear in any of the 7,000+ journals covered by *either* the *Science* or the *Social Sciences* indexes.

Even within the *Science Citation Index* itself, apart from the others, the range of cross-disciplinary coverage is amazing. Eugene Garfield, in his book *Citation Indexing: Its Theory and Application in Science Technology, and Humanities* (John Wiley & Sons, 1979), mentions a spectacular example: "From 1961 to 1969 a citation for one of the classic papers published by Albert Einstein in *Annallen der Physik* in 1906 is linked [by the *Science Citation Index*] to papers in the *Journal of Dairy Sciences, Journal of the Chemical Society, Journal of Polymer Science, Journal of Pharmacy and Pharmacology, Comparative Biochemistry and Physiology, Journal of General Physiology, International Journal of Engineering Science, Journal of Materials, Journal of the Water Pollution Control Federation, American Ceramic Society Bulletin, Journal of the Acoustical Society of America, Chemical Engineering Science, Industrial and Engineering Chemistry Process Design and Development, Journal of Colloid and Interface Science, Journal of Fluid Mechanics, Journal of Lubrication Technology, Journal of Molecular Biology, Journal of Food Science, Journal of Biological Chemistry, Journal of Sedimentary Petrology, Review of Scientific Instruments,* and the *Journal of the Electrochemical Society.*"

Students of literature or classics, particularly, should keep the *Arts & Humanities Citation Index* in mind as something to be used routinely as a supplement to both the *MLA International Bibliography* and *L'Année Philologique*. One professor of Classics, for example, was interested in the voyage of the ancient Greek explorer Pytheas. In using the *A&HCI* he found some very useful articles that had not been covered by *L'Année Philologique*—the major index of classical journals—because the *A&HCI* selectively covers geography journals, too, insofar as they have humanities subjects. Pytheas's voyages were indeed discussed in these journals, coverage of which lay beyond the scope of the conventional classical sources.

A particularly useful variation on citation searching is to "cycle" sources— that is, once you have found a first set of articles that cites your original source, you can then look to see who cited *them*. This will give you a second set; you can then see who cited this group, which will provide a third set, and so on. By pursuing this process as far as it will go you can sometimes develop a great deal of information on even the most obscure topics.

While the ISI indexes are useful in enabling you to follow the development of a debate or the progress of a scholarly discussion, they are also very useful when the various book review databases fail—for there is still a chance that a book you're interested in may have been commented on, or referred to critically or favorably, in a journal article even if it has not been formally reviewed. The ISI indexes also provide the best way to find a "review" of (or critical response to) a journal article, as these are not covered by book review indexes. They are especially good for giving a new lease on life to the material you locate through old bibliographies—if the latter refer you to somewhat dated articles, you can find out if someone has used them as background sources for a new look at the subject. It is particularly worthwhile to check if anyone has cited old state-of-the-art review articles (see Chapter 8).

These indexes sometimes play a part, too, in academic circles on questions of promotion or tenure, for departments wish to know not only whether a candidate has published, but also if he or she has been cited by other scholars in the field. (This has led, predictably, to some scholars getting their friends to cite their works to artificially inflate the count.)

Several other features of the ISI indexes are worth noting:

1. They provide the *institutional address* of the first author of each article indexed. Once you have that information, it is usually rather easy to find either a phone number or an e-mail address from Web sources or published directories.

2. They provide access to articles *through* the authors' organizational affiliation as well. You can search under the name of any institution (such as a university department) and find out who within it has published a paper in any given year. In the print format, use the *Corporate Source Index* volumes; in the Web version, use the Advanced Search option and search keywords in the Address field. For example, if you want to search for articles whose authors are in the English Department of Loyola University of Chicago, the search would be "AD=loyola u* AND AD=eng* AND AD=chicago".

3. *The Arts & Humanities Citation Index*, unlike the *SCI* and the *SSCI*, follows an editorial practice of "implicit citation," which takes effect when you do a citation (not keyword) search. In other words, when you do a citation search, this index will tell you whether a written

work, a music score, a play, a painting, a statue, an architectural drawing, etc., is *even mentioned in the text of the journal article* and not
formally cited as a footnote. Such internal references "count" as footnote references for citation indexing purposes.

4. The same *A&HCI* index, again unlike the other two, adds "enhance-
ment" keywords to titles of journal articles that are not fully informative. For example, the editors will add the word "Melville" to an article
title such as "Doing Justice to Bartleby" to make it more findable;
thus it will be searchable as though it had been written as "Doing
Justice to Bartleby (Melville)".

5. All three indexes have an additional keyword-enhancement feature,
brought about by a computer algorithm rather than by human editorial intervention; it is called KeyWords Plus. It works like this: suppose you have an article *A* that has articles *B, C, D*, and so on, cited as
its footnotes. The KeyWords Plus algorithm scans the titles of the
footnoted articles *B, C, D* et al. and extracts from them words or phrases
that it finds repeated. These "Plus" keywords are then made searchable terms on the indexing record for article *A* itself, even though the
author of *A* did not use them in his own title or abstract.

The Institute for Scientific Information also offers separate subscriptions
to two related databases, called *Journal Citation Reports (JCR)* in either a
*Science Edition* or a *Social Sciences Edition*. These provide statistical information to show the relative importance and ranking of individual journals
within their disciplinary fields. Data are given regarding the journal's "Impact Factor" (measuring how frequently an average article in the journal has
been cited in a given year), its "Immediacy Factor" (measuring how quickly
an average article is cited), and other statistical characteristics.

In producing the *SCI*, the *SSCI*, and the *A&HCI*, the publisher uses statistical studies such as these to select which journals ought to be indexed in
the first place. These three indexes give researchers some objective assur-
ance that they cover the most important scholarly journals worldwide. This
does not mean, however, that *all* significant journals articles are covered
here; quality articles often have a way of showing up rather far afield from
where they might be expected to appear—which means you will always
have to use *many* indexes, databases, and bibliographies for thorough

searching, and not just these three. (Remember, too, that none of the ISI indexes provide access through controlled subject headings or descriptors.)

The ISI publishes a number of more specialized citation indexes in particular scientific fields:

*Biochemistry & Biophysics Citation Index*
*Biotechnology Citation Index*
*Chemistry Citation Index*
*CompuMath Citation Index*
*Materials Science Citation Index*
*Neuroscience Citation Index*

As of this writing, these indexes are available only in CD-ROM subscriptions.

A noteworthy feature of the information industry these days is that other database suppliers are now venturing into citation indexing; it is no longer the exclusive domain of the ISI indexes. (Actually, citation indexes covering legal resources predate the ISI sources, but were never of much use to scholars in other fields.) The Cambridge Scientific Abstracts (CSA) Internet Database Service, for example, offers several databases, among them *Academic Search Premier, Communication Studies, Politics and International Relations, PychINFO, Sociological Abstracts,* and *Worldwide Political Abstracts* which now offer citation searching in addition to keyword and descriptor access (see Figure 10 in Chapter 4). Indeed, many databases of full-text journal articles essentially allow a form of citation searching simply by the fact that they make the keywords *of* the footnotes directly searchable, even if the files do not formally index the footnotes as a document type themselves. The various ProQuest databases are like this, as is *Nexis*; they allow keyword searching of footnotes (along with all other text words), so that you can see which previous sources have been cited by an article. The EBSCO software will also tell you which subsequent articles have cited a starting point source that you discover, to begin with, via keyword searching. A new feature of Google, too, allows you to do citation searching within thousands of scholarly books and journal articles that are now indexed as part of Google Scholar, available at http://scholar.google.com.

Citation searching as a method of subject indexing is thus gradually spreading beyond the ISI indexes, both through deliberate planning of database vendors and through unplanned happenstance. Whether the "help" screens of any particular file explain the technique or not, however, you will be a better searcher if you bring *to* any full-text database a prior awareness of the benefits of searching for footnote references to sources you already know to be valuable.

Another kind of citation searching is also an automatic feature of many popular search engines on the Internet, although these search tools provide citation links to Web sites, not to journal articles or books, which is an important distinction. (Note, however, that Google Scholar, which does cover many books and articles, has a search page that is distinct from the regular Google entryway.) One of the relevance-ranking factors in Google's search results, for example, is a consideration not just of keyword frequencies and weightings, but of how many other Web sites are linked to any retrieved sites. Google will routinely provide, at the very end of any initial display of results, the option to "repeat the search with the omitted results included." It is always advisable to click on this phrase, for you will then see the additional Web sites that "cite" (or, are linked to) your initial results.

## Note

1. The lists of disciplines covered by each ISI index are taken directly from either the indexes themselves or from the ISI Web site at www.isinet.com/isi/journals.

# 7

# *Related Record Searches*

The three indexes from the Institute for Scientific Information discussed in Chapter 6—the *Science Citation Index*, the *Social Sciences Citation Index*, and the *Arts & Humanities Citation Index* (and their merged form in the *Web of Science*)—offer an additional, and unique, way to do subject searches for articles in scholarly journals. This is "related record" searching; it can be done only in the Web or CD-ROM formats of these sources, not in their print versions.

When doing this kind of inquiry, you must first start with a keyword search in whichever ISI database you wish to consult. (If you know the names of particular authors writing on your topic, you could also use them as starting points.) Once you have a list of relevant articles rounded up via keywords, you have to call up the full-format version of each record individually; in the Web database, this display will then give you a "Find Related Records" radio button that you can click on. (The display is different in the CD-ROMs.) Clicking here will start a new search that will round up any other articles in the same database *that have footnotes in common* with your starting-point article. Note that these are not the same as subsequent articles that cite your initial source, which you would get from a citation search. The related record articles are simply other articles written independently of your starting point source—published either before it, or in the same year, or after it—which happen to share footnotes with it. The important thing is that articles sharing footnotes, especially multiple footnotes, are essentially "playing in the same intellectual ballpark." What is particularly noteworthy is that these related articles may have entirely different keywords in their titles—often, terms you would never have thought of.

The *Web of Science* version will display related records in the order of "most shared footnotes" first, with an explicit count of how many notes are shared. (Obviously articles having five or six footnotes in common will probably be of greater interest to you than those having only one.)

For example, if you are interested in the topic of medical or biological information systems, you could start the process by searching the *Web of Science* database for the keywords "(medic* or biolog*) and information"— the "*" symbol being used for truncation. This will give you a set of starting point articles with titles such as these:

"Expanding the Concept of Medical Information"
"Society and Medicine—Bridging the Information Gap"
"Diffusion and Information in Medical Care"

Clicking on the "Find Related Records" button for each of these will then turn up other articles that do not have all of the keywords you specifically asked for, such as:

"Students Can Learn Medicine with Computers"
"The Information Needs of Family Physicians"
"Status and Progress of Hospital Information Systems"

Note that among these titles the word "Computers" appears, even though only "Information" had been specified; and "Physicians" and "Hospitals" appear when only "Medic*" or "Biolog*" had been called for explicitly.

Other titles that show up in such a related record search have *no* keywords in common with the starting point articles:

"The Future of Biomedical Communication"
"Computers as Clinician—An Update"
"An Intelligent Computer-Assisted–Instruction System Designed for Rural Health–Workers in Developing Countries"
"Physicians' Use of Computer Software in Answering Clinical Questions"

If it did not occur to you to search "Biomedical," "Clinician," or "Health" (in addition to "Medic*" or "Biolog*), and "Communication" and "Computer" (in addition to "Information"), you would have missed these articles entirely in a keyword search. But a related record search finds them because they have *footnotes in common* with the titles whose keywords you started with.

Another example: a researcher looking for information on "the economics of antiquities looting" started with a keyword search on those terms and retrieved a good starting point article. A related-record search from that point then turned up other articles with titles such as these:

"Good Faith Purchasers of Stolen Art"
"Protection of Cultural Property"
"Illicit Trade in Art"

These were exactly the kinds or articles he was looking for; but he hadn't been able to think up the variety of relevant keywords they use.

Related record searches are thus a new, and very clever, way to get around the problem of synonyms and variant phrases. They effectively bypass the problem by searching for points of commonality other than title (or abstract) words within articles on the same subject—so you don't have to think up all of the possible variant terms yourself. They present you with a set of options within which you can simply *recognize* relevant articles whose keywords you couldn't specify in advance.

There are some caveats, however. If you are doing related record searches in the CD-ROM versions of the ISI indexes, your results will be limited to hits that appear only within the one disc you are using. The CD version of the *Science Citation Index* has no multi-year cumulations; each disc contains only one year's worth of data and no more. (There are some multi-year cumulative discs in the *SSCI* and *A&HCI* CD-ROMs.) This means you cannot do related record searches across many years, forwards and backwards in time, or across multiple discs—any articles you find with shared footnotes must have been published within the same year/disc as your starting point article. The cumulative Web version offers a major advantage in this regard—not only does it allow you to do searches across multiple years of the same index, it also enables you to look for shared footnotes across all three indexes simultaneously.

It is useful to think of this kind of searching in relation to the blind spots of other search methods. Suppose, for example, that you've located a good starting-point article published in 2001 within the *Web of Science* database. There are three things you can do to develop further information from it:

1. When you call up the actual article in your library (i.e., not just the citation to it in the ISI database), you can look at its footnotes. This is simply a matter of common sense. Remember, however, that footnote chasing always leads you *backwards in time*, to *previous* sources.
2. You can do a citation search from that starting point. Citation searching is the mirror-image of footnote chasing: it always takes you *forward in time*, to *subsequent* journal articles.
3. You can do a related record search. If you are using a CD-ROM version of an ISI index, then you will usually be searching, essentially, *sideways in time*, to articles that appear in the same year (technically, in the same disc) as the article you start with. If you are using the Web version, however, you are then searching *forwards, backwards, and sideways* in time for articles with shared footnotes.

While most researchers pursue footnote chasing as a matter of course, the same students routinely overlook both citation and related record searching, which often can be equally useful.

Be aware of an inherent limit in all of the ISI databases: while they provide excellent indexing of *scholarly* journals—i.e., those whose articles have footnotes—they entirely overlook thousands of popular magazines and "newsstand" type periodicals that lack this scholarly apparatus. They do indeed "see" things that are in blind spots to conventional indexes and bibliographies; but others see things that are in blind spots to them.

A repeated theme of this book is that no one way of searching does everything. (And here I would re-emphasize that keyword searching *alone* is *particularly* problematic.) You simply have to be aware of the trade-offs among the several search techniques so that your overall strategy can balance their various strengths and weaknesses against each other. Remember, though, that what you cannot do with one way of searching, you can do with another.

# 8

## *Higher-Level Overviews: Review Articles*

Researchers are especially well advised to look for a particular type or sub-
set of journal articles called review articles. These should not be confused
with book reviews. Review articles are a "type of literature" unto themselves (see Chapter 15) in which an author tries systematically to read all
the relevant literature on a subject, sometimes also to interview experts in
the field, and then to organize, synthesize, and critically evaluate the range
of information. His or her goal is to provide a state-of-the-art assessment of
knowledge in the particular field, and sometimes to indicate areas that need
further research. A literature review article is somewhat like an encyclopedia article in trying to present an overview of a subject, but there are two
important differences: (1) a review article is usually written for specialists
rather than lay people and so may assume familiarity with technical jargon;
and (2) its bibliography will usually be exhaustive rather than selective or
merely introductory.

In other words, if you are doing serious research and can find a literature-
review article on your subject, you're in great shape. The important point is
that you have to look specifically for this type of literature; if you don't
focus your search, review articles can easily be overlooked or become lost
in the retrieval of much larger sets of citations. There are several ways to
focus your inquiries.

***Web of Science*** database. The configurations of this file have been described
in Chapter 6. Briefly, it merges three smaller indexes, the *Science Citation
Index* (1945– ), the *Social Sciences Citation Index* (1956– ), and the *Arts &
Humanities Citation Index* (1975– ) into a single pool, indexing about 8,500

journals internationally in all scholarly disciplines. What is particularly relevant here is that its Search pages (either General Search or Advance Search) allow you to limit your results, via a drop-down menu of options, to any of three-dozen specific types of literature, among them:

Article
Art Exhibit Review
Bibliography
Book Review
Chronology
Database Review
Editorial Material
Film Review
Hardware Review
Item About an Individual
Letter
Music Performance Review
Poetry
Record Review
**Review**
Software Review
TV Review, Radio Review, Video
Theater Review

The crucial element to select here is simply "Review"; this is the designation, in this database, for "literature review" or "state-of-the-art" overview articles.

Using this feature of this database is the best way to find such articles quickly, across the whole range of scholarly disciplines.

**Other databases with "Review"-type limit features.** The *Web of Science* is the best overall database for finding reviews because its cross-disciplinary reach in scholarly sources is unmatched. Many other databases that are more focused on particular disciplines or subject areas, however, have comparable features allowing you to limit your searching to review articles. Several files offered by EBSCO, for example, allow limitation of searches for review articles. In *Academic Search Premier* or *MasterFILE Premier*, look in the "Document Type" drop-down menu for "Literature Review." In *PsycINFO*, look in the "Form/Content Type" menu box for "Literature Review/Research Review." If a database offers this option at all, it will usually show up in the "Advanced" search mode; once you get to this screen, look for a further menu of "Document Type" or "Form" options. Most researchers never bother to look for these; but they can be extremely useful in turning up articles that enable you to see the forest amid all the trees.

***Annual Review of . . .* (series).** Various publishers (especially Annual Reviews, Inc.) produce different series of review articles in many fields. They have titles such as *Annual Review of Anthropology; of Astronomy and Astrophysics; of Biochemistry; of Energy and the Environment; of Information Science and Technology; of Language Acquisition; of Materials Research; of Physical Chemistry; of Political Science; of Psychology; of Sociology*. A good (although somewhat dated) overview of these publications is Tony Stankus's *Special Format Serials and Issues: Annual Review of –, Advances in –, Symposia on –, Methods in –* (Haworth Press, 1995).

***Bibliographic Index*** (H. W. Wilson Company; print, 1937– ; Web, 1984– ). If your library does not have access to the ISI citation indexes or *Web of Science*, it may still have this basic Wilson index, which is a subject guide to published bibliographies, including those at the ends of books and journal articles, in more than a dozen languages. It indexes more than 2,800 periodicals and 5,000 books each year. Its criterion for including a bibliography is that it must contain at least 50 citations, so this *Index* is useful for finding review articles or literature reviews, since any article that has at least 50 footnotes is likely to be a review.

***Library Literature*** (H. W. Wilson Company; print, 1921– ; Web, 1984– ). This index covers hundreds of journals in the fields of library and information science. It is useful in finding review-type articles because reference librarians often publish for each other annotated bibliographies or bibliographic essays that discuss all the best sources (including Web sites) or finding aids on particular subjects (e.g., on women in religion; on novels set in academia; etc.). They are sometimes not picked up by *Bibliographic Index* because fewer than 50 sources are discussed. Unfortunately, nobody *except* reference librarians uses this source for this purpose; but it deserves a wider audience because the articles and annotated bibliographies to which it points are often first-rate starting points for research.

**The *Syntopicon* Index.** This comprises volumes 1 and 2 of the set *Great Books of the Western World*, 2nd ed., 60 vols. (Encyclopaedia Britannica, 1990). It provides 102 review articles on philosophical subjects, with indexing of relevant passages from all of the 517 works included in the set. A kind of shortcut to many of the indexed passages is provided by Mortimer Adler and Charles Van Doren's *Great Treasury of Western Thought* (Bowker, 1977), which provides in one volume long quotations of the actual texts of many of the philosophical and literary works that are referred to in the *Syntopicon*'s review articles.

**Institute for Philosophical Research monographs.** This organization, founded by Mortimer Adler to expand on the reviews done in the *Syntopicon*, produced several articles and full-length books that summarize the history of thought on various important ideas. Among these publications are:

- *The Idea of Freedom* by Mortimer Adler, 2 vols. (Doubleday, 1958–61). This massive 1,443-page study is skillfully digested by Charles Van Doren in "The Idea of Freedom," Parts One and Two, in *The Great Ideas Today* (1972), pp. 300–392, and (1973), pp. 232–300.
- *The Idea of Justice* by Otto Bird (Frederick A. Praeger, 1968). This book-length study is summarized in Bird's "The Idea of Justice," *The Great Ideas Today* (1974), pp. 166–209.
- *The Idea of Happiness* by V. J. McGill (Praeger, 1967); summarized by McGill in "The Idea of Happiness," *The Great Ideas Today* (1967), pp. 272–308, and updated by Deal W. Hudson's "Contemporary Views of Happiness," *The Great Ideas Today* (1992), pp. 170–216.
- *The Idea of Love* by Robert G. Hazo (Praeger, 1967).
- *The Idea of Progress* by Charles Van Doren (Praeger, 1967).
- "The Idea of Religion," Parts One and Two, by Jonathan Edward Sullivan, O.P., in *The Great Ideas Today* (1977), pp. 204–76, and (1978), pp. 218–312. (An even better overview of religious frameworks, both theistic and secular, is provided by Roy Clouser's *The Myth of Religious Neutrality* [U. of Notre Dame Press, 1991]).

- "The Idea of Equality" by Mortimer Adler in *The Great Ideas Today* (1968), pp. 302–50.
- "On the Idea of Beauty" by Donald Merriell in *The Great Ideas Today* (1979), pp. 184–222.

Each of these studies spells out very articulately what might be called "the range of options" of thought that has been covered on these most important topics. Especially recommended are the extraordinarily insightful overviews of *Freedom* by Van Doren (following Adler), *Justice* by Bird, and "Religion" by Sullivan and Clouser.

**Congressional Hearings.** These are frequently overlooked by academic researchers, but they can be real gold mines of information. Congressional investigations and oversight reviews extend into an amazing range of subject areas in the social sciences and sciences. (One estimate is that twenty hearings are held every day. For a sample of the topics covered, see Chapter 13. ) When the U.S. Congress wishes to find the best information on the current state of any situation, it generally gets it, for it can readily summon the best experts to testify. Moreover, hearings usually bring out all points of view on the subject at hand—although, of course, they can also be manipulated for political purposes. Especially important is the fact that Congress has the power of subpoena, a most useful investigative tool not generally available to other researchers. The best index to hearings since 1970 is the *CIS U.S. Congressional Index*, available in printed volumes and as a subscription Web site through *LexisNexis*. The same publisher, Congressional Information Service, also produces other indexes (both print and online) covering hearings all the way back to the beginnings of Congress. Microfiche sets of the hearings themselves, keyed to the index citations, will often be available in university or large public libraries that subscribe to the indexes.

**Congressional committee prints and CRS reports.** In addition to drawing on hearings for information, Congress can use the Congressional Research Service (CRS) of the Library of Congress, which often produces book-length "state of the situation" reports on public policy issues. The virtue of these studies is that they are strictly objective, factual, and non-partisan; CRS analysts are not allowed to advocate particular positions—they can only present to Members of Congress the range of facts and issues that need to be considered. The same print and Web index that covers hearings, the *CIS U.S. Congressional Index* (1970– ), also covers committee prints, the form in which CRS reports are sometimes made public. The *C.I.S. U.S. Congressional Committee Prints Index: From the Earliest Times to 1969* picks up earlier years. Again, research libraries that own the indexes may also own microfiche sets of the prints themselves. Another good source of CRS reports is a printed index called *Major Studies and Issue Briefs of the Congressional Research Service*, available from the UPA subdivision of LexisNexis Academic & Library Solutions; it is issued quarterly and has a 1916–1989 cumulative index. Other sources for CRS reports, as of the present writing, are Web sites maintained by one or more individual Members of Congress; these can be located by typing the phrase "Congressional Research Service reports" (in quotation marks) in Google. Note an important qualification here, however: the CRS studies mounted on these Member sites are often not updated in any systematic fashion, and so the reports as given online may not be their latest revision. A better and more up-to-date list is mounted by Penny Hill Press at www. pennyhill.com. As of the present writing, again, the Congressional Research Service (a section of the Library of Congress) is not allowed to mount its own reports online; CRS can provide its research studies *only* to Congressional offices. These same offices, however, are usually happy to obtain copies for constituents who request them; but the requests must be made to the Members' offices, not to CRS itself.

**Doctoral dissertations.** These are sometimes useful for review-type surveys of particular subject areas, especially in areas of the humanities and social sciences—although sciences are covered, too—that don't get picked up by the *Annual Review*–type series. Frequently writers will begin their dissertations with a survey of the literature of a field, to present a background and context for their own contribution to it. The best index is *Dissertation Abstracts International* or a variant form entitled *Digital Disserations*, both published by UMI, which also sells copies of individual dissertations in either microfiche, bound-paper, or electronic formats; the index is available in either print, CD-ROM, or Web versions. (Check your local library to see which form it offers.)

Review articles or overviews located through any of the above sources can often be updated by running them through the citation indexes to see if there has been any subsequent discussion of them.

The overall point to remember is that reviews, like encyclopedia articles, are often excellent starting-points for research projects; but you have to look for them specifically—otherwise they can easily get overlooked in the jumble of results from larger, unfocused computer searches.

# 9

## *Published Bibliographies*

One of the best ways to get an overview of work that has already been done on your topic is through subject bibliographies. Those that are published in book form are especially important because they usually cover citations to important studies that are not picked up by any computer databases. Indeed, published bibliographies offer several advantages over their computerized cousins: they are usually compiled by experienced scholars who can judge the relevance and importance of the items listed; they often include nuggets that can be found only by serendipity, focused browsing, and persistent searching in obscure sources not digitally searchable; and they may include types of materials and dates of coverage that are blind spots to computers. In some cases they approach the goal of offering "everything" available (up to a certain year) much more closely than do computer databases; and in others they may provide a selective distillation of only the highest quality material to consider, chosen in light of an expert compiler's deep appreciation of a subject.

A bibliography can give you much more extensive and more specific information than a library catalog; it can save you a great deal of browsing time by rounding up in one place citations to works that are widely scattered in bookstacks; and it can list journal articles on a subject all in one place, so that you won't have to repeat the same searches in dozens of relevant databases. It may also pick up "fugitive" sources such as dissertations, theses, pamphlets, manuscripts, or government documents that are not covered by most online sources. Further, it can alert you to the existence of relevant works not held by your local library but still available to you through interlibrary loan.

One of the most useful features of a published bibliography is that it will often enable you to do a simple Boolean combination search in records that are too old to be picked up by computer databases. This type of inquiry involves looking for two different subjects at the same time; and with databases such things are very easy to do. For example, I once helped a student who wanted to find comparisons of the educational philosophies of Aristotle and John Dewey. A search of a few databases combining "Aristotle AND Dewey" turned up a list of recent works discussing both men. However, through a published bibliography we could do a similar search for older material not in the online files. We simply consulted Milton Thomas's *John Dewey: A Centennial Bibliography* (U. of Chicago Press, 1962; 370 pages); this is an exhaustive list of studies about Dewey. In looking at its Index, under "Aristotle," we were immediately led to a number of works that discussed the two, some of which had not appeared on the printouts.

Another reader once asked for information about an anti-Semitic speech allegedly given by Benjamin Franklin at the Continental Congress in Philadelphia. A search of the largest database on American history, *America: History and Life*, using the combination "Benjamin Franklin and (jew* or hebrew* or anti-semitic or antisemitic)" turns up nine articles; but five of them are on Benjamin Franklin Peixotto (a U.S. consul to Romania, who concerned himself with the affairs of Romanian Jews); one is on Benjamin Franklin Davega (a Sephardic Jew in California in the 19th century); and of the three on the "right" Benjamin Franklin, only one talks about the speech. A perusal of the massive two-volume bibliography *Benjamin Franklin: A Reference Guide* (G. K. Hall, 1983–88; 1,130 pages), under its index term "Franklin, Benjamin—alleged anti-Semitism", however, leads to *seventeen* citations about the speech—and just from the annotations of the entries one can tell that it is known to be a forgery.

Remember, then, that published bibliographies enable you to find "overview" listings of relevant literature that are often much better than those provided by computer printouts—and that published sources *also* enable you to do Boolean combinations. You simply look for a bibliography on the first subject (Dewey, Franklin) and then look for the second topic (Aristotle, anti-Semitism) in its index.

One problem that keeps coming up in research is that there is often no subject heading in a library catalog that is a good match for one's particular interest. Traditionally, in the pre-computer age, libraries provided two major avenues for circumventing this difficulty: subject-classified bookstacks, which enabled researchers to look through whole books on the topic, without any filtering layers of vocabulary control; and collections of subject bibliographies, which allowed for the easy scanning of titles (sometimes of annotations as well) equally free of the constraints of artificial vocabularies. The newer methods of searching (via keywords, footnote citations, related records, Boolean combinations) that have arisen due to advances in computer indexing also solve such problems; but they are best regarded as supplements to, rather than replacements for, the traditional search avenues.

The main advantage offered by published bibliographies is that they can save you the trouble of reinventing the wheel—of doing the laborious spadework of identifying relevant sources. If a subject expert has already done the work for you, then you can start with an overview listing of sources already determined to be relevant. The disadvantage is that the compiler will almost never tell you how he or she assembled the list or what sources were consulted—you won't know what you've missed, in other words. (The fact that a bibliography gets commercially published by a reputable publisher to begin with, however, is usually an indication of some editorial quality control—it also evidences a recognition of the compiler as competent to sort through the literature.)

How do you find out if there is a good bibliography on your topic? There are two big problems that researchers usually have in this area. The first is that, in either Library of Congress or Dewey Decimal Classification schemes, *bibliographies on a particular subject are usually not shelved with the regular books on that subject.* In the LC scheme, for example, books on **Indians of North America** tend to get call numbers within the range E51–99 ("Pre-Columbian America and Indians of North America"). Bibliographies on **Indians of North America**, however, get classed in Z1209–10, a designation that probably puts them on an entirely different floor in the library. The reason for this is that rounding up all subject bibliographies in one place (at the very end of the class scheme, in Z call numbers) gives them an aggregate power that would be dissipated if they were scattered among the regular B through V classes. Having all—or most, anyway—of the bibliographies on American history right next to each other in Z1201 through Z1363 enables researchers to recognize many other search options that would never occur to them if the bibliographies were dispersed (e.g., bibliographies on American county histories are in this area, too; and many of them provide avenues for researching Native American topics). Having all of the published bibliographies, on all subjects, next to each other in Z1201 through Z8999 gives them a cumulative capacity to serve as a kind of index to the rest of the classification scheme, much like the index volume at the end of an encyclopedia.

The Dewey Decimal Classification provides an analogous situation; there, however, bibliographies are usually grouped together at the *front* of the scheme, in class 016, rather than at the end. Thus, while a regular book on civil engineering would be classed in 624, a published bibliography on the subject would be shelved at 016.624—again, such numbering probably puts the bibliographies on an entirely different floor in the library. (Individual libraries do not *have* to shelve their bibliographies in either the Z or the 016 areas; they can choose to class them directly into the various subject areas. To do this costs more money, however, since most of the "copy cataloging" that is available for them to use from various computer networks will offer records with Z and 016 call numbers already established. Having to create their own, different numbers in all of the various classes is more expensive than simply accepting what's already available. So most libraries will indeed separate the bibliographies from the monographs, and you simply have to be aware of the separation.)

The first problem in finding bibliographies, then, is this: they are usually not shelved with the regular books on a subject, and so if you browse only that subject area for your topic you will be missing all of the relevant published bibliographies. There will be no "dummy" cards on the bookshelves to tell you that they are shelved on a different floor.

How, then, do you find them? This brings up the second problem. You can find the bibliographies in a library collection by looking for the subdivision —**Bibliography** attached to the LC subject heading for your topic. The problem here, as indicated in Chapter 2, is that most people fail to find the right LC term or terms to begin with. The most common mistake is to search under general rather than specific headings. The result is that you won't find the subdivision —**Bibliography** if you're not looking at the right *heading* that it's a subdivision *of.*

The sad fact, then, is that most researchers overlook published bibliographies *twice*—they don't find them in the catalog because they look under the wrong LC subject headings, and they also miss them in the bookstacks because they don't realize the bibliographies are physically shelved in a separate area of their own. (Curiously, bibliographic instruction classes taught by librarians almost routinely fail to alert researchers to these difficulties.)

The primary solution to this problem is to find the right LC subject headings to begin with. Their —**Bibliography** subdivisions will then steer researchers to catalog records with the correct Z class numbers in the stacks.

There are actually several other ways to find out if a published bibliography exists on a subject. Researchers should keep in mind the following:

**The Library Catalog.** *Three* forms of headings in the Library of Congress system are relevant. After you have determined the proper *LCSH* word or phrase for your topic (or the one that comes closest) through the various methods discussed in Chapter 2, plug it into the following forms:

**[Subject heading]—Bibliography**
**[Subject heading]—[Geographic or Topical subdivision]—**
    **Bibliography**
**Bibliography—Bibliography—[Subject heading]**

Remember, too, that by using *browse display menus* of the subdivisions of headings, you can simply recognize the —**Bibliography** notation wherever it may appear.

Additionally, a library catalog record will usually note the presence of a bibliography at the end of a book. And such a note can appear on any catalog record under any subject heading. So even if you don't find the form **[Subject heading]—Bibliography**, you may still be able to pick out bibliographies of several pages' length under other headings if you look for this note field (Figure 13). (A *caveat* here: the note field itself may appear only in the "full" display of the catalog record—not in the default "brief" format.)

**The Z1201–Z8999 (or 016 in Dewey) stack areas.** It would be a good idea for you to just browse around these areas to get a sense of what's there. In the LC system there is a further structure to the arrangement of Z-class subject bibliographies:

Z1201–Z4890    Geographically localized subject bibliographies (by
                        continent, country, state, county, etc.) arranged in

| | |
|---|---|
| **LC Control Number:** | 76018261 |
| **Type of Material:** | Text (Book, Microform, Electronic, etc.) |
| **Personal Name:** | Hoehling, A. A. (Adolph A.) |
| **Main Title:** | Thunder at Hampton Roads / by A. A. Hoehling. |
| **Published/Created:** | Englewood Cliffs, N.J. : Prentice-Hall, c1976. |
| **Description:** | xvi, 231 p., [8] leaves of plates : ill. ; 24 cm. |
| **ISBN:** | 0139206523 : |
| **Notes:** | Includes index. Bibliography: p. 221-[226] ◄——————— |
| **Subjects:** | Monitor (Ironclad) Hampton Roads, Battle of, Va., 1862. Shipwrecks—North Carolina—Hatteras, Cape. Underwater archaeology—North Carolina—Hatteras, Cape. Hatteras, Cape (N.C.)—History. |
| **LC Classification:** | E473.2 .H57 |
| **Dewey Class No.:** | 973.7/52 |
| **Geog. Area Code:** | n-us-nc n-us-va |
| **CALL NUMBER:** | E473.2 .H57 Copy 1 |

*Fig. 13*

the order of North America, South America, Europe, Asia, Africa, Australia and Oceania, with narrower localized subdivisions within each continent.

Z5000–Z7999 Subject bibliographies (usually lacking geographical limitations or focus, arranged alphabetically by subject)

Z8000–Z8999 Personal bibliographies (on individual people, usually literary authors or historical figures), arranged alphabetically by the surname of the subject

The personal bibliographies on individual authors are usually the best sources to start with when you are looking for literary criticism of particular stories, plays, or poems. A published bibliography on an author—there are hundreds of them—will usually give you a much better overview of the range of criticism available on any particular work than any database search (such as the *MLA International Bibliography* computer file).

Note that the tripartite structuring of this arrangement will cause some scattering. Thus, bibliographies on American drama will be classed in Z1231.D7 (in the North American grouping), whereas those on English drama will appear in Z2014.D7 (within Europe); and those on drama in general (without a particular geographic focus) will appear in Z5781–85, which lies within the "D" alphabetical range for subjects in the middle group. And bibliographies on individual dramatists will appear in the Z8000s, as Ibsen in Z8431 and Shakespeare in Z8811–13.

Similarly, bibliographies on philosophy in general will appear in the "P" section of the alphabetical sequence (Z7125–30), but a bibliography on a particular philosopher, such as Socrates, will appear in Z8824.34. It's very hard to see this scattering when you're simply looking directly at the bookshelves; but if you understand the structure of the arrangement before you plunge in, you can use the collections much more efficiently. Remember in particular that all bibliographies on individual people are segregated in the Z8000s.

***Bibliographic Index*** (H. W. Wilson Co.). The online version of this index is available through WilsonWeb; it covers from 1984 forward. Annual volumes of the paper version extend back to 1937. This is a very useful source, as it lists not only bibliographies that are separately published, but also those that appear at the ends of books and journal articles. Those that are included usually contain at least 50 citations, in English or in any of a dozen other languages. The editors currently examine 2,800 periodicals and 5,000 books each year, so its coverage is excellent. It uses LC subject headings for its category terms.

A word to the wise, however: Since this index covers so many years of publications, it may list many bibliographies on your subject without indicating their quality. To prevent information overload it may be best, therefore, to ask for help at the reference desk. I once helped a student who wanted to find a bibliography on "Jacksonian democracy," but she didn't ask for this—she just asked for *Bibliographic Index*. When I discovered what she really wanted, I could refer her to a better starting point. (Nowadays that would be the two-volume *American Historical Association's Guide to Historical Literature* [Oxford U. Press, 1995], which provides an annotated list of highly recommended sources—that is, its criteria of inclusion are qualitative, not quantitative.) Often a librarian can short-circuit a potentially lengthy search in this way—but you won't know unless you ask for help in the first place. And while you can certainly ask for a particular source, it's better to *also* tell the librarian what you are ultimately trying to find.

**Encyclopedia Articles.** The bibliographies at the ends of these are often very good for providing a concise list of the standard or most highly recommended works on a subject. The trade-off is that they identify the best works to start with; but they are usually brief lists, and will not give you "everything" on specialized or narrowly focused aspects of your topic. A good trick for identifying a short list of "best" books is to compare the bibliographies from two or more different encyclopedia articles on the same subject. I recommend using the *Encyclopaedia Britannica* as one of the sets, since its bibliographies are usually evaluative—i.e., the *Britannica* writers don't just list sources; they give a running commentary on their quality in short bibliographical essays at the ends of the subject articles. To find another encyclopedia to use in comparison, consult the sources listed in Chapter 1, especially the commercial database *Reference Universe*, which indexes articles in over 5,000 encyclopedias. If the bibliography from the specialized source mentions the same titles recommended by the *Britannica*, you can be confident you've found some good starting points. (For example, I was once interested in reading a book about Confucius; but I wanted to read only *one*, and I didn't know which of the many available titles to choose. I compared the bibliography from the "Confucius" article in the *Encyclopedia of Philosophy* to that in the *Britannica*; both recommended H. G. Creel's *Confucius: The Man and the Myth* [reprinted as *Confucius and the Chinese Way*], so that's the one I read.)

**Review Articles.** These have excellent and lengthy bibliographies, and can be located by the approaches discussed in Chapter 8.

**U. S. Government Printing Office** *Subject Bibliography Series.* The U.S. federal government publishes material on an astonishing variety of subjects, and the approximately 150 subject bibliographies published (and updated irregularly) by the GPO are a good shortcut to what's available. Collectively these lists catalog more than 12,000 different books, periodicals, pamphlets, and posters. The current list can be found at http://bookstore.gpo.gov/sb/about.html. Some of the many subject covered are the following:

Annual Reports
Art and Artists
Buildings, Landmarks and Historic Sites
Census Publications
Civil War
Directories
Educational Statistics
Environmental Protection
Films and Audiovisual Information
Foreign Country Studies
Grants and Awards
Graphic Arts
High School Debate Topic
Homeland Security
Libraries
Maps and Atlases
Military History
Naval History
Occupational Safety and Health
Patents and Trademarks
Posters and Prints
Procurement
Radiation
Retirement
Small Business
Statistics
Student Financial Aid
Terrorism
Veterans
Women

***Subject Guide to Books in Print*** and ***Book Review Digest.*** The former is a good shortcut reference librarians use to find the most recent books on any subject. (The *caveat* to be observed here is that currency is not necessarily synonymous with quality.) To get a sense of the *quality* of recent books, use the subject index that appears at the end of recent volumes of *Book Review Digest* (H. W. Wilson Co.; printed annual volumes since 1905, online in

WilsonWeb from 1983 forward). This source not only lists recent books by subject, it also gives excerpts or full texts of *evaluative reviews* of the books. (Think of the subject-search capability of *Book Review Digest* as another shortcut to find quality books—like the other shortcut of comparing the bibliographies of two or more different encyclopedia articles.)

**Theodore Besterman's *World Bibliography of Bibliographies*,** 4th ed., 5 vols. (Societas Bibliographica, 1965–66). This venerable source is still sometimes useful for research in older literature not well covered by computer indexes. Arranged by subject, it lists thousands of published bibliographies worldwide. Volume 5 is a detailed index. An update is provided by Alice F. Toomey's *World Bibliography of Bibliographies, 1964–1974* (2 vols.; Rowman and Littlefield, 1977).

*Library Literature* (H. W. Wilson Co.; paper, 1921; online in WilsonWeb and FirstSearch, 1984– . WilsonWeb also offers a version with full texts of articles from 1994 forward). This is a subject index to more than 230 library journals. It is surprisingly useful for bibliographies in *all* subject areas, however, because reference librarians use these journals to communicate with each other and to publish annotated lists of sources–both print and online— on things they get asked about. (For example, one of the sources, *RSR: Reference Services Review*, has published annotated bibliographies on how to get grant money, on field guides to birds, on the impact of plastic on the environment, on touring-by-bicycle, on Afro-American movies.)

Related to the bibliography is another form of research aid, called the "guide to the literature." This is ideally more than just a list of sources (with or without annotations); it frequently provides running evaluative commentaries on the literature of a subject, in the form of expository bibliographic essays rather than annotated lists. The better ones will discuss not only finding aids and reference sources appropriate to the discipline, but also the basic texts essential to the content of the field of study. They seek to provide a whole structure of perception for the field, which is usually beyond what a bibliography does.

Some guides are more successful than others in achieving this ideal. *Research Guide to Philosophy*, by Terence N. Tice and Thomas P. Slavens (American Library Association, 1983) is a good example of what can be done. It provides overviews of the literature of philosophy from two different perspectives, by time period and by particular subject subfield (epistemology, aesthetics, moral philosophy, etc.). Within each chapter it identifies the major works that have established the boundaries of the discussion, with running commentaries on what the issues are, what the various positions are within them, and who the important writers are. Other noteworthy guides are *The Social Sciences: A Cross-Disciplinary Guide to Selected Sources*, edited by Nancy L. Herron, 3rd ed. (Libraries Unlimited, 2002), with its introductory essay overviews of various subfields; and James L. Harner's *Literary Research Guide*, 4th ed. (Modern Language Association of America, 2002). Usually such works can be found in the library catalog or in *Subject Guide to Books in Print* under a form such as **[Subject heading]—Bibliography** and **[Subject heading]—Bibliography of bibliographies**.

For general lists of what to read for self-education, a number of good "great books" lists are available. In addition to the sets of the *Harvard Classics* (various printings) and the *Great Books of the Western World*, 2nd ed., 60 vols. (Encyclopaedia Britannica, 1990), analogous rosters may be found in Charles Van Doren's *The Joy of Reading* (Harmony Books, 1985), Clifton Fadiman's *New Lifetime Reading Plan*, 4th ed. (HarperCollins, 1997), Mortimer Adler's *Reforming Education* (Macmillan, 1988; pp. 318–50), and Harold Bloom's *The Western Canon* (Harcourt Brace, 1994; pp. 531–67). An older great books list is Asa Don Dickinson's *The World's Best Books, Homer to Hemingway: 3000 Books of 3000 Years, 1050 B.C. to 1950 A.D., Selected on the Basis of a Consensus of Expert Opinion* (H. W. Wilson Company, 1953); Dickinson assembled it by collating scores of previous lists of classics. A good list of "The Great Books of the East," compiled by William Theodore de Bary, appears in the 1987 annual volume of *The Great Ideas Today* (Encyclopedia Britannica, Inc.), pp. 222–44. Online collections of copyright-free full texts of great books can be found at http://books.mirror.org, http://bartleby.com, and www.anova.org.

It is particularly useful to look for published bibliographies *in addition to* computer-generated lists. (Most researchers stop with the latter.) The bibliographies will almost always turn up valuable resources—*recent as well as old*—missed by the printouts. And it is important to *actively search* for such bibliographies, especially since they are usually overlooked for the two reasons given above. Almost every researcher has had the experience of using a bibliography that appears at the end of a book or article; but it is comparatively rare—at least from this reference librarian's perspective—for researchers to *start out* by looking for a published bibliography, as opposed to simply using one that happens to come their way as a by-product of something else they've done. A hallmark of the experts is that they actively look for such lists, especially in the early stages of their investigations. The best researchers regard the aggregate of published bibliographies as collectively forming an avenue of access to sources that is *quite different from, and not superseded by*, the alternative avenue of searching provided by computerized sources. You will be a much better scholar if you do not confuse the two.

# 10

## Boolean Combinations and Search Limitations

Several techniques of searching can be used in multiple databases, and will enable you to be much more efficient in zeroing in quickly on the best sources. Among these techniques are Boolean combinations of terms, component word searching within controlled subject strings, word truncation, proximity searches, and limitations of sets by various specifications (language, date, geographic area code, document type).

### Boolean Combinations

"Boolean" combinations derive their name from the British mathematician and logician George Boole (1815–1864); they refer to the capacities of most databases to combine multiple search elements within one inquiry. For example, a researcher interested in the topic "computer-assisted instructional techniques in the field of geography" was initially referred to the *ERIC* database, the largest index to journals and research reports in the field of education. This index has a list of controlled descriptor terms, somewhat analogous to the *Library of Congress Subject Headings* list used to standardize headings in book catalogs. The *Thesaurus of ERIC Descriptors* listed several different relevant terms for each of the two elements he wished to combine:

| | |
|---|---|
| **Programmed Instruction** | **Geographic Concepts** |
| **Learning Laboratories** | **Geography** |
| **Programmed Instruction Materials** | **Geography Instruction** |

**Computer Assisted Instruction**        **Human Geography**
                                          **Physical Geography**
                                          **World Geography**

The computerized version of this index can search all of the first-column terms at once, and all of the second column, then cross the two sets against each other to present only those citations that retrieve at least one descriptor from each column simultaneously. Had he so desired, the searcher could have introduced a third set of terms, specifying the output to only those citations having any of the additional descriptors **Secondary Schools, Secondary education, Secondary School Curriculum,** and so on. A further specification could have limited the results to only articles published within the last five years.

The computer accomplishes this operation of combining and screening terms via Boolean combinations, which are illustrated in Figure 14. If Circle A represents the set of citations retrieved by terms expressing one subject (either controlled descriptors or keywords or both), and Circle B represents another subject, then the area of overlap in Figure 14a represents those citations that deal with both subjects simultaneously. Other circles or limiting factors can be introduced for further specification. And other types of combinations are possible, as shown in Figures 14b and 14c.

In the above example, the way that the search terms are entered can also be simplified. If the terms are first specified as having to come from descriptor (rather than keyword) fields, an expression such as the following would work:

**(Programmed** OR **Learning Laboratories** OR **Computer Assisted Instruction)** AND **Geograph***

Note that the word **Programmed** by itself, being common to two of the descriptors, need not be typed in twice. The asterisk (*) after the **Geograph*** is a truncation symbol telling the computer to retrieve any terms having the same stem, equivalent here to "(**Geography** OR **Geographic**)."

Be particularly wary of how you use the NOT operator. For example, suppose you want articles on "dog food AND cat food"; in this case, if Circle A represents "dog food" and Circle B represents "cat food," then an AND combination of the two will give you the shaded area of Figure 14a. Now suppose you want either "dog food OR cat food." The OR operator

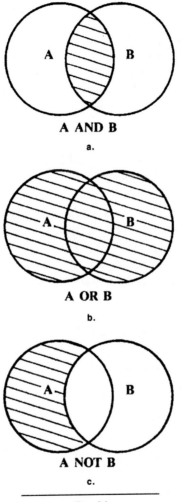

**A AND B**

a.

**A OR B**

b.

**A NOT B**

c.

*Fig. 14*

between the terms will give you the shaded area in Figure 14b. But now suppose you specify "dog food NOT cat food." The NOT operator here will give you *only the shaded area of Circle A—not the entire Circle A*—represented in Figure 14c. The area where the circles overlap contains citations that talk about *both* dog AND cat food (as in Figure 14a)—but by saying you wish to eliminate all articles that include cat food (*all* of Circle B) you

have unwittingly eliminated some entries in Circle A that *also* talk about
dog food. Be careful about using NOT as a connecting term, in other words—
you may be eliminating more than you wish.

Some databases require the capitalization of the connecting terms (AND,
OR, NOT or sometimes AND NOT) while others allow lower case entry.
Look for the "Help" icon within whichever database you are in to determine
its conventions.

## Component Word Searching within Controlled Subject Strings

The ability to search component words that are shared by multiple controlled vocabulary strings is especially useful in many situations. For example, in the *Library of Congress Subject Headings* system there are over
sixteen pages of headings that start with the term **African American(s)**;
these include such terms as the following:

**African American actors**
**African American architecture**
**African American cookery**
**African American diplomats**
**African American families**
**African American History Month**
**African American leadership**
**African American painting**
**African American parents**
**African American preaching**
**African American quilts**
**African American radio stations**
**African American students**
**African American veterans**
**African American wit and humor**
**African American women**
**African American women composers**
**African Americans—Biography**
**African Americans—Civil rights**

**African Americans—Folklore**
**African Americans—History**
**African Americans—Legal status, laws, etc.**
**African Americans—Relations with Korean Americans**
**African Americans—Religion**
**African Americans and mass media**
**African Americans in advertising**
**African Americans in mass media**
**African Americans in the motion picture industry**
**African Americans with disabilities**

Similarly, there are eight pages of headings that start with the word **Television**; among them are the following:

**Television**
   NT **Animals on television**
**Businessmen on television**
**Detective teams on television**
**Medical personnel on television**
**Sex on television**
**Violence on television**
**Television—Art direction**
**Television—Censorship**
**Television—Stage-setting and scenery**
**Television—Vocational guidance**
**Television actors and actresses**
**Television and literature**
**Television addiction**
**Television broadcasting of news**
**Television dance parties**
**Television in adult education**
**Television in politics**
**Television news anchors**
**Television personalities**
**Television plays, Hindi**
**Television programs**
   NT **Adventure television programs**
      **Documentary television programs**

**Live television programs**
**Lost television programs**
**Reality television programs**
**Television comedies**
**Television specials**
**Wildlife and nature television programs**
Television programs for children
Television weathercasting

While there are thus many separate headings with either **African American** or **Television** in them, there are also precoordinated headings that combine the two concepts, such as:

**African American television journalists**
**African American television viewers**
**African American women on television**
**African Americans on television**

The point here is that the component word search capability of online catalogs can find additional relevant records that are not included under these precoordinated headings by simultaneously crossing *all* of the various **African American(s)** headings against *all* of the various **Television** headings. In the online catalog of the Library of Congress (http.//lcweb.loc.gov), for example, you can use the "Command keyword" option under "Basic Search" to type in two Boolean commands:

ksub Television AND ksub "African American"
ksub Television AND ksub "African Americans"

The former command, as of this writing, produces 99 hits; the latter, 129. (The quotation marks around "African American(s)" assure that the words will be searched as a phrase; "ksub" is a field delimiter telling the computer to search for the following word(s) only within the subject heading [tracings] fields, not as a general keyword anywhere; this makes the search more efficient and also prevents system overload.) Although the LC catalog does allow word truncation with the "?" symbol, in practice it would be overloaded by the phrase "African American?" and so two distinct searches must be run to garner both singular and plural forms. The result of searching these Boolean phrases is noteworthy: in addition to retrieving all of the records under the precoordinated headings, these component-word combinations also turn up records with titles such as *The Oprah Winfrey Story* and *Suzanne de Passe: Motown's Boss Lady*. The subject tracings on the former title show that two headings were retrieved:

> *African Americans*—**Biography**
> *Television* **personalities**

Similarly, on the second record, two headings were found:

> *African Americans*—**Biography**
> *Television* **producers and directors**

These records, in other words, would have been missed if the researcher had used only the precoordinated terms listed in *LCSH*. In a sense, this technique of searching for individual elements *within* subject strings is a fifth way to find the right *LCSH* terms for a topic, over and above the four discussed previously in Chapter 2. Note, however, that this is not simply a conventional keyword search of transcribed terms from titles or from any other elements within the books themselves. Rather, it is a keyword search of terms within artificially created phrases—subject headings—that were *added to* the catalog records by librarians (rather than transcribed from the titles or tables of contents). The controlled vocabulary terms had to have been added, to begin with, for these records to be found, because their titles do not contain terms specifically designating either the **African American** or the **Television** subject content.

Searching for individual component words that appear within many different subject heading phrases is very useful whenever there are large clusters of related headings. (**Art, Business, Indians**, and **Women** are other component words that each appear within scores of different *LCSH* phrases.)

## Word Truncation

Word truncation is a feature of online searching that you should use routinely. It has already been mentioned in passing, but deserves greater elaboration.

This is the feature that enables you to find, simultaneously, all of the words having the same root stem. In most databases, the asterisk (*) is the truncation symbol; some others, however (including the Library of Congress online catalog) use the question mark (?); *LexisNexis* uses the exclamation point (!). Thus, the form "eviden*" will retrieve both "evidence" or "evidentiary" at the same time; and the form "child*" will retrieve "child," "child's," "children," and "children's" all at once. There is a caveat, however: sometimes truncated forms will retrieve more than you want. In these examples, "eviden*" will also find "evidently"; and "child*" will also find "childlike" and "childish"—which may add unwanted chaff to your search results. Use truncation—but, as always, be aware of the trade-offs of any search technique you employ.

## Proximity Searches

Beyond the word-combining capabilities of the standard Boolean commands AND, OR, and NOT, some databases allow more nuanced retrieval through word proximity searching. In these instances you can tell the computer not just to find the same words anywhere on the same record, but also in proximity to each other. This lessens the frequency of retrieving the right words in the wrong contexts. For example, the *Periodicals Contents Index* database —a commercial subscription service not freely available on the Net (see Chapter 5)—is a keyword index to over 4,500 journals internationally from 1770 to 1995. In addition to the standard Boolean operators it also offers two forms of proximity searching. As its "Help" screen indicates, you can type in phrases such as "genetic near.5 engineering" or "atomic energy near.7 nuclear power," and you will find the specified phrases either before of after each other, within a distance of whatever number of intervening words you choose. You can also specify the order of the terms, again within a word range of your choice, as in "genetic fby.3 engineering" or "atomic energy fby.3 nuclear power" ("fby" meaning "followed by").

Proximity searching is also allowed in many databases through the use of quotation marks; in such cases you can distinguish, for example, "philosophy of history" from "history of philosophy"—a difference that would not be pinned down by a simple Boolean combination of "philosophy AND history." Most Google searching on the Internet is greatly improved by using phrases in quotation marks rather than strings of terms whose relationship to each other is otherwise unspecified. Also within Internet searching, note especially that the AltaVista and AllTheWeb engines are the only two (as of this writing) that allow NEAR proximity searching, from their Advanced Search screens. This kind of searching is often useful when you are trying to pin down a quotation you do not fully remember. For example, one researcher vaguely remembered a saying of Benjamin Franklin having something to do with the pitiable state of anyone alone on a rainy day who doesn't know how to read. An advanced AltaVista search of "franklin NEAR rain* NEAR read" turned up Franklin's answer to the question of what kind of man deserves the most pity: "A lonesome man on a rainy day who does not know how to read." (Note that AltaVista's advance search mode also allows word truncation, with the asterisk symbol.)

## Limitations of Sets

Some databases also allow limitations of search results by language, by date of publication, or by other features. The "Help" screens of any database will usually provide the necessary information on how to do this. Some of these "limit" options are unusually important, and should be actively employed.

## Limiting by Time Periods

Two of the best files for coverage of history journals, *America: History and Life* and *Historical Abstracts* (see Chapter 4), offer especially useful limit possibilities. Not only can you specify publication dates, you can also specify any "Time Period" of coverage you want—that is, you can ask for articles on the subject of science education in France, for example, but limited to only those articles discussing its practice in the decades of 1880, 1890, 1900, and 1910. (This will eliminate from your results all of the articles talking about French science education in Napoleonic times, or in all of the decades after World War I.) These two databases allow time-period specifications either *by decades* or *by entire centuries*; these are extremely useful limit features when you are doing any kind of historical research. (As always, make sure to go to the Advanced Search screen if it is not the initial default display in your library's configuration; you will not see the Time Period limit option on the Simple Search menu. The icons to click on for any of the limit features, in either of these databases, all look like little magnifying glasses. See Figure 15.)

## Limiting by Geographic Area Codes

A particularly useful, but generally neglected, limit feature within online book catalogs is the capacity to specify geographic area codes. This is best illustrated by examples. One researcher, for instance, wanted to retrieve a set of any books on the folklore of Indians of North America. This is complicated by several factors. One is that the notion of "folk" cultural practices is divided among many different *LCSH* terms, among them:

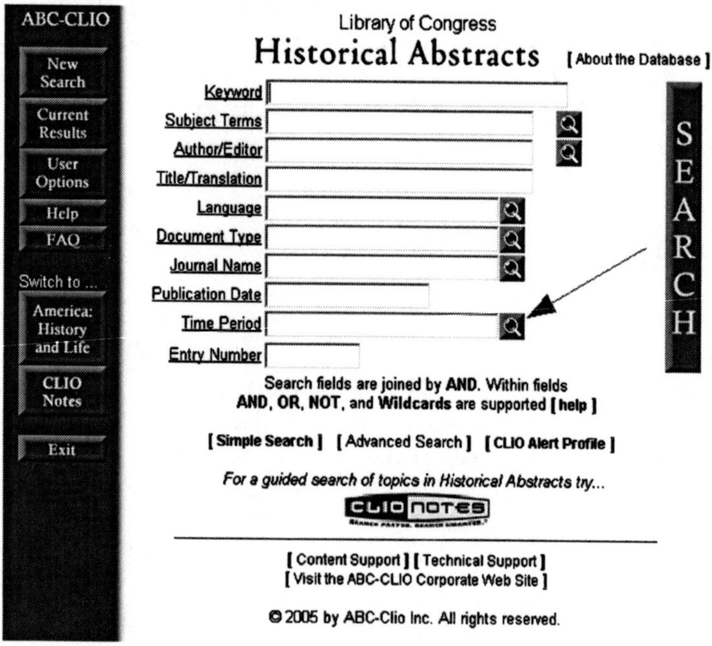

*Fig. 15*

**Folk art**
**Folk artists**
**Folk dance**
**Folk dancing**
**Folk drama**
**Folk festivals**
**Folk literature**
**Folk music**
**Folk poetry**
**Folk singers**
**Folk songs**
**Folklore**

Another complication is that there are many different terms within *LCSH* for North American Indian groups. While there is a general heading **Indians of North America**, there are also numerous Narrower Term cross-references from it, such as:

**Algonquian Indians**
**Athapascan Indians**
**Caddoan Indians**
**Off-reservation Indians**
**Ojibwa Indians**
**Piegan Indians**
**Reservation Indians**
**Sewee Indians**
**Shoshoni Indians**
**Tinne Indians**

The further problem is that several of these Narrower Terms themselves lead to *further* narrower headings; thus, under **Algonquian Indians** one finds a list of *over fifty* additional groups, such as:

**Abenaki Indians**
**Cheyenne Indians**
**Fox Indians**
**Narragansett Indians**

**Ojibwa Indians**
**Potawatomi Indians**
**Wampanoag Indians**

The important point here, as Chapter 2 explained, is that the many narrower terms are *not included* by the more general terms such as **Indians of North America** or even **Algonquian Indians**, and so must be searched separately. Obviously it would be very difficult to round up all of the many scattered cross-referenced terms to begin with; and combining them all with a lengthy series of Boolean OR operators would inevitably overload the system.

This is where component word searching can combine with geographic area codes to solve the problem. I will take the online catalog of the Library of Congress as the exemplar here, as it is freely available on the Internet (go to http://lcweb.loc.gov, then click on "Search Our Catalogs"). Let me first note a useful trick mentioned above, but not elaborated. Searchers in this catalog can specify in which fields, on the catalog records, they wish their desired terms to be found. The major field delimiters are these: KSUB for the subject headings field; KTIL for the title field; and KPNC for the author names field. Other codes can be found in a drop-down menu within the Guided Search option. (They can be typed in either uppercase or lowercase.)

The best way to do Boolean combinations in the LC online catalog is to first chose the Basic Search option, and then the drop-down menu within it for "Command Keyword." Within the search box here, one could then type in the following phrase:

KSUB folk? AND KSUB indians and K043 n

Theoretically, this would tell the computer catalog to look for any appearance of the words **folk** or **folklore** as parts of subject headings, combined with any appearance of the term **Indians** within any subject headings, combined further with the geographic area code (designated by K043) for any record whose subject concerns North America (designated by the **n**). In practice, however, truncating "folk?" will overload the system; and so the search actually has to be done in two stages, specifying "folk" and "folklore" separately.

The use of the geographic area code for North America neatly solves the problem of excluding all records having to do with Indians of South America.

The important distinction to note is that, in the area-code system (unlike the subject-heading system), the broader codes *do include the narrower codes within them.* Thus the code **n** will retrieve not just works about North America as a whole, but also further subdivisions such as **n-cn** (Canada), **n-us-ut** (Utah), **n-us-wy** (Wyoming), and **n-mx** (Mexico).

The major geographic area codes are these:

| | | |
|---|---|---|
| **n** | = | North America |
| **s** | = | South America |
| **cl** | = | Central (or Latin) America |
| **e** | = | Europe |
| **a** | = | Asia |
| **f** | = | Africa |
| **u-at** | = | Australia |
| **po** | = | Pacific Oceania |
| **d** | = | Developing Countries |
| **xd** | = | Western Hemisphere |

Within the large continental categories, individual countries or regions can be further specified, for example:

| | | |
|---|---|---|
| **a-cc** | = | China |
| **a-ja** | = | Japan |
| **a-su** | = | Saudi Arabia |
| **e-fr** | = | France |
| **e-gx** | = | Germany [**e-gw** and **e-ge** for the former West and East Germany] |
| **e-it** | = | Italy |
| **e-ru** | = | Russia (Federation) [**u-ur** = old Soviet Union] |
| **n-cn** | = | Canada |
| **n-us** | = | United States |
| **n-us-al** | = | United States - Alabama |
| **n-us-il** | = | United States - Illinois |
| **n-us-usp** | = | West (United States) |

The complete list of codes and subdivisions is published in the booklet *MARC Code List for Geographic Areas* (Library of Congress, Cataloging Distribution

Service, 2002). Since you will probably not have this publication at hand, the easier way to determine the geographic area code for any region is to simply call up a recent catalog record for a book on that area. A display of the full format of the record will show you a field designating the appropriate code(s). For example, in Figure 16, W. R. Smyser's book *Germany and America: New Identities, Fateful Rift?* (Westview, 1993) shows two codes, **n-us** and **e-gx**. Remember, then, that displays of records in the full format will bring to your attention *not just subject tracings but also geographic area codes.*

When typing a geographic area code into a search box, you may have to include it within quotation marks. KSUB "n–us–il" is an example.

Unfortunately, as of this writing, these codes are not displayed on records in either the large *WorldCat* database in the FirstSearch system or the comparable *RLG Union Catalog* in the Eureka system; nor do these files allow *limits* by geographic area codes, even if you know what they are. The only very large database that allows for such manipulation is the Library of Congress catalog.

## Limiting by Document Types

Many commercial databases allow for limitations by other considerations, such as "by language" or "by year(s) of publication." A particularly useful—but, unfortunately, generally neglected—parameter is that of document type. The best researchers can achieve amazingly on-target results through exploitation of this option. Within the *ERIC* database for educational resources (as mounted in the CSA Internet Database Service; see Chapter 4), for example, you can limit your retrieval to any of several very specific types of resources:

books
collected works general
collected works proceedings
collected works serials
creative works
dissertations/theses doctoral dissertations
dissertations/theses masters theses
dissertations/theses practicum papers

| | |
|---|---|
| **LC Control Number:** | 93011276 |
| **Type of Material:** | Text (Book, Microform, Electronic, etc.) |
| **Personal Name:** | Smyser, W. R., 1931- |
| **Main Title:** | Germany and America : new identities, fateful rift? / W.R. Smyser ; with a foreword by Paul Nitze. |
| **Published/Created:** | Boulder, Colo. : Westview Press, 1993. |
| **Description:** | x, 139 p. ; 24 cm. |
| **ISBN:** | 0813318610<br>0813318629 (pbk.) |
| **Notes:** | Includes index. |
| **Subjects:** | United States—Foreign relations—Germany.<br>Germany—Foreign relations—United States.<br>Germany—Foreign relations—1990-<br>United States—Foreign relations—1989-1993.<br>United States—Foreign relations—1993-2001. |
| **LC Classification:** | E183.8.G3 S585 1993 |
| **Dewey Class No.:** | 327.73043 20 |
| **Geog. Area Code:** | n-us— e-gx— ◀——————— |
| **CALL NUMBER:** | E183.8.G3 S585 1993<br>Copy 1 |

*Fig. 16*

guides general
guides classroom learner
guides classroom teacher
guides non-classroom
historical materials
information analyses
book/product reviews
journal articles
legal/legislative/regulatory materials
non-print media
computer programs
machine-readable data files
numerical/quantitative data
opinion papers
reference materials general

reference materials bibliographies
reference materials directories/catalogs
reference materials geographic
reference materials vocabularies/classifications
reports general
reports descriptive
reports evaluative
reports research
speeches/meeting papers
tests/questionnaires
translations
multilingual/bilingual materials

Similarly, within the *PsycINFO* database (see Chapter 4) you can limit by several publication types:

All Books
Authored Book
Edited Book
Chapter
Journal Article
Peer Reviewed Journal
Secondary Publication
Dissertation Abstract
Report

Within the *Web of Science* database (Chapter 6) you can limit by these publication types:

Article
Abstract of Published Item
Art Exhibit Review
Bibliography
Biographical Item
Book Review
Chronology
Correction

Correction, Addition
Dance Performance Review
Database Review
Discussion
Editorial Material
Excerpt
Fiction, Creative Prose
Film Review
Hardware Review
Item About an Individual
Letter
Meeting Abstract
Music Performance Review
Music Score
Music Score Review
News Item
Note
Poetry
Record Review
Reprint
Review
Script
Software Review
TV Review, Radio Review, Video
Theater Review

Within this menu, "Review" is unusually important, as it designates "literature review" or "state-of-the-art"–type overview articles (see Chapter 8). It is especially important to look for this kind of document type within the "Advanced Search" screen menu available in most commercial databases, as the *Web of Science* is not the only database that allows for its specification.

With options such as these, teachers searching *ERIC* can zero in on curriculum guides ("guides classroom") or tests; psychology grad students using *PsycINFO* can look immediately to see if doctoral dissertations have already been done on their topics; and general researchers can use in *Web of Science* to quickly locate review articles in any academic field. Without the document-type limiting features, the best material could easily be lost within large jumbles of mostly irrelevant hits—especially since the *form* of any document will usually not be revealed by its title or abstract keywords.

## Combining Keywords and Citation Searches

Before leaving the consideration of Boolean combinations, I want to draw one particular option to your attention. It appears, again, in the *Web of Science* database (which covers arts and humanities, and social sciences, as well as science topics). This is the capability of combining keywords with citation search results. For example, a search for articles on the topic "changing paradigms in the concept of property" can be done in very interesting ways. One approach, of course, is simply to look for a simple combination of the keywords "property" and "paradigm*"; and this does produce relevant hits such as articles entitled "Information, Incentives, and Property Rights—The Emergency of an Alternative Paradigm" and "Symposium—Toward a 3rd Intellectual Property Paradigm."

There are other ways to search this topic, however. Anyone who writes about paradigms in a scholarly journal probably cites, in a footnote, the book that put this term into prominence: Thomas Kuhn's *The Structure of Scientific Revolutions*. Similarly, a scholarly discussion of private property is likely to cite the classic work on that subject, John Locke's *Second Treatise on Civil Government*. When footnotes are introduced as searchable elements, a researcher then has a larger variety of elements that can be combined:

**#1.** the word "property" itself appearing in the title of an article
**#2.** a footnote referring to John Locke's work on property
**#3.** the word "paradigm*" appearing in the title of an article
**#4.** a footnote referring to Kuhn's book on paradigms.

One can thus combine the results of several separate searches "(#1 OR #2) AND (#3 OR #4)" to find a number of relevant articles that do not have both keywords in their titles. The article titled "The Concept of Property in Private Constitutional Law — The Ideology of the Scientific Turn in Legal Analysis," for instance, has the word "Property" in its title, but not "Paradigm." The latter concept is "included" however, because this article cites Kuhn's work in a footnote.

Similarly, the article "Paradigms as Ideologies—Liberal vs. Marxian Economics" does not have the word "Property" in its title; but it does have a footnote citing Locke's *Second Treatise*. And the articles "A Consent Theory of Contract" and "The Constitution and the Nature of Law" have neither relevant keyword in their titles; but each article cites both Kuhn and Locke in its footnotes. (A related record search [see Chapter 7] on some of these titles will lead to other relevant articles such as "Property Rights and Economic Theory—A Survey of Recent Literature.")

The ability to search footnote citations, and to combine them with either keywords or other footnote references, is an option that few researchers think of; but it can provide extraordinary results, and if you want to be an expert searcher you should watch for opportunities to employ this search technique.

## Boolean Combinations Without Computers

Combining terms, or sets of terms, via computer searches is an extremely useful capability, especially if you employ refinements such as word truncation, proximity searching, and set limitation. But it is also important to remember that you have additional, and very powerful, mechanisms for effectively combining two or more search elements without using the postcoordinating power of software systems. The other mechanisms are precoordinated subject headings in the *Library of Congress Subject Headings* system, particularly in online-catalog browse displays; index pages in published bibliographies; and classified bookstacks enabling you to do focused browsing.

Remember, as discussed in Chapter 2, that thousands of precoordinated headings have been devised that, in effect, already combine two or more search elements into a single subject string of terms, such as the following:

**Women in aeronautics**
**Sports for children**
**Theater in propaganda**
**Minorities in medicine—United States—Mathematical models**
**Education and heredity**
**Doping in sports**

**Architecture and energy conservation—Canada—Awards**
**Erotic proverbs, Yiddish**
**Church work with cowgirls**
**Hallucinogenic drugs and religious experience in art—Mexico—**
   **Zacatecas (State)**
**Odors in the Bible**
**Smallpox in animals**
**Miniature pigs as laboratory animals**
**Television and children—South Africa**

Many of the strings within the *LCSH* system, again, are created by use of standardized subdivisions, and these linkages often show up in online browse displays without being recorded in the red books list of subject headings:

**United States—History—Civil War, 1861–1865—Regimental**
   **histories**
**World War, 1939–1945—Underground movements—France**
**Juvenile delinquency—Case studies**
**Corporations—Charitable contributions—Japan—Directories**
**Hospitals—Job descriptions**
**Potatoes—Social aspects**
**Mexican-American agricultural laborers—United States—**
   **Bibliography**
**Cancer—Psychological aspects**
**Bird droppings—Pictorial works**
**Toilet training—Germany—Folklore**
**Flatulence—Humor**

There are hundreds of thousands of actual and potential precoordinated headings in any catalog that uses the *LCSH* system. Reference librarians are trained to literally *think in these terms*. To the extent that you understand the possibilities and probabilities that there may be a precoordinated heading for your subjects, you can in effect do Boolean combinations even in old card catalogs. This is an especially important skill to have if you need to do research in material too old to be in a database that allows for postcoordination. Indeed, even within computer catalogs, the ability to exploit *browse displays* will often enable you to surpass any results you could achieve through combining separate terms on your own, because the browse menus enable you to *recognize* combinations that you could never have specified in advance. In Chapter 2 I gave the example of how the various precoordinated subdivisions of **Yugoslavia** greatly aided one researcher in getting an overview of unanticipated options. Let me give another example here.

I once had to help a classics professor find out how ancient writers transcribed animal sounds. There is a heading **Animal sounds** within *LCSH*, but the books it retrieved turned out not to be on target for this inquiry. I therefore suggested that we simply look through all of the various subdivisions displayed under the heading **Greek language**. There were many screens to scroll through, quickly; but doing so brought to our attention the unanticipated string **Greek language—Onomatopoeic words**. This heading led to a particular dictionary that, among other things, gave transcriptions of animal sounds. While it can be said that a postcoordinate search of these two elements would have produced the same result, the problem is that it did not occur to either the professor or me to use **Onomatopoeic words** *as* the second element until I saw it displayed in front of me in an array of precoordinated search options. In other words, the information science theory often does not work in real situations. The larger the file, the more browse menus of options are needed by fallible human researchers who cannot guess in advance *which* terms need to be entered *into* Boolean combinations in the first place. As noted in Chapter 2, most researchers would kill to have browse menus, such as those found in good library catalogs, within Google or other Internet search-engine displays; but they are not there and they never will be. Internet search engines cannot create such structured menus "on the fly"; they have to be created by intelligent human catalogers. Library catalogs thus frequently solve the problem of giving you "overview" perspectives on the literature of a topic—perspectives that cannot be duplicated by any Internet engines—which, of course, cover Web sites rather than books to begin with. (Book records, however, will soon be appearing in Google searches; but the Google software will not be able to show browse displays of subject headings and their subdivisions.) Even within their limited domain of coverage, however, the simple *ranking* algorithms of the various Web search engines do not and cannot accomplish the more difficult tasks of *categorizing resources* or *providing structured displays of search aspects within a large topic*—which enable you to simply *recognize* relevant options that you could not guess in advance. An awareness of the power of precoordinated browse displays of headings within online library catalogs will thus greatly enhance your ability to orient yourself quickly within new and unfamiliar subject areas.

Yet another mechanism exists for combining two subjects without using a computer; as noted in Chapter 9, published subject bibliographies provide this search capability. The trick here is simply to find a bibliography on the first topic of interest, and then to look for the second topic within its index. This search technique is especially useful when looking for a particular topic in connection with a literary author or an historical figure, as there are thousands of excellent book-length bibliographies available on such individuals. For example, a scholar looking for material comparing the philosophy of Sartre with that of Christianity could turn to Francois H. Lapointe's *Jean-Paul Sartre and His Critics: An Annotated Bibliography (1938–1980)*, 2nd ed. (Philosophy Documentation Center, 1981). He could then simply turn to its index to see which of the studies is listed under "Christianity." (There are eleven.) Similarly, a researcher looking for material discussing both Samuel Beckett and Alberto Giacometti turned to Catherine Andonian's 754-page *Samuel Beckett: A Reference Guide* (G. K. Hall, 1989) and simply looked under "Giacometti" in its index, to find four articles. (A search on the *MLA International Bibliography* online turns up three.)

Yet another non-computer mechanism exists for effectively combining two subjects: focused shelf-browsing. The example of "traveling libraries in lighthouses" is relevant, as discussed in Chapter 3. In this case, after exhausting all of the computer databases I could think of, with no luck, I went directly to the bookstacks to the group of texts on "Lighthouse Service" (VK1000–VK1025) and quickly looked through all the volumes on those several shelves, looking for "libraries" as an index entry or a text word within the books. I found fifteen directly relevant sources. The trick here, then, is similar to that with published bibliographies: *first find the classification area of the bookstacks for the first subject; then look for the second subject within that limited range of shelves*. This focused browsing technique, too, enables you to cross subjects that cannot be brought together by Boolean searches in computers.

The moral of the last several paragraphs can be summarized briefly: do not rely exclusively on Internet searches for in-depth research, as they are too limited in both the content covered and the search techniques they allow.

The same can be said even for the large arrays of commercial databases that are not freely accessible on the open Internet. Don't allow yourself to be boxed in exclusively by computerized resources; if you want to be a good researcher you need to be aware of *all* of the options available.

## How to Identify Which Databases Exist

To find out which subscription databases exist, the best thing to do is to talk to the reference librarians in your local public or academic library. They can show you lists of which ones the library subscribes to, and which are freely searchable through the library. Beyond that, a published directory of databases exists; it is the annual *Gale Directory of Databases* (Gale Research), and it lists, describes, and subject-indexes over 10,000 online commercial files as well as 7,000 CD-ROMs and other local-use databases. Gale also publishes the irregularly revised *CD-ROMs In Print* listing, which covers over 20,000 CDs. None of the databases listed in either publication are freely available on the open Internet; they are all purchase or subscription files that will usually be freely accessible only within libraries.

# 11

## *Locating Material in Other Libraries*

If your own library does not own the sources you've identified through subject heading searches, keyword searches, citation or related record searches, or those done through published bibliographies, there are three major resources that will usually enable you to identify which other libraries do own them. Beyond those three, however, thousands of other sources may be useful.

### Determining Library Locations of Desired Items

The first place to look is the *WorldCat* database. It is available in the FirstSearch system and now as a free-access site in Google and Yahoo. (It may soon be accessible through other Internet search engines.) The database itself is essentially the combined library catalogs of over 45,000 libraries in eighty-seven countries. It has over 52,000,000 records. In addition to books, it also records maps, prints, photographs, sound recordings, slides, newspapers, motion pictures, videotapes, manuscripts, recommended Web sites, and other formats. Whatever gets cataloged in any of the participating libraries winds up in the pot for everyone to search. For each item library locations are provided. (This database forms the basis for most interlibrary lending.) To get into this file in Google, use the advanced search page and specify the domain as "worldcatlibraries.org."

The second resource, the *RLG* (Research Libraries Group) *Union Catalog* in the Eureka system, is somewhat similar. Often available in larger libraries, this file effectively combines the catalogs of more than 160 of the largest research libraries in the United States, along with the catalogs of eight foreign national libraries, including those of Great Britain, France, Germany, Russia, and Australia. Like the WorldCat, it includes all formats of material: books, serials, maps, manuscripts, films, music scores, electronic resources, photographs, posters, microfilms, and sound recordings. It lists over 45,000,000 titles with library locations. The publisher of this file has been experimenting with a more generally accessible version, on the open Web at www.redlightgreen.com; as of this writing it is not yet settled whether it will be a free source or a subscription file.

You can search the subscription forms of both databases by author, by subject heading, or by keywords. You can also limit by specifications of language, format, or date of publication. Neither file, however, allows the use of geographic area codes. The quality of cataloging, especially in *WorldCat*, varies rather widely; and so the use of *Library of Congress Subject Headings* is not as consistent as one would wish. A particularly useful feature of the *RLG Union Catalog* is that its software will show you *browse displays* of authors' names and subject headings, which often enable you to recognize name forms or search terms, from menus, that you otherwise would not have thought to use.

The third major source is much smaller, and exists only in printed form. It is the *National Union Catalog: Pre-1956 Imprints* or *NUC* (London: Mansell, 1968–81). This is a 754-volume set listing more than 12,000,000 entries (both catalog records and cross-references), with library locations, for works published before 1956 as reported by about 1,100 libraries in North America. Although many "cyber" librarians now look upon it with open contempt as a bibliographic "dinosaur," my own experience is that it is not superseded by either *WorldCat* or the *RLG Union Catalog*. Granted, the latter databases are now the first places to look for library locations of items not in your local collection. The *NUC* continues to be useful, however, in research libraries—that is, large libraries that must deal with the exceptional questions that cannot be answered by any computer searches, or by small print collections.

The *NUC* is arranged alphabetically by authors' names (including corporate authors), with other entries recorded by titles when no names are apparent. It cannot be searched by subject. Like the databases, it includes all formats of material. (Some supplementary post-1956 volumes exist; but these are indeed largely superseded by the electronic files.) A major reason for saving the *Pre-'56 NUC* is that it has never been digitized, and the *WorldCat* database lacks many of the entries, library locations, and cross-references found in it. For example, within my own experience I've found that the following works recorded in the *Pre-'56 NUC* are not, as of this writing, in *WorldCat* at all:

- *Anais et d'Orbeville* (3 vols., 1808)
- Mayeur de Saint Paul, Francois Marie. *L'Autrichienne en goguette* ([Paris?], 1789)
- Siebe, Josephine. *Henriette Goldschmidt* (Leipzig, 1922)

The *Pre-'56 NUC* has also provided what turned out to be crucial cross-references that are not in *WorldCat*:

- From "Abbott, Frank D." (editor) to title *Presto Buyers Guide to the American Pianos* ... The *NUC* also provides a library location, the Newberry Library, for this work that is not given in *WorldCat*. (Although "Abbott" appears on the *WorldCat* record, as of this writing it is not in a searchable field.)
- From the *International Conference on Light* (1928) to the *International Congress on Light* (1932). (The *RLG Union Catalog* does not provide a linkage between these forms, either; there, however, the two can be found adjacent to each other in an "author" *browse display*, but they would still remain unlinked if the inquirer did only keyword searching.)

The *Pre-'56 NUC* also provides many locations not in *WorldCat*, for example:

- *Briefe von C. F. Gauss an B. Nicolai* (Leipzig, 1877) is listed at the New York Public Library (not in WorldCat) as well as the U.S. Naval Observatory Library.
- For Valentin Boltz's *Illuminierbuch* the *NUC* records a 1913 reprint at the Newberry Library, different from the original 1562 copy listed there in *WorldCat*; and the *NUC* lists additional Chicago and Boston locations not given on any of the several *WorldCat* entries.
- For Jose Silvestre Rebello's *Correspondence between Senhor Jose Silvestre Rebello . . . and Citizen Antonio* Gonsalves da Cruz . . .

(Philadelphia: Stavely & Bringhurst, 1824), *WorldCat* records only the Boston Athenaeum and the Massachusetts Historical Society as holding this volume; the *NUC* also lists the American Philosophical Society in Philadelphia (entry in Vol. 483)—as well as a Spanish language version of the book by a different publisher (Philadelphia: John F. Hurtel, 1824), with a library location (entry in Vol. 751, p. 320). The latter book and location are not in *WorldCat* at all.

In short, the *Pre-'56 NUC* continues to have entries, cross-references, and library locations not found in any online source. (The cross-references it provides, that are not in the electronic files, are its strongest feature; if you follow these to determine alternate forms of names or titles, you can then often enter these discoveries back into *WorldCat* or the *RLG Union Catalog*, for better results there.) The problem is not that the *NUC* is superseded— it is not—but rather that, unfortunately, too many librarians nowadays are prejudiced against print-format resources, and lack adequate experience in actually using the set.

One very important point about the *National Union Catalog: Pre-1956 Imprints* is that it is made up of two different alphabetical sequences, and both must be consulted. The first extends from A to Z in volumes 1 through 685; volumes 686 through 754, however, provide an entirely separate A–Z sequence with about 900,000 entries, cross-references, and additional library locations not found in the first alphabet. (The reason is that the first sequence took decades to publish, and in the meantime the project continued to receive reports of new entries and locations that fell within letters of the alphabet that had already been printed. These additional reports form the second sequence. Tables of additional library locations in these volumes, at the end of each, are separate from the alphabetical entries.) The most common library location symbols are listed on the endpapers of each volume; the full list is printed in volumes 200, 560, and 754.[1]

Catalogs that merge the files of several libraries are called "union lists." One trick to be aware of in using any of them, whether online or printed, is to *try slightly variant spellings of names or titles* if the one you start with does not work. In my own work, for example, I've found works by "Lesse*m*" that were initially asked for under the name "Lesse*n*"; "B*u*lle*t*tino di Pisano" when "B*o*lle*t*ino" was cited; and "Abern*e*thy" when the original footnote read "Abern*a*thy." This approach works *with surprising frequency.*

Although *WorldCat*, the *RLG Union Catalog*, and the *Pre-'56 NUC* all list manuscripts, there are two additional union lists specifically for unpublished material. That is, they will tell you which archives or manuscript repositories in the United States hold whose papers. The first is the *National Union Catalog of Manuscript Collections* (*NUCMC*—pronounced "nuckmuck" by librarians). This is freely available on the Internet at www.loc.gov/coll/nucmc; there is also a printed version of it. The other is *ArchivesUSA*, which is a subscription service from ProQuest/UMI that is often freely available within library walls. Each provides locations of papers that are not recorded in the other. If neither works, try also the *Dictionary of Literary Biography*, or *American National Biography*, or *The Oxford Dictionary of National Biography*. All of these titles exist as both printed sets and subscription databases; each usually identifies the locations of the biographees' manuscripts.

For locating copies of journals, especially older titles, two printed sources are especially noteworthy in their capacity to turn up entries not listed in *WorldCat* or the *RLG Union Catalog*. They are the *Union List of Serials* (*ULS*) and *New Serial Titles*. The former is a five-volume set published by the H. W. Wilson Company (3rd ed., 1965) listing about 227,000 titles and cross-references for journals that began publication before 1950, as reported by 956 U. S. and Canadian libraries. The latter is a series of multi-volume cumulative supplements to it (1950–1970, 1971–75, 1976–80, etc.); after about 1980 it can be considered superseded by the online catalogs. Both of these printed sets should be checked if the serial title you want is not listed online; indeed, in such cases you should also check the *Pre-'56 NUC*, which records still other old serial titles.

Any number of specialized union lists cover journal holdings in particular regions (e.g., *California Union List of Periodicals*, *Journal Holdings of the Washington-Baltimore Area*); or on particular subjects (e.g., *Union List of Military Periodicals*; *Education Journals: A Union List*). There are also union lists of serials from some other countries (e.g., *British Union-Catalogue of Periodicals*, *Catalog Collectif des Periodiques*). And then there are combinations of subject and area holdings (e.g., *Union List of Statistical Serials in British Libraries*; *Art Serials: Union List of Art Periodicals and Serials in Research Libraries in the Washington DC Metropolitan Area*). Such publications are usually given the form subdivision **—Union lists** within the *Library of Congress Subject Headings* system; as of this writing, in LC's own online catalog, there are over 2,700 entries that have this form designation. These specialized lists often provide library locations that do not show up in the larger databases and catalogs. For example, the old periodical *Filmplay Journal* (1921– ) is not recorded in *WorldCat, RLG Union Catalog, Pre-'56 NUC*, or *Union List of Serials*; but it is listed, with a library location, in *Union List of Film Periodicals: Holdings of Selected American Collections* (Greenwood Press, 1984).

Other sources for locating copies of desired books are the Web sites of second-hand book dealers. Three sites in particular are always worth searching:

- www.bookfinder.com
- www.addall.com
- www.abebooks.com

The first two are "meta" search engines that cover the holdings of tens of thousands of bookdealers all over the world. Supposedly they also cover abebooks.com automatically; but my experience is that, sometimes, a direct search of abebooks will still turn up titles not found through either bookfinder or addall. (I've also found that these Web sites sometimes find books not listed in either *WorldCat* or the *RLG Union Catalog*.)

An additional Web site for searching the library holdings of selected national libraries around the world is Karlsruher Virtueller Katalog (KVK) at www.ubka.uni-karlsruhe.de/hylib/en/kuk.html.

## Determining Which Libraries Have Special Collections on Your Subject

No matter how good the coverage of *WorldCat, RLG Union Catalog,* and the many other union catalogs and databases, libraries will always have many items that are recorded only on their own premises. It is foolish to think that "everything is online." If, then, you cannot pinpoint the location of a desired item through a union list, the next best thing is to identify a collection that is *likely* to have it. There are several good sources for determining the existence and location of specialized subject collections, both in the United States and internationally. The overall sources are the following:

1. *Subject Collections*, compiled by Lee Ash and William G. Miller (New York: Bowker, revised irregularly). This is the basic guide to well over 65,000 special collections in more than 5,800 university, college, public, and special libraries and museums in the United States and Canada. Entries are arranged alphabetically according to *Library of Congress Subject Headings* (with additional subject terms as needed); each provides the address of the library, an estimate of the number of items in the collections, and, frequently, descriptive notes.

2. *Repositories of Primary Sources*. This is a free Web site maintained by the University of Idaho at www.uidaho.edu/special-collections/ Other.Repositories.html. It lists "over 5,500 Web sites describing holdings of manuscripts, archives, rare books, historical photographs, and other primary sources for the research scholar."

3. *Directory of Special Libraries and Information Centers*, edited by Alan Hedblad (Detroit: Gale, revised irregularly). This describes more than 34,000 facilities in the United States and Canada; it lists them in alphabetical order and has a detailed subject index. A particularly useful feature is its geographic index, which will tell you quickly which libraries are in your area.

4. *Subject Directory of Special Libraries and Information Centers*, edited by Alan Hedblad (Detroit: Gale, revised irregularly) is a companion set to the above *Directory of Special Libraries*. This one lists the names of the libraries in subject-classified order (e.g., Business/Finance Libraries, Law Libraries, Health Sciences Libraries).

5. *World Guide to Special Libraries* (Munich: K. G. Saur, revised irregularly). This lists more than 32,000 libraries internationally under about 1,000 subject terms; it also has an alphabetical index of library names.

6. *Directory of Special Collections in Western Europe*, edited by Alison Gallico (London and New York: Bowker-Saur, 1993). This is a list of approximately 700 special collections in the arts, humanities, sciences, and social sciences. Details are given as to time periods covered, languages, formats, and accessibility (including loan policies); contact names and addresses, phone and fax numbers, hours, and availability of catalogs are also covered. (Most of the listed libraries now have Web sites to provide updated information.) Entries are arranged by country, then alphabetically by institution. Indexes are by subject and

geographic location; the subject indexes are in English, French, German, and Spanish.

7. *Directory of Information Sources in the United Kingdom* (London: Aslib, revised irregularly). Volume 1 is a listing of over 6,800 information centers; volume 2 is a very detailed subject index to their areas of coverage.

8. *Directory of Literary and Historical Collections in the United Kingdom* (London: Aslib, 1993). This is a one-volume listing of 1,030 institutional libraries in the U.K. with a detailed subject index.

9. *Historical Research in Europe: A Guide to Archives and Libraries* at http://webcat.library.wisc.edu:3200/HistResEur/.

As with union lists, there are also many specialized guides to libraries in particular regions within the U.S. and to those in other countries (e.g., *Special Collections at Georgetown*; *Special Collections and Subject Area Strengths in Maine Libraries*; *Special Collections in German Libraries*). The librarians in your area can tell you which ones exist locally. A good shortcut is to search for such publications under the *LCSH* forms **Library resources—[Place]** and **[Subject heading]—Library resources**.

## Interlibrary Loan and Document Delivery

The United States, Canada, and Great Britain are particularly blessed with excellent interlibrary loan (ILL) networks. If you cannot find the book or article you want within your area, and it is not online in any system available to you, be sure to ask your librarians about the possibilities of borrowing the item from another facility, or of acquiring a photocopy. Some libraries nowadays also have access to document delivery services that provide copies of articles for a fee; a Web site from Northwestern University provides a good overview of options at www.law.northwestern.edu/lawlibrary/illweb/. It is best to first ask through a library; if this doesn't work, or if the item cannot be borrowed or photocopied by interlibrary services, or is not covered by document-delivery operations, then contact the holding institution directly. Sometimes it will have photocopy or microfilming procedures outside the ILL network; or, upon request, it can give you the names of local researchers for hire who can make photocopies for you.

The overall point to keep in mind is that if you have identified a good source that is not available in your local library, don't give up. The same local library is likely to have the means of identifying which other libraries either have the desired item or are likely to have it.

## Note

1. I cannot resist recording the reference to the disgruntled note, famous among reference librarians, recorded in the *NUC* in the entry for James Wolveridge's *Speculum Matricis* (vol. 671); and the bibliographic ghost recorded in entry NP0576549 (vol. 471), which is not owned by the University of Oregon. Similar peculiarities add dashes of color to otherwise stodgy reference works. The way to tell if your library has the first (1980) printing of *The New Grove Dictionary of Music and Musicians* is via the presence of a decidedly unconventional spelling of the word "fugue" in vol. 7, p. 783, col. 1, l. 2; the obscenity is corrected in subsequent printings. Also in the 1980 *New Grove* set, two hoax entries slipped past the editors, for the fictitious composers Guglielmo Baldini and Dag Henrik Esrum-Hellerup; in later printings these spaces are filled by illustrations. A hoax entry also appears in the 1971 edition of *Music Since 1900*, entered under 27 April 1905; subsequent printings reproduce the entry with an explanatory disclaimer note. In the *Congressional Record* of September 27, 1986, p. S14050, col. 1, a memorandum in support of a bill to outlaw indecent communications by means of telephone includes a full-paragraph transcription of a dial-a-porn message, thereby making the *Record* itself a printed means of indecent communication. Chapter 42 of Niels Horrebrow's *Natural History of Iceland* (London: A. Linde, 1758), entitled "Concerning Owls," reads in toto: "There are no owls of any kind in the whole island." And all male readers will wince, and some feminists cheer, at the singular particulars of the death of the son and heir of Sir John Hussey Delaval, later created Baron Delaval, as succinctly recorded in G. E. Cokayne's *Complete Peerage*, vol. 4, p. 139, note (b).

# 12

# *People Sources*

So far we have examined seven major avenues of subject access to information: controlled vocabulary searches, systematic and focused browsing of subject-classified full texts, keyword searches, citation searches, related record searches, searches through published bibliographies, and those done via computers (accessing either library-subscription databases or open Web sites). Computer searches use elements of some of the other methods but add the possibility of post-coordinate Boolean combinations. The eighth major avenue—talking to people—is the one most favored by journalists, but it is also valuable for anyone else.

It is particularly important for academic researchers not to overlook this method, as most academicians have developed an overly strong print bias, often unconsciously assuming that if needed information cannot be found in print, then it cannot be found at all. In recent years this bias has expanded along parallel lines to include Internet sources, but the underlying assumption is the same: "If it can't be found on the Web, or in print, then the information doesn't exist." This belief has the undesirable result of inducing people to change their questions to fit whatever information they *can* find online or in print—even if it's not what they really want—and to diminish the scope of their papers accordingly.

Such an assumption can be very detrimental to quality research. Even the most recent print resources may be several months old due to the time lag involved in submission, review, acceptance, and publication of manuscripts; and Internet sites are often limited in subject coverage and untrustworthy in authority. Even if such drawbacks did not exist in the alternative sources of information, however, people sources would be valuable in any event because someone who has firsthand experience with a subject can usually provide you not just with information that has never existed in print or online, but also insight into how you should be framing your questions in the first place.

It may seem obvious to state this; and, indeed, I have found few people who would say they disagree with these observations. Still—and this is the problem—many people who intellectually know that doing good research must take them outside the walls of a library and beyond the reach of Web search engines will not *act* as though they know it. When it finally comes to *doing* research, they are very shy about going beyond print and electronic sources to find what they want.

Part of the difficulty lies in the way "research methods" courses are taught in colleges. Very often they are confined to the presentation of a relatively few sources on a prescribed bibliography; and correlative assignments are frequently made with the stipulation that "you have to use the sources on this list," coupled with "don't bother the reference librarians—you should do your research on your own." Alternatively, today, many such classes confine themselves exclusively to presentations on "how to critically evaluate Web sites"—as though anything not on the open Web isn't worth talking about to begin with. Unfortunately, students tend unwittingly to learn more than they should from such experiences: they learn that "doing research" equals "playing library games"—or "using the Internet" *alone*—and that talking to people is "bothering" them, and may even have a faint scent of "cheating" to it. Professors seem unaware of the long-term damage this does, not only to their students' subsequent academic careers but also to the future satisfaction of their curiosity about topics of personal interest. Being told not to talk to people, for purposes of a particular class assignment, often produces the kind of result Mark Twain referred to in an anecdote about a cat:

> We should be careful to get out of an experience only the wisdom that is in it—and stop there; lest we be like the cat that sits down on a hot stove-lid. She will never sit down on a hot stove-lid again—and that is well; but also she will never sit down on a cold one anymore.

Reference librarians notice the limiting effects of such "learning" all the time, in the reluctance students—and their professors, too—display in asking for much-needed reference help in all other situations.

Genuine learning should obviously be a broadening rather than a limiting experience; and in doing research the most important lesson to learn is that *any* source is fair game. One should always go to wherever the information needed is most likely to be, and often this will be in someone's head rather than on a computer screen or in a book. (Remember, too, however, that you can travel full circle from talking to an expert to getting back into the literature—for usually the expert will know the *best* written sources, or can offer shortcuts that will make library or Web research more efficient.)

Talking to people can provide unanticipated insights into your area of research, feedback on problem points, and a structure or frame of perception that written or online sources often cannot match. Conversations can reveal quickly which areas of inquiry are valuable and worth pursuing, and which are likely to waste time. People sources can also often identify quickly what are the "crackpot" positions, with concealed agendas and ideologies, that may be very hard to discern otherwise if the subject field you're entering is entirely new to you.

Experts, enthusiasts, and buffs are available without direct personal contact (at least initially) through thousands of listservs and discussion groups available on the Internet. A good starting point to find a group relevant to your topic is through the Google home page; click on the "Groups" tag just above the initial search box. Another good listing is available through GeniusFind's Chats & Forums link at www.geniusfind.com/Chats_and_Forums.htm. These services enable you to throw out a question to a wide variety of people interested in a particular subject area; usually you will receive direct e-mail responses from anyone interested enough to contact you. As with other people sources, such contacts can provide you with either direct answers or possible leads. For example, I once had to find out if the U.S. Army had ever used the phrase "Certified Disability Discharge" in reference to veterans' status. At the time I could not find this exact phrase in either print or online sources, but I did discover a veterans' information homepage on the Web, and I sent my question to the group's e-mail address. The experts on the other end found some knowledgeable "old timers" to talk to who clarified the use of the term.

As wonderful as Internet sites can be, it is best not to be naive in using them. One student, for example, sent a request to a Shakespeare discussion group, asking for the sources of such quotes as "Alas, poor Yorick" and "Double, double, toil and trouble"—and he even gave the list members a deadline for responding! Needless to say, such an inquiry evoked several replies that can only be deemed less than charitable. Keep in mind that, while the enthusiasts who populate the various discussion groups are generally very helpful, they are often not kindly disposed toward questions creating the appearance that a student is simply trying to circumvent the work of real engagement with the subject of their list.

What is even more important to remember is that, right from the start, not every expert is available on the Internet—there are hundreds of millions of knowledgeable people in different subject areas who simply do not participate at all in listservs or discussion groups. (This may seem to be a commonsense observation—but the view from a reference desk is that too many researchers are oblivious to it.) And even those who do participate will not choose to respond to every inquiry that gets tossed into their pool. (Most of these people have actual *lives*.) In other words, there is a vast ocean of experts who can still be reached only by telephone, letters, or direct e-mail.

No matter what your means of contacting people, a word of caution is in order: a judicious mixture of personal, print, and online sources is often the ideal in doing good research. Just as academics often overemphasize print and Web sites, so journalists tend to overemphasize personal contacts to the outright neglect of print sources. Each group can learn from the other.

Contrary to widespread assumption, it does not take special training or credentials to do research by interview. Indeed, one notable research company in Washington charges its clients hefty fees by the hour to find information on anything from the market for golf carts in the United States, to eggplants, to abrasives, to the marketability of rubber-soled shoes in Eastern Europe—and without its researchers having any more background in these areas *than you do right now*. The president of the company has said:

> The information [that clients want] is usually somewhere in the federal government. The problem most people have is that they don't know how to find it. They make 10 calls, get transferred around and still don't get to the right person. So they get frustrated and give up. . . .
> We have a former French pastry chef and an ex-seminarian. We look for people who make others want to talk to them and aren't intimidated by getting into a new topic every day.
> Sometimes you're better off if you're not a hotshot specialist. Then it's easy to know how hard it might be to find something. Ignorance is bliss in a lot of research projects.[1]

The fact that people without "credentials" can charge more than $75 per hour for making telephone calls points up two very important things: the technique of talking to people *does* produce good results, no matter what the subject; and *anyone can do it*, including *you*.

The key factors for success are not experience and credentials but rather your attitudes and assumptions. All you have to do is start somewhere, then follow through in asking questions. In other words, just jump in and do it. *It's okay.* The main stumbling block most researchers have is their own inhibiting belief that other people will not respond. But most interviewees are flattered that you would consider them knowledgeable in some area, and they will usually answer helpfully. Experience will show that the odds are in your favor—telephone or other contacts will usually be friendly, and people will sometimes volunteer much more information than you originally request. And even if you do run into a jerk or two along the way, ask yourself, *So what?* If someone is not helpful, don't take it personally—just work around that person and get other names to talk to. Persistence routinely solves even the jerk problem.

If you start with *any* negative assumptions—"I'll be *bothering* someone"; "Why would they talk to *me*?"; or "They'll be *too busy*"—you will be foolishly defeating yourself before you begin. If the reasons for not making a phone call seem stronger than the reasons to go ahead and do it, then you'll be dooming yourself to unnecessary failure. Most of the "reasons" will only be rationalizations to justify your own unwarranted shyness. Your attitude should be, simply, "What have I got to lose?" The answer is "Nothing"— or at worst a minuscule charge for a long-distance call; and frequently you'll spend much more than that amount on amusements that are much less important to your well-being than good information is.

I've known researchers who use fictional heroes to good effect. When confronted with a puzzle, they would ask themselves questions along the line of, "What would Sherlock Holmes [or Perry Mason, James Bond, Nancy Drew, Amelia Peabody, Miss Marple—take your pick] do in this situation?" The detectives we admire so much in novels are not limited by print or electronic sources in solving their mysteries; neither should we be in solving ours!

The results are likely to repay you amply in time saved on complicated library or Web searches. For example, one student looking for information on the little-known winner of the Nobel Peace Prize one year could find nothing on him in library resources at the time he won the award; but calls to Amnesty International and the Washington Office on Latin America turned up whole files of information.

Talking to people can provide you with a quick overview of a whole field; it can give you not only the answer to a question but the larger context in which the question should be asked. For example, someone who was looking for information on the U.S. market for padlocks imported from India first did considerable library research, but only in talking to knowledgeable people in the field did he really get oriented. He was told that there are several different grades of padlocks, which have different markets; that it's best to concentrate on small areas, as data on large areas are unreliable; that there were forthcoming national standards for padlocks, which imported items might have to meet in another year or two; that he should first have the locks tested for quality (using current military specifications as interim standards, if applicable to the grade of item being imported) and to have a written contract that all other locks will be comparable, before paying for any; that he should incorporate to prevent personal liability in case a lawsuit should result from the sale of a defective lock; that he must consider not only the price of the items but also the shipping charges and import duties; and that big chain stores would certainly be able to buy more cheaply than he, so his best bet would be to market through independent "Mom and Pop"–type hardware stores.

The experts that this researcher talked to not only provided him with answers, they also alerted him to *whole new areas of questions* he had to consider, none of which he had thought of on his own. It's impossible to get this kind of corrective feedback from printed sources or Web sites, as they allow no interaction with their readers, nor can they be modified on the spot to accommodate slightly different inquiries. For this kind of thing you just have to talk to someone who has experience. (Note, too, that an array of concerns such as those listed in this example would not be easily elicited by e-mail correspondence—for the simple reason that few contacts would want to do that much typing! The same information flows much more easily over the phone. That is an important distinction: telephone calls, or—much better —in-person interviews, work much more effectively than e-mails.)

Another example: I once had to identify, quickly, the company that built a bank vault which allegedly survived the collapse of the World Trade Center. The Library of Congress had just been given a special appropriation, in the wake of the September 11th attacks, to acquire a super-secure vault for its own treasures, and needed to know what kind of vault to acquire. One of the LC administrators remembered reading a newspaper article about some gold bullion being removed from a vault that had survived the collapse of the twin towers, and wanted information about that particular product. From the ProQuest database of full-text newspapers I could quickly find the newspaper article (*Wall Street Journal*, November 1, 2001, p. A12) reporting on the recovery of the gold; the article identifies the owner of the vault as the trading arm of the Bank of Nova Scotia, specifically its "ScotiaMacotta unit." Unfortunately, the reporter consistently misspelled the company's name, which is actually ScotiaMocatta; and this threw off my keyword searching for the next twenty minutes. In any event I soon found the correct spelling, and through various business directories I discovered the company's New York telephone number—which proved to be nonworking. However, since I also had the parent company's name, Bank of Nova Scotia, I could come at the problem through their office; doing so resulted in several telephone referrals until I finally found one man who knew that the head of all of the company's security operations, including all of its bank vaults, was situated in Toronto. When I called this Director of Protective Services, he proved to be very helpful, and he immediately gave me the name of the bank vault manufacturer and offered to provide further contacts. But he also gave me some other very important information that I hadn't asked for: the media reports of the vault's survival were misleading. The vault in question, he told me, was not within the twin towers; it was actually located on two levels of #4 World Trade Center, a nine-story building off to the side. This smaller building itself only partially collapsed, and none of the events of that terrible day threatened the structural integrity of the vault. (It was surrounded by an underground parking area at levels 3 and 4 below ground, and the many cars in the area were not damaged either, other than to be covered by layers of dust.) This fact was not at all apparent from the original newspaper article, which did leave the impression that the vault had directly withstood the collapse of the twin towers themselves.

The point here, for researchers, is simple but important: even when I had the full resources of the largest library in the world at my disposal, with hundreds of commercial databases freely available inside, and even when I also had the full Internet available on top of all the library resources, the information that I really needed turned out to be only in the head of someone sitting in a Toronto business office. And not only could he provide the information I specifically asked for, he could also point out an unsuspected problem in the assumptions with which I was working. This kind of thing happens all the time for researchers who go "outside the boxes" of both libraries and the Internet, and talk directly to knowledgeable people.

Note also, however, that the library resources were extremely helpful in providing the starting point for the necessary string of telephone calls, especially since the initial *Wall Street Journal* article was not freely accessible on the open Internet.

Some recalcitrant souls will undoubtedly still be intimidated by their lack of "credentials," even though lack of training is truly irrelevant to their success. For academics, it is hoped that the obvious will allay their fears: they already have credentials precisely because of their university affiliation. The best way to start off a telephone conversation with a potential source is to mention this right up front: "I'm a student/grad student at _____ University, and I'm not sure who to talk to—maybe you could help or direct me to the right person. I'm trying to find information on _____." Non-academics can say something similar: "My name is _____ and I'm with _____, although I'm not calling in that connection. I'm kind of on a fishing expedition, and I'm hoping you or someone else there might be able to point me in the right direction. I'm trying to find information on _____; do you know of someone there who might be able to get me started on this?"

In obtaining information from people, the "secret" that is so hard for so many people to believe is precisely this: *There is no secret. Just make the call anyway and be honest about your reasons. It's okay to ask for help. The odds are that you will succeed if you are simply persistent in developing a chain of referrals.*

When using the phone, a few things should be kept in mind to make your calls more productive. First, if the nature of your inquiry is particularly complex, do a little homework first. At least talk the reference librarians of your local library to see if they can suggest some overview or orientation sources. An expert will be more helpful if you convey the impression that you've already done some work on your own and are willing to do more—and that you're not simply dumping the whole problem into his or her lap to solve for you. (This applies to Internet inquiries and e-mails as well as to phone calls.)

Second, explain the purpose of your research—that is, what you're *ultimately* trying to do and what you'll use the information for (e.g., personal curiosity, term paper, publication, broadcast, etc.). Be open and honest. It will help here if you can say which sources you have already tried, and why you thought this phone call was necessary to get beyond their inadequacies.

Third, try to be as specific as you can. If you ask specific questions, you're likely to get on-target answers; but if you ask only vague, general questions, you're likely to get only vague, general answers.

Fourth, respect the expert's intellectual property rights. Don't simply "milk" a person for information and then pass if off as your own—be careful not to infringe on your source's own potential use of the information. People who burn their sources in this way not only ruin their own chances for follow-up contacts, they also make the sources hesitant about helping other researchers. Anyone who uses "the network" has a responsibility to leave it in good or better shape for the next person.

Fifth, when you talk to people about a subject you're not familiar with, it is very important to ask for more contacts. Few researchers will rely exclusively on one printed source; it is similarly unwise to rely on only one spoken (or e-mailed) viewpoint. People's memories of events, and their opinions, tend to be self-serving; it is therefore advisable to seek a balance of perspectives. (A related problem in some inquiries is that of "shrinkage of testimony." Private investigators and journalists frequently run into this. Sometimes a source will be very garrulous and free with statements when you first talk to him; but if he is later subject to cross-examination by an unsympathetic interrogator, or if he comes to realize he will somehow be held accountable for his opinions, he may have much less to say. This points up the advantage of a printed source: it will be the same no matter how often you refer to it. There is also, of course, a corresponding disadvantage: the situation may have changed dramatically since the words were printed.)

And sixth, after you have talked to someone who has been helpful—especially if the person has gone out of his or her way for you—it is very important to write a thank-you note. There are several reasons for this:

- A written record of your interest in a subject will help your source remember you, and to contact you again if additional information turns up; the same record will enable your source to use *you* as a contact for information in your shared area of interest. This is how mutually beneficial contact networks are built up.

- You will frequently find that days later, when you are finally writing your report, new questions will occur to you that you did not think to ask the first time. When you call your source again for further clarification, he will be more responsive if he's already received a good thank you in writing, for such notes are useful to him in concrete ways. They provide proofs of good job performance he can readily refer to in justifying raises, program extensions, and so on.
- The *lack* of a thank-you note can positively hurt you when you want to use a source again. I am aware of more than one instance in which contacts who had no obligation to help researchers nevertheless went out of their way to provide information—sometimes a great deal of it—and never received any thanks for their efforts. The result was that, in each case, the contacts "dried up" when the same researchers sought them again for more information.

When you are paying someone to help you, you can call that person at any time. But when you are getting information for free, you must at all costs avoid the impression of being thankless or pushy. It is therefore advisable to consider the sending of timely thank-you notes not simply as a nice thing to do, but rather as *an integral part of the research process*. If you haven't put word of thanks *in writing*, you have not finished your contact with that source.

The problem remains, then, that even if you do want to talk to someone who knows about your subject, how do you find that person? Where do you start? If your own circle of acquaintances doesn't get you far enough, many sources will be useful, among them the following:

*Encyclopedia of Associations* (Gale, annual). Associations, professional societies, amateur hobby groups, and nonprofit organizations are excellent switchboards for connecting researchers with highly qualified sources. Indeed, the very purpose of most societies is to disseminate information and provide means for people with common interests to interact with each other; and so they will welcome inquiries that enable them to tell you more about themselves and their areas of interest. The annual *Encyclopedia* from Gale is available in both print and subscription online formats. It is the best listing there is of such groups, describing more than 22,000 nonprofit American membership organizations of national scope. Each entry provides the address, telephone number, e-mail address, Web URL, and the name of the organization's top official, plus a detailed description of the society's areas of interest and purpose. There is also information on the society's publications, and dates and city locations of upcoming conventions. (Further or updated information will be available via the organization's own Web site.) The printed volumes have detailed indexes by keywords and by geographic areas.

There is a society for everything under the sun. The following brief list gives only the slightest hint of the range and diversity of such groups:

American Accordionists' Association
American Society of Abdominal Surgeons
Baker Street Irregulars [Sherlock Holmes buffs]
Bald-Headed Men of America
Federation of Historical Bottle Collectors
American Bottlers of Carbonated Beverages
International Chinese Snuff Bottle Society
Dance [more than 250 organizations]
Antique Doorknob Collectors of America
Estonian Educational Society
International Franchise Association
Frog Pond Frog Collectors Club
Gemological Institute of America
Association of Gravestone Studies
Great Books Foundation
Society for Austrian and Habsburg History
Insurance [more than 100 groups]
Society for Siberian Irises
Brewster Society [collectors of kaleidoscopes]
American Kitefliers Association
Congress of Lung Association Staff
Manuscript Society
American Medical Informatics Association
Milton Society of America
International Nanny Association
Institute of Outdoor Drama
National Frozen and Refrigerated Food Association
National Quartz Producers Council

American Registry of Radiologic Technologists
Restless Legs Syndrome Foundation
National Alliance for Research on Schizophrenia and Depression
Stuntwomen's Association of Motion Pictures
Tall Clubs International
American Institute of Ultrasound in Medicine
Veterinary Medicine [more than 150 societies]
Brotherhood of the Knights of the Vine [vintners and grape growers]
Window Covering Manufacturers Association
Women Executives in Public Relations
National Ice Cream and Yogurt Retailers Association

The *Encyclopedia of Associations* is a publication everyone should browse through; it's of interest not only for research but also for finding people who have the same hobby as you. Two other complementary sets are also published by Gale: *Encyclopedia of Associations: International Organizations* and *Encyclopedia of Associations: Regional, State, and Local Organizations*. An additional useful volume is Charles S. Mack's *The Executive's Handbook of Trade and Business Associations: How They Work, and How to Make Them Work Effectively for You* (Quorum Books, 1991). Two volumes from CDB Research round out the list, *Directory of British Associations & Associations in Ireland* and *Directory of European Professional & Learned Societies*.

**Yellow Pages.** This incredible subject directory of the resources in your own area is one of the best starting points for handling many questions, yet it is often overlooked by those who think research can be done only in libraries or on the Internet. An added feature is a detailed subject index, which is the necessary key to the controlled vocabulary subject headings used in the book. Remember, too that your local library may have a set of yellow pages for other cities throughout the country, if you prefer paper formats to Internet versions. A good Web site that includes both white and yellow pages for many cities, both domestic and foreign, is www.infobel. com/teldir/. Note, however, that only current information will be found online—sometimes researchers need the earlier directories rather than their most recent versions.

***Directories in Print*** (Gale, irregular.) Print, CD-ROM, and online subscription versions are available. While it is certainly true that most "directory" type questions for specific information are now best handled by searches of the open Internet—almost all companies and organizations now have their own Web sites providing up-to-date contact information—the one big problem with such online searching is the difficulty of gaining *overview* information on the *range* of organizations that may be relevant to your inquiry. If you have a particular one already in mind, go directly to its Web site; but if you want to identify what other, similar sources may be out there, *Directories in Print* can be very useful. It is a descriptive, annotated guide to print and electronic "Directories, Buyer's Guides, Rosters and Other Address Lists of All Kinds." It lists *and categorizes* some 16,000 publications in 26 broad subject areas, with indexes by Alternative Formats, Subjects, and Keywords. Directories from the United States, Canada, United Kingdom, and Australia are included. Just as there is an organization for everything under the sun, so, too, there is a directory of contacts on any subject. The following is just a brief sampling of available directories:

*National Directory of Adult Day Care Centers*
*Auto Museums Directory*
*Opportunities for Study in Hand Bookbinding and Calligraphy*
*Directory of Conventions Regional Editions*
*Crematories Directory*
*Earthworm Buyer's Guide*
*Directory of Professional Genealogists*
*Sunday Telegraph Golf Course Guide to Britain and Ireland*
*Grants, Fellowships, and Prizes of Interest to Historians*
*Directory of Historical Organizations in the United States and Canada*
*Mail Order Business Directory*
*Marketsearch: International Directory of Published Market Research*
*Museums Directory*
*British Performing Arts Yearbook*
*Official ABMS Directory of Board Certified Medical Specialists* (American Board of Medical Specialists)
*National Catalog of Occult Bookstores*
*Seasonal Employment* (National Park Service)

*The Specialty Travel Index: The Special Interest and Adventure Travel Directory*

*Directories in Print* also lists local directories for specific areas under names of countries, regions, states, and cities in its subject index.

**Current British Directories** (CDB Research Ltd, irregular). This lists 3,000 directories by title, with indexes by publisher and subject.

**Washington Information Directory** (CQ Press, annual). This is a subject guide to government agencies in the executive branch, to Congress and its committees and subcommittees, and to private and nongovernmental organizations—e.g., embassies, think tanks, lobbyists—in the Washington, DC, area. It describes each organization, gives a summary of its area of interest, and provides specific phone numbers, addresses, and Web URLs. Chapters include sources in twenty broad categories:

Advocacy and Public Service
Agriculture and Nutrition
Business and Economics
Communications and the Media
Culture and Recreation
Education
Employment and Labor
Energy
Environment and Natural Resources
Government Operations
Health
Housing and Development
International Affairs
Law and Justice
Military Personnel and Veterans
National Homeland Security
Science and Technology
Social Services and Disabilities
Transportation
U.S. Congress and Politics

Each chapter has further subject subdivisions, and there is a detailed index to the whole volume.

The value of having this information network at your call (and it *is* available to anyone) is incalculable. The U.S. federal government is an especially good place to begin looking for subject experts, as it employs thousands in mid-level positions. These people spend their careers keeping abreast of information in limited areas, and all of these subject specialists can be reached by phone. (Note that you should first seek the specialists themselves in the department or agency—not the librarians in the agency library.) They are quite helpful—and, in fact, *you* are helpful to *them*, since in answering inquiries from the public they justify their jobs, programs, and salaries. These are important considerations in an era of downsizing. They can also refer you to excellent private and nongovernmental contacts. The researcher mentioned above who was working on padlocks started out with the *Washington Information Directory* and then just followed a chain of referrals from the Commerce Department to various private sources.

**Leadership Directories, Inc.,** *Yellow Book* **directories.** These include fourteen titles: *Congressional Yellow Book, Federal Yellow Book, State Yellow Book, Municipal Yellow Book, Federal Regional Yellow Book, Judicial Yellow Book, Corporate Yellow Book, Financial Yellow Book, News Media Yellow Book, Associations Yellow Book, Law Firms Yellow Book, Government Affairs Yellow Book, Foreign Representatives Yellow Book,* and *Nonprofit Sector Yellow Book.* All fourteen are also available in a subscription Web site called *The Leadership Library.* These sources are much more detailed than the *Washington Information Directory*—they provide information down to the level of individual bureaucrats, editors, administrators, local officials, and scholars.

**Carroll Publishing Company directories.** These titles are somewhat like those from the Leadership Library; they include *Carroll's Federal Directory, Carroll's Federal Regional Directory, Carroll's State Directory, Carroll's Municipal Directory,* and *Carroll's County Directory.* A Web subscription version of all of these sources, to which many libraries subscribe, is also available.

**Authors of books or articles you've already read.** Writers who have published something on a particular subject often keep up-to-date on new developments in the field. Such people can be located through Google (or other) searches of various institutional Web pages, or through published directories in libraries. The *Web of Science* database, covering over 8,500 academic journals internationally (or its print equivalents—see Chapters 5 and 6), is particularly useful in this regard; it will give you the institutional address of the authors of the journal articles it indexes. From that information it is usually only a short step to a phone number or an e-mail address.

**Faculty of local universities.** The professors at institutions of higher learning are experts in an astonishing variety of topics, and most maintain regular office hours in which they are available for consultation or simply "chewing the fat." An advantage to researchers here is that there is no problem in getting past secretaries during these office hours—the scholars are there to be available to all comers.

These resources should be more than adequate for leading you to knowledgeable people in any field. Two additional sources with useful "how to" tips are John Brady's classic *The Craft of Interviewing* (New York: Vintage Books, 1977) and Risa Sacks's *Super Searchers Go to the Source: The Interviewing and Hands-On Information Strategies of Top Primary Researchers—Online, On the Phone, and In Person* (Medford, NJ: CyberAge Books, 2001).

A further word of advice has to do specifically with talking to reference librarians. Just as it is useful to match your book-retrieval techniques to the library's storage techniques, so it is often advisable to match the way you ask questions to the way librarians think (and any group that can put books on "moonshining" under **Distilling, Illicit** obviously does not think like most people).

Actually, it is the librarian's professional responsibility to find out what you're ultimately looking for—which may not be what you request initially—through a reference interview; so if you wind up being directed to an inappropriate source it may be more the librarian's fault than your own. Still, whatever the reason for any misdirection, you will nevertheless want to avoid it; and if you can make the librarian's job a little easier by knowing the sort of information he or she is listening for, then you will be the one to benefit. Going with the grain is more efficient than going against it.

Three examples of what to be aware of:

- A woman asked a librarian, "Where are your books on nineteenth-century English history?" The reference interview, however, elicited that fact that what she really wanted was, specifically, biographical information about her ancestor Samuel Earnshaw. Once this had been determined, the librarian could refer her directly to the multi-volume set *Modern English Biography*, which contained the necessary information. (*Biography and Genealogy Master Index* also provided other sources.) Had the librarian simply directed her to the library's bookstacks on nineteenth-century English history, the woman would have wasted much time.
- Another woman asked a graduate library assistant, "Where is *Chemical Abstracts*?" Further questioning could not elicit her ultimate aim, so she was indeed referred to *CA*. After about an hour, however, she came back and the assistant asked if she'd found what she needed. She had not. "What I'm really trying to find," she revealed, "is information on the side effects of Valium." Once the graduate student knew this, she could refer her directly to the *Physician's Desk Reference* manual, which the woman had never heard of.
- A student asked a reference librarian, "Where are your books on English literature?" After some discussion the librarian finally determined that he specifically wanted critical articles on Sir Walter Scott's *Heart of Midlothian*. The student could then be referred to *English Novel Explication: Criticism to 1972* (among other sources), which lists articles exactly on that topic. Had the librarian simply referred him to the PR (English literature) section of the classified bookstacks, the student would have wasted a lot of time there and still would not have found what he needed. (Journal articles on a particular subject are difficult to find through browsing bookstacks.)

In each of these cases—librarians could cite thousands more—the inquirers asked *not for what they really wanted but for what they thought the library could provide*. The problem is that most people have grossly inadequate assumptions about what can or cannot be found in a library. Other tend to think that the few resources or databases they've heard about, or the jumble of information that comes up in Google searches, constitute the full array of the best sources that exist. *They are usually wrong.*

Frequently professors and graduate students are more inefficient than anyone else. This hearkens back to a point made earlier, that a large number of them have never done any critical thinking about the dictum passed on to generation after generation of graduate students all over the country: "You shouldn't have to ask a librarian for help; if you can't find it on your own, you're no scholar." Researchers who have less "learning" and more common sense will not thus cut themselves off from a major source of help. The "find it on your own" imperative not only prevents scholars from asking for help, it also encourages them to settle for whatever they do find on their own, even when it's not exactly what they want. Even worse, when scholars can't think of a likely source through their own devices, this mentality encourages them to give up searching in the first place and to pretend that they don't really need what they think they can't get. Or just as bad, it encourages them to put inordinate trust in computer or Internet searches, which they wrongly assume will cover "everything."

That dictum is bad advice. Phrase positively, however—and understood positively—it is good advice: "The more you understand about library sources and retrieval systems, the better the scholar you will be." To the extent that you learn the range and depth of what you can expect from a library, you will allow yourself to ask more questions—and especially specific questions—you might otherwise think could not be answered efficiently. You will then find yourself asking, "Where can I find biographical information on my ancestor Samuel Earnshaw, who lived in nineteenth-century England" rather than "Where are your books on nineteenth-century English history?" You will ask, "Where can I find information on the side effects of Valium?" rather than "Where is *Chemical Abstracts*?" You will inquire, "Where can a find criticisms of Scott's *Heart of Midlothian*?" rather than "Where are your books on English literature?"

What is most useful to a reference librarian is to know what you are *ultimately* trying to find. A good way to clarify your thoughts on this is to ask yourself, "If there were an absolutely perfect article already written on my subject, what would the title of that article be?"

In going *outside* the library to talk to people, however, you will need some good directory information, and while much of it can indeed be found on the Internet, not all of it resides there; many excellent "overview" directories are not freely available online, but may be freely consulted (either in print or electronic forms) within library walls.

The rule to remember in all of this is that somewhere along the line in your research you should ask yourself, "*Who* would be likely to know about this subject? Whose *business* is it to know? In whose *interest* would it be?" These questions, plus a browsing familiarity with the resources listed above, can get you started on some very valuable pathways, and lead you to important information not recorded in any print or online source.

# Note

1. Leila Kight, quoted in the *Washington Post* (April 15, 1980), p. B5.

# 13

## *Hidden Treasures*

Five types of resources contain an incredible wealth of information in all subject areas, but are so neglected by most conventional databases and indexes that they are virtually unknown to most researchers. Discovering any one of them, however, can provide you with the reader's equivalent of tapping into Alaska's north-shore oil reserves. The five are:

- Microform sets (some of which have Web or CD-ROM counterparts)
- Web collections of documents (both subscription and free sites)
- Government documents
- Archives, manuscripts, and public records
- Special collections

CD-ROMs sets of documents are analogous to microform collections but are fading into obsolescence, being largely superseded by subscription Web sites. The advantage of either CD or Web collections, of course, is that they allow keyword searching of the full texts of their component documents. Migration to the Web is not happening with the majority of microform sets, however; and libraries that opt for online versions, where available, have to accept the trade-off that increased keyword access is probably being achieved at the expense of losing long-term preservation capability.

Most of these sets of documents—the microforms, government documents, archives/manuscripts, and special collections—have several points in common:

- In addition to being neglected by most library catalogs and databases, they are usually housed in quarters that are physically separate from a library's general collections.
- They are not shelved or stored in a way that allows efficient subject access through general or focused browsing, or their formats do not allow browsing to begin with.
- They are accessible only through a variety of special databases or bibliographies, not through a single convenient source; and the identification of the best indexes may be a separate treasure hunt in itself.

It takes extra steps to get into these materials, in other words, and few people bother with non-Web materials because to those lacking prior experience in these areas the paths are obscure and the destination isn't foreseeable. Researchers who have enough faith to venture off the beaten track, however, are usually well-rewarded.

You simply have to suspect in advance that microform or Web collections, government documents, archives or manuscript resources, and special collections will indeed yield remarkable results; and then you must actively look for them, for you cannot expect the normal channels of research to turn up adequate references to them. In seeking these materials it is especially important to ask for help, for frequently the best initial access is through an experienced custodian's knowledge of what is likely to be found in the collections.

The ways to identify special collections have been discussed in Chapter 11 and so will not be repeated here.

## Microform Sets and Counterpart Web Sites

Many researchers are initially deterred from using microforms by the mistaken assumption that they cannot make quick photocopies on paper from such formats. Such copies, however, can be made very easily; any library with microfilm or microfiche holdings will also have reader-printer machines.

Hundreds of large, prepackages research collections exist in a bewildering variety of subject areas, and there is likely to be one or more of interest to any scholar. A good starting point, even though dated, for microforms is Suzanne Dodson's *Microform Research Collections: A Guide* (2nd ed.;

Meckler Publishing, 1984). It lists many of the major sets and describes them in detail; it also has a good subject index. The annual *Guide to Microforms in Print: Subject* (K. G. Saur) includes collections as well as individual titles, but does not describe or annotate them. A useful online list is the *Guide to the Microform Collections in the Humanities and Social Sciences Division* (Library of Congress) at www.loc.gov/rr/microform/guide/; this has good annotated descriptions and a good subject index. Most of these collections are commercially available sets that are duplicated in many other research libraries.

Two additional online lists, identifying hundreds of microform research collections, are offered by Primary Source Microfilm at http:// microformguides.gale.com/index.shtml and Scholarly Resources, Inc., at www.gale.com/scholarly.htm. These sites also provide digital versions of the various *Guides* that accompany the sets, which list all of the individual titles within them. By consulting these free Web sites you can not only get an overview of much of the range of existing collections—you can also determine if individual titles within them are interesting enough to lure you into a library, to read the microfilms. Other online lists of microfilm/Web collections are searchable at:

- www.proquest.co.uk (click on the "Chadwyck-Healey" and "UMI" links)
- www.lexisnexis.com/academic/2upa/upaMnu.asp (University Publications of America).

Although there is a trend to digitize sets that already exist in microformats, most such collections do not have digital counterparts. Further, no single source will tell you which microform sets do have subscription Web versions. Nevertheless, if you can identify a particular microform collection to begin with, the catalog record for it—as it appears in either your local library catalog, or in *WorldCat* or the *RLG Union Catalog*, or in the Library of Congress online catalog—may contain a note field identifying a Web counterpart. If your local library subscribes to the Web version, the link may be a "hot" one that you can simply click on.

Once you've determined which collections exist, you can search for them by title in your own library's catalog. (Most catalogs add the word "microform" as a format indicator to the title field of any relevant catalog records—

so you can also search for this keyword directly, limiting it to title appearances.) If your local library doesn't own the set you want, the *FirstSearch* and *RLG Union Catalog* databases (see Chapter 11) can usually identify other libraries' holdings.

The range and variety of the collections that exist can be suggested by a brief listing of some of their titles:

*African Library*

*American Architectural Books*

*American Natural History*

*American Fiction, 1774–1900; 1901–1910* (Web version: *Early American Fiction 1789–1875*)

*American Periodical Literature, 1741–1900* (Web version: *American Periodicals Series*)

*American Poetry, 1609–1900* (Web version: *American Poetry 1760–1900*)

Archives of the Soviet Communist Party and Soviet State

*Black Biographical Dictionaries, 1790–1950* (Web version: *African American Biographical Database*)

*Botany Library on Microfiche*

*British and Continental Rhetoric and Elocution*

*Civil War Unit Histories*

*City Directories of the United States* [1786–1901] (partially in Web version)

*Crime and Juvenile Delinquency*

*Declassified Documents* (Web version: *Declassified Documents Reference System*)

*Early American Imprints, 1639–1800; 1801–1809* (Web version: *Evans Digital Collections Online*)

*Early English Books, 1475–1640; 1641–1700* (Web version: *Early English Books Online*)

*Eighteenth Century Collection* (Web version: *Eighteenth Century Collections Online*)

*French Revolution: Critical Works and Historical Sources*

*Gerritsen Collection of Women's History* (Web version available)

*Goldsmiths'-Kress Library of Economic Literature* (CD-ROM and Web versions available)

*Herstory*

*History of Medicine*

*History of Photography*
*History of Women*
*Human Relations Area Files* (recent material on Web; backfile on microfiche)
*Indians of North America*
*Kentucky Culture*
*Landmarks of Science*
*Labor Union Periodicals*
Microbook *Library of American Civilization*
*Musicache*
*The Negro: Emancipation to World War I*
*Records of Ante-Bellum Southern Plantations*
*Reports of Explorations Printed in the Documents of the United States Government*
*Russian Revolutionary Literature*
*Slavery: Source Material and Critical Literature*
*Source Materials in the Field of Theatre*
*Southern Women and Their Families in the 19th Century: Papers and Diaries*
*Spanish Drama of the Golden Age*
*Travels in the Confederate States*
*Travels in the Old South I, II, III*
*Travels in the West and Southwest*
*Western Americana, 1550–1900*
*Witchcraft in Europe and America*

Each of these sets may contain hundreds or thousands of publications. Many other collections exist, too; especially noteworthy are the complete sets of books published within various countries up to a certain date (usually more than a century ago, for copyright reasons); the various exhaustive collections of old literature, drama, or poetry for particular countries; and many collections of national and international government publications. A closer look at three of the above sets will give some indication of the riches that are included.

***Goldsmiths'-Kress Library of Economic Literature.*** This is a huge collection of 4,267 reels of microfilm containing 62,345 titles of monographs and serials: books published between 1460 and 1850 and serial literature (466 titles) whose publication began prior to 1850. (Entire runs of serials are included even when they extend after 1850.) The material is in more than ten European languages. The *Guide* to the set suggests its range:

> In addition to the standard, well-known works used in studying the history of economics and business, the microfilm library contains unusual and exceedingly rare items which offer unique possibilities for comparative and cross-cultural research in the history of economic thought. Moreover, the collection is extremely rich in materials on political and social history in particular, and on history in general. Individual works are seldom confined to a single academic discipline, as the period antedates modern academic specialization. The micropublication thus constitutes a major research source for all social scientists and historians, as well as for economists.

Among the subjects covered are mercantilism, agriculture, emigration, European colonial expansion, slavery, demography in eighteenth-century England, the textile industry, socialism, trade unionism, piracy, dietary habits in various European countries, early business and technical education, commerce in Italy, penology, trade manuals, numismatics, the economy of eighteenth-century Scandinavia, Irish-English relations, social conditions, population, transport and transport technology, and even theology. As of this writing, CD-ROM and Web versions are now available.

*Human Relations Area Files.* This is a huge, ongoing collection of ethnographic source materials (mainly published books and articles, although some unpublished manuscripts and reports of field research are included) for worldwide, comparative, cross-cultural study of human behavior and society as represented in approximately 350 cultures. It is useful to students of anthropology, sociology, psychology, politics, literature, home economics, comparative religion, art, and agricultural development—and for anyone else who wishes to compare the perceptions, customs, social institutions, values, beliefs, and daily life of all peoples of the world, past and present. The set of documents is now split between microfiche and electronic formats. The microfiche set of 23,381 fiche, published in 42 installments from the 1950s until 1993, contains the bulk of the collection; installments 43 through 49 were published in CD-ROM format. A Web version incorporating all installments from 43 forward is now available; this subscription also includes some, but not all, retrospective conversions and updates of the fiche material. Information about the entire collection is online at www.yale.edu/ hraf/collections.htm. The source documents are arranged in about 350 groups, each representing a different culture; and each culture is analyzed, insofar as the documentation permits, in more than 600 topical categories (e.g., mortality, recorded history, food production, architecture for various functions, humor, entertainment, trial procedures, recruitment of armed forces, old-age dependency, sexual practices and norms, views on abortion, drug use, division of labor by sex, sanitary facilities, power development, interpersonal relations, art, religion, political organization, etc.). Within each category is found all relevant descriptive documentation drawn from more than one million pages of source material. (Foreign-language documents are translated into English.) The standardization of categories under each culture allows for ready comparisons of information, which in many cases can be statistically significant. All of the cultures are listed in the accompanying publication *Outline of World Cultures* (available online at www. yale.edu/hraf/collections_body_ethnocultures.htm), while the subdividing topical categories are listed in *Outline of Cultural Materials* (www.yale.edu/ hraf/collections_body_ethnotopics.htm).

**Microbook *Library of American Civilization*.** According to the guidebook that accompanies this microfiche set, it:

> contains more than 6,500,000 pages of materials relating to all aspects of American life and literature, from the beginning to the outbreak of World War I. Included are pamphlets, periodicals, documents both public and private, biographies and autobiographies of persons both known and obscure, fiction and nonfiction, poetry, collected works and papers, material of foreign origin relating to America, and many rare books not generally available.

It is essentially a large historical library of approximately 10,000 books in a filing cabinet, covering early exploration, colonial history and records, politics and government, military history, foreign policy, constitutional history, law and law enforcement, the frontier, the South, local history, Indians and other minorities, agriculture, the city, business, labor, religion, education, reform, intellectual history, science and technology, literature, the various useful and performing arts, architecture, manners and customs, and so on. There are separate author, title, and subject index volumes.

Most of the other microform sets are equally amazing. Two important points to remember, however, are:

1. In most cases, *none* of the many individual items within a collection will be separately recorded in your library's computer catalog. The only indication in your local catalog will be a record of the printed *Guide* that accompanies the set and lists its contents; it will usually be found under the headings **[Subject]—Bibliography** or **[Subject]—Microform catalogs**. If you miss these entries, you will in effect miss all of the possibly thousands of relevant sources in the collection.

2. Many—not all—of the individual microform works within collections are recorded (with their reel numbers) in the *RLG Union Catalog* or *WorldCat*. In other words, if you find a record in these databases that says the work you want is available on a particular reel within a microform collection, check your local libraries to see if they own that collection.

One microform set that is not generally regarded as a separate collection unto itself is the aggregate of more than a million American doctoral dissertations available for purchase from University Microfilms International (UMI/ProQuest). The only library that owns a full set of them is the Library of Congress, where all of them can be read for free, onsite. Some researchers have justified trips to the Library just to use this collection, as the cost of ordering many individual titles from UMI may be greater than that of a plane ticket to Washington. Online indexes, *Dissertation Abstracts* or *Digital Dissertations*, allow keyword searching of citations and abstracts, but not the full texts of the dissertations themselves. (Abstracts are searchable only from mid-1980 forward; prior to that date, the databases contain only citations without abstracts.) The *Digital Dissertations* version of the index allows researchers, for a fee, to email themselves electronic copies of the full texts of any dissertations from 1997 or afterward.

Another equally amazing set not usually regarded as one aggregation is the collection of National Technical Information Service (NTIS) reports on microfiche. These are millions of research studies funded by the U.S. government. Again, the Library of Congress is the only facility that owns all of them, for free reading onsite; however, individual titles may be ordered directly from NTIS (see below, in the Government Documents section).

## Web Collections

Many collections of published documents and other material (manuscripts, photographs) exist in subscription-based Web sites, without any corresponding microform sets; in a sense, these sets are somewhat like "invisible Web" resources (see Chapter 5) because neither type of resource is directly accessible via conventional search engines such as Google or Teoma or AskJeeves. The difference, however, is that invisible Web sites are indeed freely accessible if you can find them in the first place, while subscription Web sites can be entered only through site-licensed terminals within library walls, or via paid passwords.

Subscription sets are similar in content to the microform collections, with the obvious difference that they allow keyword searching of the full texts of their component documents. Scores of such collections already exist, and more are continually being produced. A sampling of these databases includes:

*AMDOCS: Documents for the Study of American History* (free invisible Web site)
*American Civil War: Letters and Diaries*
*American Film Scripts Online*
*American Memory* (free invisible Web site; see below)
*Ancestry Plus*
*Black Thought and Culture*
*British and Irish Women's Letters and Diaries*
*Digital Library of Classic Protestant Texts*
*Documenting the American South*
*Early Encounters in North America: Peoples, Cultures, and the Environment*
*Heritage Quest*
*History Resource Center*
*Internet History Sourcebooks Project* (free invisible Web site)
*Making of America* (Cornell) (free invisible Web site)
*Making of America* (Michigan) (free invisible Web site)
*North American Immigrant Letters, Diaries, and Oral Histories*
*North American Theatre Online*
*North American Women's Letters and Diaries, Colonial to 1950* (see below)

*Oral Histories Online* (see below)
*Women and Social Movements in the United States*

There is no single listing of subscription online research collections; descriptions of individual subscription databases can be found through some of the microfilm publishers' sites listed above, and at the Alexander Street Press site www.alexanderstreetpress.com/products/index.htm.

Google searches of the titles of the free (non-subscription) collections will also turn up the entry portals to their otherwise invisible contents. A good online listing of free research collections is maintained by the University of Idaho at www.uidaho.edu/special-collections/Other.Repositories. html. This list, however, simply identifies the collections at the level of their "top" pages; to see if any of them have actual digitized full texts freely online—many of them do—you have use the search box within each site individually.

Web sites—whether subscription-based or free—can indeed provide remarkable resources. A closer look at three of the above sites will indicate some of the riches available.

**American Memory.** This is a free site maintained by the Library of Congress at http://memory.loc.gov. It includes about nine million scanned images from over 120 historical collections in the Library, with links to other Web sites. Among the digitized collections are the following:

*Emergence of Advertising in America*: over 9,000 images relating to the growth of advertising in the U.S.

*Built in America: Historic American Buildings Survey and Historic Engineering Record*: a collection of "more than 350,000 measured drawings, large-format photographs, and written histories for more than 35,000 historic structures and sites dating from Pre-Columbian times to the twentieth century." The online version includes "digitized images of measured drawing, black-and-white photographs, color transparencies, photo captions, data pages including written histories, and supplemental materials."

*Federal Theatre Project*: 13,000 images of items including photographs, stage and costume designs, playscripts, and administrative records.

*Map Collections*: a selection of copyright-free maps of cities and towns, military battles and campaigns, cultural landscapes, transportation and communication, etc.

*Sheet Music*: more than 62,500 historical pieces of sheet music registered for copyright from 1820–1885.

*Slave Narratives*: more than 2,300 first-person recorded transcripts of accounts of slavery, with over 500 photos of former slaves.

*Variety Stage*: a documentary collection of materials on vaudeville and other popular entertainments from 1870–1920, including play scripts, handbills, motion pictures, sound recordings, and photographs.

*Woman Suffrage*: collections of 167 books and pamphlets, as well as photographs and cartoons.

The Library is prevented by law from digitizing works that are still under copyright protection, so the materials found in *American Memory* are usually more than ninety-five years old.

***North American Women's Letters and Diaries, Colonial to 1950.*** This is a subscription file from Alexander Street Press; it is not freely available on the Web, but many research libraries subscribe to it and offer free access within their walls or via university-issued passwords. According to the publisher's description, "the collection includes approximately 150,000 pages of letters and diaries from colonial times to 1950 . . . drawn from more than 1,000 sources. . . . Represented are all age groups and life stages, a wide range of ethnicities, many geographical regions, the famous, and the not so famous. . . . Six tables of contents allow the user to browse the collection from different entry points, including personal life events and a chronology of historical events. Full-text searching is extremely precise. [Texts are indexed] by numerous fields, including race, occupation, recipient's gender, geography, marital and maternal status, and more. . . . Questions like these can be answered quickly and easily:

"Show me:

- All diary entries and letters written between 1820 and 1900 that discuss childbirth.
- All materials written from 1941 to 1945 that mention war.

- All correspondence from women in the Northeast to their husbands in the Northwest during the Gold Rush.
- All letters written by African Americans who were educators.
- All letters sent by Abigail Adams that mention Boston.
- All diary entries by suffragettes that have women's rights issues as subjects.
- Diaries and letters, written by women younger than twenty, which mention marriage."

New material is continually added. The real strength of this collection lies in its exceptionally detailed indexing, which enables users to categorize and sort material according to scores of different criteria—which could not be done at all in a strictly keyword database.

*Oral History Online.* This is another subscription-based service from Alexander Street Press. It is an index that identifies over 10,000 oral histories in over 2,500 collections, and directly links to more than 60,000 pages of full texts, 1600 audio files, and 600 videos. Each oral history is indexed in dozens of standardized categories. The publisher's description of possible searches include:

- "List all oral history interviews conducted with miners in Pennsylvania between 1950 and 1960.
- Detail all oral histories pertaining to health workers.
- Identify all collections that have material relevant to substance abuse.
- Determine which collection contains an interview with James T. Hiram.
- Find all interviews with survivors of the Titanic disaster."

The collection will grow continually.

## Government Documents

The term "document" is synonymous with "publication"; it can refer to just about any format, including monographs, magazines, reports, pamphlets, broadsides, maps, prints, photographs, posters, kits, CD-ROMs, Web sites, and so on. Also included in government documents are many finding aids and reference sources such as catalogs, indexes, directories, dictionaries, and bibliographies.

The U.S. federal government—with whose publications this section is concerned—also produces films, sound recordings, audiovisuals, and microforms.

The range, variety, and depth of coverage of these materials are amazing. They are particularly thorough in scientific and technical areas, and in all of the social sciences—especially regarding issues of public policy. There are even surprising contributions to the humanities as well (e.g., from the Smithsonian Institution, the Library of Congress, and the National Endowment for the Humanities). In using government documents, you can ask almost the same questions—and expect to find answers—as you can in using the more well-known research tools.

The main publisher of U.S. government documents is the Government Printing Office (GPO). In recent years, however, this agency has made a concerted effort to produce fewer materials in paper format, and to publish most of its output directly on the Web. In addition, in those cases in which the GPO formerly published printed materials for other federal agencies, it is now encouraging those agencies to bypass GPO involvement and to publish their own offerings, too, directly on their own Web sites. There is a trade-off here: this policy is likely to be disastrous for long-term preservation purposes, but in the short run it makes much more material readily accessible to larger audiences.

In looking for *current* information from the U.S. government, then, the Web is the first place to check, at the following sites:

- FirstGov, the U.S. government's official Web portal: www.firstgov.gov. (Remember, again, that the publications of individual agencies may now be accessible from the agencies' own portals, listed here, rather than from the GPO.)
- Government Printing Office: www.gpoaccess.gov. Pay particular attention to the site's "A–Z Resource List," which provides a good overview of the important federal publications that are now online, with dates of retrospective coverage.
- FedStats, a gateway to statistics from over 100 federal agencies: (www.fedstats.gov).
- U.S. Census Bureau: (www.census.gov).

- FedWorld (maintained by the National Technical Information Service): www.fedworld.gov.
- Congressional Research Service (CRS) reports are indexed by Penny Hill Press, which also sells copies of the documents, at www. pennyhill.com.

Since it is almost impossible to speak systematically of the subjects of government publications, let me offer a brief menu of titles, simply to suggest how surprising their range and variety is:

*Camper's First Aid*

*Report of the United States Commission on International Religious Freedom*

*Miro: Selected Paintings*

*Treaties in Force*

*Health Information for International Travel* [serial]

*Professional Boxing: Issues Related to the Protection of Boxers' Health, Safety, and Economic Interests*

*Poisonous Snakes of the World*

*The African American Mosaic: A Library of Congress Resource Guide for the Study of Black History and Culture*

*Library of Congress Music, Theater, Dance: An Illustrated Guide*

*The Tradition of Science: Landmarks of Western Science in the Collections of the Library of Congress*

*The Tradition of Technology: Landmarks of Western Technology in the Collections of the Library of Congress*

*Cataloging and Classification Quality at the Library of Congress*

*Doing Research at the Library of Congress: A Guide to Subject Searching in a Closed Stacks Library*

*Environmental Planning for Small Communities: A Guide for Local Decision-Makers*

*Polish Genealogy and Heraldry*

*Preparing Your Child for College: A Resource Book for Parents*

*Guide to Federal Government Sales*

*How to Buy Surplus Property from the Department of Defense*

*How to Sell to Government Agencies*

*Selling to the Military*

*Backyard Bird Problems*
*Migration of Birds*
*Falconry*
*Fifty Birds of Town and City*
*Ducks at a Distance: Waterfowl Identification Guide*
*The Education System of Switzerland*
*Rotorcraft Flying Handbook*
*Occupational Outlook Handbook*
*How Basic Research Reaps Unexpected Rewards*
*Handbook of North American Indians*
*Small Scale Beekeeping*
*Underground Railroad: Official National Park Handbook*
*Sex and the Spinal Cord Injured*
*The Science of Fingerprints*
*Handbook of Forensic Services*
*ATF Arson Investigative Guide*
*A Basic Guide to Exporting*
*An Office Building Occupant's Guide to Indoor Air Quality*
*Guide to High Speed Patrol Car Tires*
*The Murals of Harold Weston*
*The Effects of Nuclear War*
*United States Senate Catalogue of Fine Arts*
*Soldier's Manual and Trainer's Guide: Broadcast Journalist*
*Low-Cost Wood Homes for Rural America: Construction Manual*
*A Descriptive List of Treasure Maps and Charts in the Library of Congress*
*Nutritive Value of Foods*
*The Calibration of a Burn Room for Fire Tests on Furnishings*
*Modern Written Arabic*
*Diplomatic Hebrew*
*What You Should Know About Smoke Detectors*
*Survival, Evasion, and Escape*
*Substance Use in Popular Movies & Music*
*Project MKUltra: The CIA's Program of Research in Behavior Modification*
*The Naval War of 1812: A Documentary History* (2 vols.)
*Radiologic Technology Medical Service*
*A Barefoot Doctor's Manual*
*A Study of Lumber Used for Bracing Trenches in the United States*

*Artillery Through the Ages*
*Wildlife Portrait Series*
*The Ship's Medicine Chest and Medicine Chest at Sea*
*The Star of Bethlehem* [LC bibliography]
*Occupational Diseases: A Guide to Their Recognition*
*Soil Taxonomy*
*The Translation of Poetry*
*The Black Population in the United States* [serial]
*Family Folklore: Interviewing Guide and Questionnaire*
*Angler's Guide to the United States Atlantic Coast* [also *Pacific Coast*
    volume]
*Marine Life Posters*
*The Martian Landscape* [with 3-D stereo viewer]
*A Guide to the Study and Use of Military History*
*Literary Recordings: A Checklist of the Archives of Recorded Poetry and
    Literature in the Library of Congress*
*Catalog of Federal Domestic Assistance*
*North American Industry Classification*
*Standard Industrial Classification Manual*
*A Study of Global Sand Seas*
*NOAA Diving Manual*
*Small Business Location and Layout*
*Raising a Small Flock of Sheep*
*Defining Death: A Report on the Medical, Legal, and Ethical Issues in
    the Determination of Death*
*Fermentation Guide to Potatoes*
*The Bark Canoes and Skin Boats of North America*
*How to Buy a Christmas Tree*
*How Trees Help Clean the Air*
*The Hammered Dulcimer in America*

Many of these publications are themselves but the tip of a "subject iceberg"—whenever you find one document on a subject that interests you, you can usually figure that there are many others waiting to be discovered (see especially the *Subject Bibliographies* series, described below). The Government Printing Office and other federal agencies publish tens of thousands of titles each year. Note, however, that not all such publications stay in print indefinitely—as with commercial publications, many are available for sale only for a few years, after which they can be found in libraries' collections of government documents.

If you have not used government documents before, you almost have to make a leap of faith to start looking for them; but it is probable that you will be pleasantly surprised. (Students who use such documents will almost invariably find that none of their classmates has found the same sources.)

A number of reasons account for the general neglect of government publications by academic and other researchers; let me extend a few points made at the beginning of this chapter.

- Although the government spends millions of dollars a year to publish these materials, it spends very little to advertise or market them. Some enterprising private companies republish documents, in paper or online, for a wider audience—which is perfectly allowable, since virtually nothing printed by the Government Printing Office is copyrighted— but such efforts pick up only a fraction of what is available.
- Libraries that own large collections of government documents often shelve them separately rather than integrate them into the general collections. This is done because the best access to documents is provided by their own special indexes, which are keyed to Superintendent of Documents (SuDocs) call numbers rather than Library of Congress or Dewey Decimal numbers; and the alphanumeric patterns of SuDocs numbers are such that they cannot be interfiled with such traditional shelf-arrangement schemes. The result is that you will not find documents through the two major avenues of subject access to the library's books: the computer catalog and shelf browsing. (Even in its own section a documents collection cannot be browsed very efficiently because the SuDocs scheme arranges items according to the agencies that produced them and *not* according to the *subjects* of the documents. This is the difference between an archival scheme of arrangement and a subject-classification scheme.)
- Documents are not covered by the most commonly used databases, indexes, and catalogs; and those available online often lie within "invisible" Web sites.
- Documents are not sold in most bookstores.
- Courses in government publications are not required in library schools.

One result is that not all librarians themselves are aware of their potential. This is unfortunate for researchers, because you probably won't be referred to documents in the first place unless you chance upon someone with experience in using them.

There are two types of government-documents collections: regional depositories and selective depositories. The regionals are required by law to receive and permanently retain copies of *all* federal documents available through the depository program. Selective depositories are just that—they can choose which categories of publications they wish to receive and can weed their collections. A printed directory of which depositories are in which cities—including a list of where the regionals are—is available in any public library; the same information is available on the Web at www.gpoaccess. gov. Note that although more and more *current* publications are now being published directly online, the depositories will contain the rich *retrospective* collections of millions of older documents.

Law school libraries are usually selective depositories, but they generally confine their selections to series of law-related materials and administrative decisions.

It is noteworthy for researchers that all depositories (including those at law schools) must admit the general public to their documents collections. The law that allows them to receive free federal publications stipulates that access must be open to all; schools that try to permit only their own students to have access to the documents can lose their depository status. In other words, you can use the demand "I want to use your documents collection" to get in the door of law or medical libraries that are otherwise closed to you.

For those who wish to undertake systematic research in U.S. government documents there are a variety of databases and indexes that have different strengths and weaknesses and must therefore be used in combination.

***Catalog of U.S. Government Publications.*** This is the title of the online version, searchable at www.gpoaccess.gov/cgp/advanced.html; it includes entries for publications listed from 1994 forward, with hot links to full texts (when available). The corresponding printed index is the *Monthly Catalog of U.S. Government Publications*, sets of which are still required for retrospective searches. In either format, this is the basic "umbrella" index to government publications, excluding NTIS reports (for which, see below). It is intended to be a complete list, with (in paper form) cumulated annual indexes, to all federal publications. An online subscription version called *GPO*, with coverage of over a half million entries back to 1976, is available through the FirstSearch system (see Chapter 4). For earlier decades of coverage you will want to use the *Cumulative Subject Index to the Monthly Catalog of United States Government Publications 1900–1971*, 15 vols. (Carrollton Press, 1973–75) and the *Cumulative Subject Index to United States Government Publications 1895–1899*, 2 vols. (Carrollton Press, 1977). There is also a *Cumulative Title Index to United States Public Documents 1789–1976*, 16 vols. (U.S. Historical Documents Institute, 1971–79) and a *United States Government Publications Monthly Catalog: Cumulative Personal Author Index 1941–1975*, 5 vols. (Pierian Press, 1971–79). A cumulative approach through corporate author or agency name is provided by volumes 606–624 of the *National Union Catalog: Pre-1956 Imprints*, which segment has also been republished as a separate set. The *WorldCat* and *RLG Union Catalog* databases can also be useful, but they do not entirely supersede the printed sources. Several other indexes and catalogs for historical approaches are ably discussed in Joe Morehead's *Introduction to United States Government Information Sources* (Libraries Unlimited; revised irregularly), which is the bible for documents researchers.

**CIS Indexes.** Congressional Information Service (CIS) produces a variety of subscription databases, print indexes, and microfiche sets of federal publications in the legislative, executive, and judicial branches of government. All of these provide finer and more careful indexing than the government's own *Catalog*. CIS is now a subsidiary of *LexisNexis*, so Web versions of its indexes (usually with direct links to online full texts) are now available exclusively via that source. Note that the CIS components of *LexisNexis* are not part of the standard subscription to the latter database, but must be added via supplemental subscriptions (see Chapter 5). Although digital versions of many of the CIS indexes used to be available on CD-ROMs, the company has discontinued this form of publication. In other words, libraries that do not have subscriptions to the Web version of the CIS indexes via *LexisNexis* must now rely on the various paper copy publications. Each index is keyed to a microfiche set of the actual documents indexed (although it is possible that libraries may subscribe to the indexes without the fiche documents). The several CIS paper-format indexes covering legislative branch publications include the following:

*CIS Index.* This is the best index to U.S. Congressional publications—House and Senate hearings, committee prints, reports, and documents—as well as legislative histories from 1970 forward.

*CIS US Congressional Committee Hearings Index*, providing retrospective coverage for the years 1833–1969.

*CIS Index to Unpublished US House of Representatives Hearings*, providing retrospective coverage for the years 1833–1968.

*CIS Index to Unpublished US Senate Hearings*, providing retrospective coverage for the years 1823–1976.

*CIS US Congressional Committee Prints Index*, providing retrospective coverage for the years 1830–1969.

*CIS US Serial Set Index*, providing retrospective coverage of miscellaneous Congressional reports and documents from 1789 to 1969.

*CIS Index to US Senate Executive Documents & Reports*, providing retrospective coverage from 1817 to 1969.

*Congressional Member Organizations & Caucuses: CIS Guide to Publications and Policy Materials.* This is an index to the publications of about 120 coalitions, caucuses, study groups, and conferences within the U.S. Congress, including such groups as the Democratic Policy Committee, the Congressional Black Caucus, the House Republican Conference, and the Congressional Hispanic Caucus.

Indexes to executive branch publications include the following:

*CIS Index to US Executive Branch Documents*, covering (as of this writing) 1789–1932.

*CIS Index to Presidential Executive Orders and Proclamations*, covering 1789–1983.

*CIS Federal Register Index*, covering 1984–1998, including executive orders and proclamations after 1983 (This index has now been discontinued.)

*Reports Required by Congress: CIS Guide to Executive Communications*, covering from 1994 forward. These are publications filed by federal agencies reporting on their compliance with Congressional legislative intentions; they are usually not published by the GPO and are not easily accessible outside the microfiche set of documents corresponding to this index.

For the judicial branch, CIS publishes a number of microfiche sets of documents, such as *U.S. Supreme Court Records & Briefs* (1897 forward) and *U.S. Reports* (1790 forward), but without specialized indexes.

It is worthwhile to step back for a moment and focus specifically on U.S. Congressional hearings, because these are frequently potential gold mines of information for those researchers who have the initiative to seek them out. The U.S. Congress has an astonishing range of oversight interests and responsibilities that generate detailed inquiries; these investigations monitor all areas of U.S. society and world relations. Most people are aware, simply from newspaper coverage, of Congress's investigations of 9/11 readiness, regulatory reform, military spending, Social Security problems, nuclear energy, dependency on foreign oil suppliers, foreign-policy directions, and so on; but the many hearings it conducts on smaller issues are underpublicized and underutilized. The value of hearings is that they assemble top experts and interested parties on all sides of an issue to testify on the current state of problem, or the background to its development, and to recommend specific courses of action. Often they include extensive documentary material in appendices. This kind of overview is not often available anywhere else. Some examples of hearings include:

*Acid Rain*
*Assessing the Impact of Nasal Radium Treatments*
*Halting the Spread of HIV/AIDS: Future Efforts in the U.S. Bilateral and Multilateral Response*
*Youth Violence and Gangs*
*Violence in Video Games*
*Exploitation of Young Adults in Door-to-Door Sales*
*Scientific Fraud*
*Review of Production and Marketing Challenges Facing U.S. Fruit and Vegetable Industries*
*Employee Privacy: Computer-Use Monitoring Practices and Policies of Selected Companies*
*Status of the African Elephant*

*Elephant, Rhino, and Tiger Conservation*
*Desert Tortoise Habitat Conservation*
*Rail Freight Transportation Issues in Montana*
*Childhood Leukemia Clusters in Fallon, NV*
*The Nursing Shortage*
*Methamphetamine and Date Rape Drugs*
*Under the Influence: The Binge Drinking Epidemic on College Campuses*
*Mold: A Growing Problem*
*Stumbling onto Smut: The Alarming Ease of Access to Pornography on Peer-to-Peer Networks*
*Prostate Cancer*
*Cranial Deformities: Giving Our Kids a Fighting Chance*
*The Role of Basic Research in Economic Competitiveness*
*Airworthiness of the DC-10*
*Life on Mars?*
*Preservation of Petroglyphs in Albuquerque, New Mexico*
*Contaminated Frozen Strawberries in School Lunches*
*Competitiveness in the Glassware Industry*
*Shaping Our Responses to Violent and Demeaning Imagery in Popular Music*
*Medical and Psychological Impact of Abortion*
*Hearing on the Rights of Artists and Scholars to Freedom of Expression and the Rights of Taxpayers to Determine the Use of Public Funds*
*Superconductivity*
*Samoan White-Collar Crime*
*Atlantic Swordfish Oversight*
*Oversight Hearing on Arctic Snow Geese*
*Mailing of Dangerous Martial Arts Weapons*
*Degradable Six-Pack Rings*
*Persecution of Albanian Minority in Yugoslavia*
*Public Safety Issues Surrounding Marijuana Production in National Forests*
*Organ Transplants, Choices and Criteria, Who Lives, Who Dies, Who Pays?*
*Global Change Research: The Role of Clouds in Climate Change*
*Turn It Down: Effects of Noise on Hearing Loss in Children and Youth*
*New Research on the Potential Health Risks of Carpets*

*Racial Discrimination in Awarding Toyota Dealerships*
*Breastfeeding in the U.S.*
*Sleep Disorders*
*The Effects of Traffic Radar Guns on Law Enforcement Officers*
*Insurance Redlining Practices*
*Auto Repair Fraud*
*Parental Kidnapping*
*Sex and Violence on TV*
*Street People*
*Severe Storms Research*
*Effect of Pornography on Women and Children*

As should be obvious from even this very brief list, Congressional hearings provide rich materials for both advanced scholarship and student term papers, and researchers who browse through the basic *CIS Index* will have an advantage in selecting topics that their classmates will overlook entirely. *Thousands* of topics are covered by hearings every year.

The federal government is also one of the best sources for statistics on any subject imaginable; and here, too, Congressional Information Service provides the best index:

**American Statistics Index (ASI).** This is an annual hardbound print index, with monthly supplements and quarterly cumulations. Although it began publication in 1974, its first volume covers statistics back to the early 1960s. *ASI* is the best overall index to all of the statistical publications of the U.S. federal government, whether from executive, legislative, or judicial branches. It provides detailed subject access to *every* statistical table, list, or publication produced by the government. Especially useful are its many category indexes (e.g., "By State," "By Industry," "By Occupation," "By Sex," etc.), which greatly facilitate finding comparative figures. Through the *ASI* you can find answers to such questions as "How much advertising do Chicago TV stations sell?"; "How much of the coal used in U.S. coke plants comes from Fayette County, Pa.?"; "How many children of unemployed parents are on welfare in California?"; "How much did the chemicals industry invest in pollution control equipment in New Jersey?"; and "How many people are killed each year in bombing incidents and what are the motives of such incidents?"[1]

CIS also produces two related indexes: *Statistical Reference Index (SRI)* and *Index to International Statistics (IIS)*. The first is a wide-ranging index to statistics produced by non-federal U.S. agencies such as state and municipal governments, universities, trade and industry groups, think tanks, private pollster companies, and so on; the latter covers the statistical publications of approximately 100 international agencies such as the United Nations system, the European Union, the Organization for Economic Cooperation and Development, the Organization of American States, and so on.

As with the other CIS indexes, any library that owns the *ASI, SRI,* or *IIS* may also own a corresponding microfiche set that provides the full texts of the documents indexed; but remember that none of these fiche sources will be individually recorded in the library's online catalog. (*SRI* is particularly useful to business researchers, as it often provides rankings of companies by name; and its fiche will also include full texts of various market studies.)

The only current online access to these CIS statistical indexes is through optional modules that can be added to a subscription of the *LexisNexis Statistical* database; a CD-ROM version, called *Statistical Masterfile,* is no longer produced. If your library does not have the LexisNexis modules, you will have to used the printed indexes. (Be sure to look at the various category indexes at the end of each volume.)

**Statistical Abstract of the United States.** This annual volume from the Government Printing Office is a smorgasbord of statistical information on thousands of subjects. In most cases you will want to look here first, before getting into any of the *ASI, SRI,* or *IIS* indexes. *Statistical Abstract* all by itself will answer many questions, without reference to complicated indexes or microfiche sets of documents. An online version is available at: www2.census.gov/prod2/statcomp/index.htm. (See also the section on "Statistics" in Chapter 14.)

**Statistical Resources on the Web.** The University of Michigan maintains an unusually good Web site for turning up government (and other) statistical sources on the Internet; the site is available at: www.lib.umich.edu/govdocs/statsnew.html.

**U. S. Government Periodicals Index** (Congressional Information Service, 1992– ). Although publication of this source began in the early 1990s, its subject coverage extends back to 1988. It is an index by subject and author to all of the articles in 170 magazines and journals published by the federal government. Most of these titles are not indexed elsewhere, and topical coverage spans everything from abortion to zoology; a good overview list of some of the subjects covered can be found at: www.lexisnexis.com/academic/ 3cis/cise/USGovernmentPeriodicalsIndex.asp. The online version, called *LexisNexis Government Periodicals*, includes the entire run of the print version; it is available as an add-on subscription to *LexisNexis*. Anyone who uses *Readers' Guide to Periodical Literature, ArticleFirst*, or *PAIS* would find this source useful in the same ways. Earlier years, 1970 to 1987, are covered by the old *Index to U.S. Government Periodicals* (Chicago: Infordata), a printed set for which there is (as of this writing) no online equivalent.

***Subject Bibliography* series.** This online source provides an excellent shortcut in documents research; it is a listing of 12,000 books, periodicals, pamphlets, and other GPO publications categorized in 150 subject areas (see Chapter 9 for a sample listing). Free access is available at: http://bookstore. gpo.gov/sb/about.html; or type in "Subject Bibliography" in the search box at www.gpoacces.gov. The site also provides a detailed index to the 150 bibliographies.

***Government Reports Announcements & Index (GRA&I)*** (Department of Commerce, National Technical Information Service [NTIS], 1946– ). Every year the federal government spends millions of dollars on grants and contracts for research; and each recipient of such funding is required to submit a report of results. The *GRA&I* is the ongoing, overall index to these reports. A free online version covering 1990 to date is available at www.ntis. gov/search/; a subscription version available from Cambridge Scientific Abstracts, Dialog, and other vendors extends coverage back to 1964. Each citation includes a detailed abstract.

NTIS studies cover virtually all subject areas in science, technology, and social sciences; there is even surprising coverage in the humanities, too. Since more than 50,000 titles are added annually, you can expect to find a government-funded research report on just about anything. There are studies of air pollution, anchor chains, drug abuse, educational philosophy, food contamination, foreign military forces, Greenland's ice cap, junction transistors, leadership, personnel management, poisonous animals and insects, quark models, seafloor spreading, sex behavior, and garbage collection in Machala, Ecuador. There is even a study of one of Lord Byron's poems—it was done as a Master's Thesis at the Air Force Institute of Technology—and since government money paid for it, it got picked up by NTIS.

The vast majority of the over two million NTIS reports are not depository items in documents collections, although the *GRA&I* itself is, if the depository library chooses to receive it. Nor are the full texts of the reports freely available online; they are for sale from the NTIS Web site. (The only virtually complete set of NTIS reports that can be read without charge is at the Library of Congress, available to onsite researchers.)

**National Security Archive.** The National Security Archive is an independent nongovernmental organization founded by investigative reporters; its purpose is to make available copies of any previously secret or classified documents released by the federal government through Freedom of Information Act requests. Its collection now contains more than two million pages in 200 collections, available for onsite research at its office in Washington, DC. More than a score of these collections have been published in microfiche sets, available in many academic libraries; many of the same collections are available in a subscription Web site, the *Digital National Security Archive* from ProQuest. Further information about the organization and its collections is available at www.gwu.edu/~nsarchiv/.

*Declassified Documents Reference System.* This is an ongoing set of documents published by the Primary Source Media division of Thomson Gale, available in both Web and paper subscription versions. It is an index to declassified federal documents, accompanied by either microfiche or online full texts of the indexed sources. Coverage began in 1982; about 75,000 documents are included at present. Further information is available at www. galegroup.com/psm/; type "declassified" into the "Quick Title Search" box.

The Web sites and indexes listed above are the major avenues of access to government documents; several other sources, however, deserve particular mention.

- There are federally produced maps, charts, and aerial photographs of every section of the United States and many regions of the rest of the

world. A good overview site is searchable at www.firstgov.gov/Topics/
Maps.shtml.

- The National Technical Information Service offers a subscription service called *World News Connection* that provides English-language
  translations of current foreign newspapers, magazine articles, wire
  service reports, television and radio broadcasts, and political speeches.
  Many academic libraries subscribe to it; further information is available at http://wnc.fedworld.gov/.

- There are many researchers who, understandably, throw up their hands
  at the prospect of documents research in a library. Often it is the case,
  however, that those who balk at library research are whizzes at using
  the telephone to find what they need. A very useful but obscure guide
  to phone numbers and addresses for seekers of federal publications
  and reports is the Defense Technical Information Center's *How to Get
  It: A Guide to Defense-Related Information Sources* (revised irregularly), available in paper copy from DTIC at www.dtic.mil/dtic/htgi-
  notice.html. This 500-page directory lists contacts for all sorts of
  information in federal (and other) sources for reports, maps, pamphlets, documents, translations, and databases; it also tells you where
  to order copies, what restrictions on access apply, and where particular types or series of documents are indexed. It is especially good at
  explaining report numbers—if all you have is a citation with such a
  number, this guide will tell you what it means, which agency produced it, and whom to contact for a copy of the report.

- Government documents produced by cities and counties are often
  extremely useful for local information. An excellent index, by subject
  or by locale, is the *Index to Current Urban Documents* (Greenwood
  Press, 1972– ). This index was published in annual paper-copy volumes from volume 1 (1972–73) through volume 28 (1999–2000); an
  accompanying microfiche set of all of the indexed documents was
  also produced. As of volume 29 (2001) and afterwards, however, the
  set is no longer published in paper and microfiche; from this year
  forward the entire set is available only in an online subscription, including both the index and the documents, the latter in PDF format.
  Information is available at www.urbdocs.com/support/faq.asp. These
  urban documents include planning studies for stadiums, environmental studies, plans for developing downtown areas, reports on local

educational systems, statistical studies of crime, and so on. Nearly 300 U.S. and Canadian city and county jurisdictions are covered.

- One of the persistent problems that documents researchers have is that of trying to cite federal publications in a formal manner; many style manuals do not adequately deal with documents. A solution is available in *The Complete Guide to Citing Government Information Resources*, 3rd ed. (Congressional Information Service, 2002).

## Archives, Manuscripts, and Public Records

It is useful to consider unpublished primary sources as falling into two classes: archives or manuscript collections that have been assembled in special historical repositories, and current sources that are still with the people or agencies that originally created or received the records. Both offer gold mines of information.

Research in archives or historical manuscript collections is unlike research in books or journal articles in libraries. The latter sources are comparatively well cataloged and indexed, and there is subject access to individual items. Not so with unpublished sources—there may be broad subject access to large groups of items but not to the individual papers or documents within the groups. A major reason for this is that most individual unpublished sources are simply not worth the time and expense it would take to catalog or index them fully, for most of them make sense only within the context of the other items they are stored with. The strategy for working with such materials involves four levels of searching:

1. Identifying which repositories have collections or archival manuscript materials that are relevant to your subject.
2. Determining if there is a separate repository guide or Web site that will give you an overview of the particular repository you're interested in.
3. Finding out if the repository has an archival inventory or manuscript register for a particular series of documents you wish to examine.
4. Browsing through the documents themselves, which will be grouped according to who wrote or received them, or which agency produced them—often regardless of what their subject may be.

At the first level, several good open Web sites, subscription databases, and printed guides will help you identify which collections exist.

*National Union Catalog of Manuscript Collections (NUCMC).* NUCMC began in 1959 as an ongoing set of printed volumes, produced by the Library of Congress, identifying whose unpublished papers are located in which repositories in the United States. The printed set ceased publication in 1993; thereafter it continues in online form as part of a larger database produced by the Research Libraries Group, the *RLG Union Catalog of Archival and Mixed Collections (AMC File)*, which retrospectively picks up *NUCMC* entries back to 1986/87. In other words, records reported to the *NUCMC* before 1986 are not in this database. (They are searchable elsewhere, however, in either the printed volumes of the set, or in the *ArchivesUSA* database; see below). The combined *NUCMC/AMC* database is freely searchable at www.loc.gov/coll/nucmc. Chadwyck-Healey has published two cumulative indexes to most of the older, printed volumes: *Index to Personal Names in the National Union Catalog of Manuscript Collections, 1959–1984* (2 vols., 1988), and *Index to Subjects and Corporate Names in the National Union Catalog of Manuscript Collections, 1959–1984* (3 vols., 1994).

*ArchivesUSA.* This is a subscription database from Chadwyck-Healey; it is an index to over 140,000 collections of manuscripts and primary source materials in 5,500 repositories in the United States. It includes over 5,000 online links to finding aids and 2,350 links to repository home pages; it also provides detailed subject indexing of the finding aids of over 58,000 collections. Unlike the *NUCMC/AMC* database described above, this file contains the entire *NUCMC* from 1959 to the present in electronic form.

**Repositories of Primary Sources.** This is a free Web site maintained by the University of Idaho at www.uidaho.edu/special-collections/Other. Repositories.html. It is a listing of over 5,500 Web sites describing holdings of "manuscripts, archives, rare books, historical photographs, and other primary sources for the research scholar." Its coverage is worldwide. Basically, it will link you to the home pages of any of these thousands of repositories, which then provide more detailed listings of their local holdings. (It is not a mechanism for searching all of the sites' holdings all at once.)

**State Archives Referral List.** The office of the Secretary of State of Georgia maintains an online listing of archival offices of all 50 U.S. States, D.C., Puerto Rico, and the Virgin Islands. The best way to find this site is to do a Google search on the phrase "State archives referral list."

**Archival Internet Resources.** This is an "index of archival indexes" around the world, at www.tulane.edu/~lmiller/ArchivesResources.html.

**Search Systems Free Public Records Directory.** This is the largest directory of free public records sites on the Internet. It links to over 21,000 sites containing "business information, corporate filings, property records, unclaimed property, professional licenses, offenders, inmates, criminal and civil court filings, and much more." It is available at www.searchsystems.net.

Printed sources at the first level include *Subject Collections: A guide to special book collections and subject emphases as reported by university, college, public, and special libraries and museums in the United States and Canada*, compiled by Lee Ash and William G. Miller (Bowker, revised irregularly). This is a subject guide to more than 65,000 collections in over 5,800 institutions. Although its focus is on book rather than manuscript collections, oftentimes libraries having particular subject strengths in their book collections also collect relevant manuscript materials. The Modern Language Association has also published two relevant sources, John A. Robbins's *American Literary Manuscripts: A Checklist of Holdings in Academic, Historical, and Public Libraries, Museums, and Authors Homes in the United States*, 2nd ed. (1977), a directory of 2,800 authors' papers in 600 repositories; and James Thorpe's *The Use of Manuscripts in Literary Research*, 2nd ed. (1979).

The first of two British sources at this level is the *Index of English Literary Manuscripts* (a multi-section set still in progress, being published in England by Continuum/Mansell and in New York by Bowker); Volume 1 covers 1450 to 1625; Volume 2, 1625 to 1700; Volume 3, 1700 to 1800; Volume 4, 1800 to 1900. The second is the *Location Register of Twentieth-Century English Literary Manuscripts and Letters: A Union List of Papers of Modern English, Irish, Scottish, and Welsh Authors in the British Isles*, 2 vols. (G. K. Hall, 1988).

Another very good way to locate the papers of particular authors is through the ongoing *Dictionary of Literary Biography* (Gale); its entries routinely identify where the papers of the biography subjects are housed. *American*

*National Biography* and *The Oxford Dictionary of National Biography*, the two standard biographical encyclopedias for American and British subjects, both published by Oxford University Press, perform similar services. The large *WorldCat* and *RLG Union Catalog* databases also list manuscripts and archival resources. All of these sources can locate manuscripts that do not show up in *NUCMC* or *ArchivesUSA*.

At the second level of research, the *Guide to the Federal Records in the National Archives of the United States*, 3 vols. (National Archives and Records Administration [NARA], 1995) may serve as an example of a particular repository guide. The printed set has now been put online and updated at www.archives.gov/research_room/federal_records_guide/. This site describes the various Record Groups held by the National Archives; these groups of government records are arranged not by subject but rather according to the agency or bureau that produced them. If you wish to find out which agencies' records have material on your subject, you must use some imagination in thinking how the federal government would have become involved with your area of interest—for, with rare exceptions, there are no subject or name indexes to the records. For this reason alone you must work closely with the archivists, who have a good sense of what types of things can be found in the various agencies' documents. The same rule applies at other repositories: use the expertise of the staff as much as you can, and be sure that they understand clearly—not just in vague, general terms—what you are *ultimately* trying to research. Although many guides to collections may now be appearing on the Web, direct contact with the archivists onsite is still usually an important element in this kind of research.

The British equivalent of NARA is The National Archives, holding official governmental records for England, Wales, and the United Kingdom; this agency combines the former Public Record Office and the Historical Manuscripts Commission. Its site can be searched at www.nationalarchives.gov.uk/.

The third level of guide is that of the archival inventory or manuscript register; usually it is a locally produced finding aid that describes one particular collection with an introductory note followed by a listing of the parts of the collection down to the box or folder level (but rarely to the level of individual items within boxes or folders). Most of these inventories and registers are themselves unpublished, although there is now an effort among major archives to put their finding aids online. An excellent printed list of which ones exist is Donald L. DeWitt's *Guides to Archives and Manuscript Collections in the United States: An Annotated Bibliography* (479 pages; Greenwood Press, 1994); it lists more than 2,000 inventories, checklists, and registers (at this third level), as well as repository guides at the second level. DeWitt has also compiled *Articles Describing Archives and Manuscript Collections in the United States: An Annotated Bibliography* (459 pages; Greenwood Press, 1997). Each volume has an excellent subject index, and together they are capable of bringing to your attention many collections, and articles describing them in depth, that you will not find through Web searches.

Chadwyck-Healey publishes ongoing microfiche collections of the finding aids of a variety of manuscript collections in the U.S. and the U.K. Their *National Inventory of Documentary Sources in the United States* has three components: Part 1, *Federal Records* (including the National Archives, Presidential Libraries, and Smithsonian Institution Archives); Part 2, *Manuscript Division, Library of Congress*; Part 3, *State Archives, State Libraries, State Historical Societies, Academic Libraries and Other Repositories*. The British set is the *National Inventory of Documentary Sources in the United Kingdom and Ireland* (covering collections in over 200 repositories, as of this writing, with quarterly additions). These sets do not publish the actual manuscripts located in these repositories; rather, these are copies of the finding aids and manuscript registers *of* the collections. (The indexing information of the *United States* section of the *National Inventory*—but not the full texts of the actual microfiche guides—is searchable in the *ArchiveUSA* database. This online file, in other words, can serve as the index to the microfiche set of the finding aids.)

Some of the guides and finding aids that are published in these Chadwyck-Healey microfiche sets are now also directly searchable on the Web sites of the various repositories themselves.

As helpful as the archival inventories and manuscript registers may be, only at the fourth level of research—reading through the documents themselves—can you really know what is in a collection. Although some manuscript material is being published online, through repositories' Web sites, the vast majority of manuscript material can be read only onsite when you actually visit the particular collections that interest you. You cannot do archival or manuscript research quickly; you must be prepared for much browsing and many dead ends before you come to any nuggets. Plan your time accordingly.

If you plan to visit an archival or manuscript repository, it is especially important to read as many secondary or published sources as you can on your subject *before* you inquire into the unpublished sources. Since these are not cataloged or arranged by subject, you will have to have in advance a rather clear idea of what you are looking for in order to recognize it when you're browsing. (It is especially useful to know in advance the names of any people connected with your area of interest; names are easy to look for in the records.) If you are planning a research trip, it is a good idea to write or e-mail the archives in advance, stating what you are interested in and asking for suggestions on what to read before you come in personally.

Once you are at the repository and are looking through the boxes of manuscripts or documents it has, *it is essential that you replace in the correct box any material you photocopy.* The individual papers are *not cataloged,* so if you misplace an item it is *permanently lost for other researchers.*

As with the other three levels, some of this fourth-level material—actual records, not just finding aids—is now appearing on the Internet. An example is the *Online Archive of California,* a site that leads to tens of thousands of digital images of primary sources on the history of that State, at www.oac.cdlib.org/.

Research in public records—those that are still with the agency that produced or collected them and not yet sent to an archival repository—is another very valuable avenue of inquiry for studying individuals, businesses, or government itself. A good guide to finding such records is *The Investigative Reporter's Handbook: A Guide to Documents, Databases, and Techniques,* 4th ed., edited by Brant Houston, Len Bruzzese, and Steve Weinberg (Bedford/St. Martin's, 2002). A good source for doing background checks for criminal records of individuals is a commercial service called *rapsheets* at www.rapsheets.com.

Other useful sources for locating manuscripts or archival records are discussed in Chapter 14, in the sections on "Biography," "Business and Economics," "Genealogy and Local History," and "Primary Sources."

It should be obvious at this point that few researchers would get very far into microform sets, Web collections, government documents, or archival/manuscript sources (and the same could be said of special collections) if left only to the most widely used Web search engines or library indexes and databases. What is required is that you actively seek out these collections.

This will often mean making a leap of faith that the effort will be worthwhile; but you should give it a try anyway—the results may be spectacular.

## Note

1. These examples come from some of the publisher's own promotional literature.

# 14

## Special Subjects and Formats

Although the various methods of searching discussed so far are all applicable in any subject area, some topics present unusually complex arrays of research resources, and require more particular overviews of individual sources. Those discussed in this chapter have proven themselves useful in providing answers to many specialized questions.

### Biography

Two excellent starting points for biographical information on individuals, both prominent and obscure, are the *Biography and Genealogy Master Index* (Gale) and *Biography Index* (H. W. Wilson); both are available in subscription-online and print formats. The former is an index to thousands of biographical dictionaries, who's who compilations, and subject encyclopedias having biographical articles; it is an excellent starting point for locating biographical write-ups on both famous and obscure people from all parts of the world, from all time periods. It currently indexes nearly 14 million sketches. *Biography Index* is the largest ongoing index to biographical books, pamphlets, and journal articles; it indexes biographical articles from 2,700 periodicals and more than 1,500 books every year. The subscription database format covers material published from 1984 forward (as of this writing); the printed volumes go back to 1946.

K.G. Saur has published a number of *Biographical Archive* sets for various parts of the world. Each of these is an index to hundreds of old biographical encyclopedias or works of collective biography; and each printed index is keyed to a microfiche set of the actual articles from all of the various sources. The indexes, in other words, can refer you either to paper copy sets (if your library owns them) or to cumulative microfiche collections published by Saur. The *American Biographical Archive*, for example, provides single-alphabet indexing of over 500,000 names from 536 sources published between 1702 and 1975; the corresponding microfiche set reproduces 742,000 articles. Individuals from the earliest period of North American history up to about 1970 are covered. The other sets in the series are these:

*African Biographical Archive*
*Archives Biographiques Francaises*
*Archivio Biografico Italiano*
*Archivo Biografico de Espana, Portugal e Iberoamerica*
*Australasian Biographical Archive*
*Baltisches Biographisches Archive*
*Biografisch Archief de Benelux*
*Biographisches Archiv der Antike*
*British Biographical Archive*
*Chinese Biographical Archive*
*Deutsches Biographisches Archiv*
*Griechisches Biographisches Archiv*
*Indian Biographical Archive*
*Judisches Biographisches Archiv*
*Polskie Archiwum Biograficzne*
*Russisches Biographisches Archiv*
*Scandinavian Biographical Archive*
*South-East Asian Biographical Archive*
*Turkisches Biographisches Archiv*

As of this writing, a subscription database containing the full texts of all of the biographical articles is being developed by Gale Research under the title *World Biographical Information System Online.*

A good overview of the less extensive biographical sites that are freely available on the Web, including Biography.com, can be found through the *Librarians' Index to the Internet* at http://lii.org/search/file/people, and through refdesk.com at www.refdesk.com/factbiog.html.

*Current Biography* (H. W. Wilson) is a printed set that gives extensive biographical information about people currently in the news; since the set began publication in 1940, more than 25,000 articles have been published; 19,500 provide photos. There is a printed cumulative index to the whole series from 1940 to 2000. Libraries may also have the set available in an online version; but the print set is more likely to be available. *The New York Times Biographical Service* (1969– ), which reproduces biographical articles from that paper, is somewhat comparable. (Remember, however, that the full text of the *NYT* back to 1851 is available in an online subscription from ProQuest.)

The largest quick-reference sources on American biography are the multivolume sets *American National Biography* (Oxford, 1999 & Suppl.), the older *Dictionary of American Biography* (Scribner's), and the *National Cyclopedia of American Biography* (James T. White Co.). The first set is also available in a subscription Web version; it is the standard biographical encyclopedia for Americans. The *National Cyclopedia* is especially good for picking up noteworthy people (e.g., business executives, military officers, clergy) who are otherwise neglected by the history books. Its articles tend to be authorized or approved by the biography subjects themselves. For British historical figures, the best set is the *Oxford Dictionary of National Biography* (Oxford, 2004), a 60-volume set that is also available in a subscription Web version.

If these sources don't cover the individuals you want, often the various national or specialized encyclopedias pick up obscure people. Robert B. Slocum's two-volume *Biographical Dictionaries and Related Works*, 2nd ed. (Gale Research, 1986), is a bibliography of more than 16,000 biographical sources categorized by country and by occupation; it can alert you to many sources not covered by the *Biography and Genealogy Master Index* or the Saur *Biographical Archive* sets. The *ARBA Guide to Biographical Dictionaries* (Libraries Unlimited, 1986) is a comparable but smaller annotated listing of 718 biographical sources.

Genealogical Web sites are also good for turning up information on obscure individuals; see the Genealogy and Local History section, below.

Old city directories, such as those published by the R. L. Polk Company, can often be used to construct mini-biographies of individuals. Among the questions they can often answer are: Is the individual married? If so, what is the spouse's name? If a widow, what was the husband's name? Who else resides at the same address? Who are the neighbors? What is the individual's occupation, and where is he or she employed? Is the individual a "head of house" or a resident? Retrospective searching of earlier volumes can also indicate how long an individual has been employed at a job, what were his previous jobs or business associations, how long the person has lived at an address, who were previous neighbors, and so on. (Researchers who want to milk old directories to the last drop should study pages 158–60 of Harry J. Murphy's *Where's What: Sources of Information for Federal Investigators* [Quadrangle/New York Times Book Company, 1976]; Murphy quotes a previous publication listing about fifty questions city directories can answer.) The drawback is that Polk directories are no longer published for large cities; they are mainly good for small towns and suburbs. The various directories now published for large cities are strictly "criss-cross": you have to start out with either a phone number or an address, and the directory will give you the names connected with either (without any biographical or occupational information). (Google offers a somewhat similar capability for phone number searching: if you simply type in the number, in quotation marks, it will tell you the name and address of its holder.)

A profusion of full-text retrospective publications are now online in a variety of commercial services (e.g., several U.S. newspapers going back more than a century in ProQuest, or the *American Periodicals Series* database providing texts of 1,100 nineteenth century magazines). All such databases, available through library subscriptions, can be mined for biographical information.

## Book Reviews

Virtually all of the commercially available databases that cover journal articles—the Wilson indexes (including *Readers' Guide Retrospective*), the *Web of Science*, *Periodicals Contents Index (PCI)*, and so on—also index book reviews. Remember that *PCI*, covering over 4,500 journals internationally from 1770 to 1995, is a particularly rich resource for turning up such sources. *Book Review Digest* (H. W. Wilson) adds paragraph-length extracts from the reviews themselves; it is available in print format from 1905 forward, and online (as of this writing) from 1983. Two excellent sources for scholarly reviews of older books are the printed sets *Combined*

*Retrospective Index to Book Reviews in Scholarly Journals 1886–1974*, 15 vols. (Carrollton Press, 1979–82) and *Combined Retrospective Index to Book Reviews in Humanities Journals 1902–1974*, 10 vols. (Research Publications, 1982–84). Neither is available online. I have found many reviews listed in these two sets that I could not identify in any database.

Note that book reviews are generally not the best sources for students who want literary criticism or scholarly analyses of individual books, stories, plays, or poems; for these, see the section on Literary Criticism, below.

## Business and Economics

The Web is now the first place to check for information about individual companies, nonprofit organizations, or industries. These are particularly good starting points:

- *Business.com* at www.business.com. This is a very large search engine and business directory, with multiple subcategories for drilling down into hidden Web sites.
- The Library of Congress's *Business Reference Services* at www. loc.gov/rr/business/. This site categorizes Web sites by subject (with links), provides of list of relevant commercial databases (although not entry into them), and a bibliography of useful reference books and library resources.
- GeniusFind's *Economy and Business* link at www.geniusfind.com/ Economy_and_Business.htm. This is another roster of links to deep Web sites not directly searchable by Google or the other standard engines.
- Librarians' Index to the Internet section on Business, Finance, and Jobs at http://lii.org/search/file/busfinjobs.
- Rutgers University Libraries' Business Research Guide at www. libraries.rutgers.edu/rul/rr_gateway/research_guides/busi/business. shtml. Scroll down the to the "Company Research" section for a particularly good overview of options within library resources, which may be duplicated in your local university or public library.

Since Web directories—even the good ones, like these—can be somewhat overwhelming, it is good to remember a particular useful printed resource, the *Encyclopedia of Business Information Resources* (Thomson/Gale, revised frequently). This is a directory of print and electronic sources, and people contacts, listed alphabetically under very specific subjects (e.g., Boat Industry, Computers in Accounting, Condominiums, Dental Supply Industry, Economic Entomology, Financial Ratios, House Organs, Inheritance Tax, Location of Industry, Molasses Industry, Office Design, Patents, Retirement, Solar Energy, Sweet Potato Industry, Theater Management, Youth Market, etc.). Under each heading is an evaluated listing of electronic, print, and live sources, including names of associations and industry groups, with Web URLs, e-mail addresses, phone numbers, and other contact information.

In researching an individual company it is useful to approach the task with some "overview" assumptions in mind, which may not be obvious to those just starting out in this area. The first thing to do is to situate the firm into one of three categories: those that sell stock and are *publicly owned*, those that don't sell stock to the public and are *privately owned*, and those that are *nonprofit* organizations. (*Foreign-owned* companies are a fourth group.) Another distinction to keep in mind is that information can be of two types: what the company says about itself, and what others say about it. For the former you will consult such things as annual reports and filings with governmental regulatory agencies. For the second you will want to read articles in business (or other) magazines and newspapers, or commercially prepared research reports (which may be freely available via library subscriptions). Business-reference sources—both online and print—tend to be excerpts or compilations of the self-reported public record filings, or indexes to the articles and reports generated by others, or some combination.

Business databases are extremely varied. There is a general trend in commercial databases to provide, either directly or via hot links, access to full texts of government filings, journal articles, newsletters, and research reports. Overviews of the range of these resources, with descriptions of their scope, can be found at the above Web sites. Amid the profusion of files, three are particularly good starting points: *Wilson Business Abstracts, ABI Inform,* and *Business and Company Resource Center.* The first database, from the H. W. Wilson Company, is an index to 600 high-quality business journals since 1986, with abstracts of articles from 1990 forward. *ABI Inform,* from ProQuest, indexes 1,800 business periodicals worldwide, with coverage from 1971; it includes quick access basic information on more than 60,000 companies. The *Business and Company* file, from Thomson/Gale, is an integrated database that brings together "company profiles, brand information, rankings, invest-ment reports, company histories, chronologies, and periodicals."

In researching company histories there are a few shortcuts to be aware of. In addition to the above databases, an ongoing printed set from Gale, the multivolume *International Directory of Company Histories*, provides three- to five-page histories of over 4,500 of the world's largest companies. The set is also available in an online subscription as part of the *Gale Virtual Reference Library*. A good researcher's trick in doing company histories is first to find the founding date of the firm (often provided in standard direc-tories such as *Standard & Poor's Register* or *Ward's Business Directory*), then to check for articles in business journals and newspapers at important "anniversary" years for the company (especially their twenty-fifth and for-tieth years); often there will be write-ups on the company's histories at those points. For very old firms, founded in the United States between 1687 and 1915, Etna M. Kelley's *The Business Founding Date Directory* (Morgan & Morgan, 1954), available in research libraries, may be helpful; its *Supple-ment* (1956) covers foundings up to 1933.

The best guide for job hunters is the annual *What Color Is Your Para-chute?* by Richard Nelson Bolles (Ten Speed Press). Its basic advice is first to decide where you want to be, then get to know the person or persons who can hire you. (This really does work much better than sending out scores of re-sumes or relying on want ads and posted job vacancies. I've gotten three jobs myself–including my present one–by following what this book says to do.)

The field of business research is very large and very changeable. When you are doing work in this area, don't just go to the Web sites and other sources listed above, or provided by any other list; be sure to talk to the business reference librarians at your library, too, and ask them for other suggestions.

## Copyright Status Information

The Harry Ransom Humanities Research Center at the University of Texas at Austin maintains an online WATCH registry (Writers, Artists, and Their Copyright Holders); this is a directory of sources providing information on the copyright status of works that you may wish to quote, along with con-tact information for obtaining permissions. The site can be found at http://

tyler.hrc.utexas.edu/. Another site to check is the Copyright Clearance Center at www.copyright.com.

## Genealogy and Local History

The best book for genealogists to start with is Val D. Greenwood's *Researcher's Guide to American Genealogy* (Baltimore: Genealogical Pub. Co., revised irregularly); the best free Web site is *Cyndi's List of Genealogy Sites on the Internet* www.cyndislist.com/. The former is truly required reading if you want to trace your family history; it will alert you not just to whole ranges of sources that you otherwise would not think of, but also to the questions that you need to ask in the first place. The latter is a listing of more than 230,000 links categorized in over 150 topical areas.

There are two excellent commercial databases to genealogy, which are likely to be available through local libraries, and which provide access to sources not freely accessible on the open Internet. The first is *Ancestry Library Edition* (formerly *AncestryPlus*; Thomson/Gale), which is an enhanced and expanded version of the freely available *Ancestry.com* site; the second is *HeritageQuest* (ProQuest). The latter includes the *PERSI* or *Periodicals Source Index*, a subject index to 6,500 genealogy and local history periodicals and newsletters written in English and French (Canada) from 1800. It can be searched by names of individuals, locations, or by general keywords. (The coverage of American history in this database, at the local level, is astonishing—it should be used routinely in conjunction with the more widely known *America: History and Life* database from ABC-CLIO.)

Oftentimes material on particular families or individuals can be found in local or county histories; two good sources for these are P. William Filby's *A Bibliography of American County Histories* (Genealogical Publishing Company, 1985) and Arthur P. Young's *Cities and Towns in American History: A Bibliography of Doctoral Dissertations* (Greenwood, 1989). Another good approach to local history is through old fire-insurance maps. The commercial database *Digital Sanborn Maps 1867–1970* (ProQuest) is an online file reproducing more than 660,000 maps of over 12,000 American cities and towns. University Microfilms (a subsidiary of ProQuest) offers a set of the maps in microfilm format as well. The Sanborn company produced unusually detailed maps of urban areas; they can often show you who owned the land on which you now live, where your ancestors lived in the given city at the time of the map (some cities have as many as seven maps published at different times), how many rooms each building had, the number of windows, the kind of roof, and the materials the walls were made of. (Such data were important for fire-insurance purposes.) You can use these maps to identify which businesses were located in a community (when and exactly where), the location and denomination of churches, and where the grocery stores, banks, hotels, and saloons were. These maps can shed light on the characteristics of the neighborhoods in which your ancestors lived, and how the areas changed over the years.

## Illustrations, Pictures, and Photographs

The Internet now provides a number of large, freely searchable archives of illustrations. Among the first sites to check are these:

- Google's "Images" file at www.google.com (click on "Images"; this file alone contains over 900 million images.)
- Altavista image search at www.altavista.com (click on "Images.")
- Alltheweb pictures search at www.alltheweb.com (click on "Pictures.")
- Visual Collections at www.davidrumsey.com/collections/index.html.
- Fagan Finder Image Search Engines at www.faganfinder.com/img/.
- Corbis at www.corbis.com (a commercial site with over 4 million images.)
- The Library of Congress's Prints & Photographs Online Catalog at www.loc.gov/rr/print/catalog.html.
- The New York Public Library's Digital Gallery at www.nypl.org/digital/.

The *Library of Congress Subject Headings* system has a number of standard subdivisions that are useful for finding pictures in books:

**[Subject heading]—Illustrations**
               **—Pictorial works**
               **—Portraits**
               **—Caricatures and cartoons**

In searching for older books, also try two additional subdivisions that formerly appeared under names of places:

**[Name of place]—Description—Views**
**     —Description and travels—Views**

The Wilson databases also note whether a journal article is accompanied by illustrations.

Facts on File publishes a wide variety of three-ring loose-leaf binders with copyright-free illustrations, pictures, diagrams, charts, and maps, all intended for easy photocopying. Among these titles are:

*African-American Experience On File*
*American Government On File*
*American History On File*
*Animal Anatomy On File*
*Charts On File*
*Chemistry Experiments On File*
*CIS and Eastern Europe On File*
*Design On File*
*Earth Science On File*
*Environmental Issues On File*
*Forensic Science Experiments On File*
*Genetics and Cell Biology On File*
*Geography On File*
*Health On File*
*Historical Maps On File*
*Human Anatomy On File*
*Life Sciences On File*
*Maps On File*
*Middle East and North Africa On File*
*Nature Projects On File*
*Physics Experiments On File*
*Religions On File*
*Science Experiments On File*
*Timelines On File*
*Weather and Climate On File*

The various specialized encyclopedias are also frequently useful for pictures (see Chapter 1), as is the technique of doing focused browsing in subject-classified books in the library's stacks (Chapter 3).

## Literary Criticism

The first source that students often go to for literary criticism is the subscription database *MLA International Bibliography*, which is the largest online index to literary criticism journals. This isn't the best way to start, however, since the results retrieved here will be spotty due to very inconsistent indexing in the database (e.g., not all articles on Captain Ahab are indexed under "Moby-Dick"). Better overviews of the critical literature can usually be obtained by finding a published bibliography devoted to the particular author, then checking its index for the particular story, play, or poem title you have in mind. For example, a student who wishes to find analyses of John Donne's *Holy Sonnet #10* ("Death Be Not Proud") will find four articles on it indexed under "Death Be Not Proud" in the *MLA*. (The same researcher will probably miss an additional article discoverable by combining "Holy Sonnet" and "10 or ten"—another example inconsistent indexing.) If the student checks his library catalog under **Donne, John, 1572–1631—Bibliography**, however, he may find two compilations by John R. Roberts, *John Donne: An Annotated Bibliography of Modern Criticism, 1912–1967* and *John Donne . . . 1968–1978* (University of Missouri Press, 1973 and 1982). The first lists five articles about the sonnet; the second, sixteen.

Similarly, a student interested in Edgar Allan Poe and cryptography would get different results looking in the *MLA* database, on the one hand, and in J. Lesley Dameron and Irby B. Cauthen's *Edgar Allan Poe: A Bibliography of Criticism 1827–1967*. In this case, the former online resource serves to update the latter published source—but the important point is that the database does not include everything listed in the printed source.

A neglected but very useful index to 146 printed bibliographies of literary criticism is Alan R. Weiner and Spencer Means's *Literary Criticism Index*, 2nd ed. (Scarecrow Press, 1994). This source enables you to search for critical articles on particular plays, poems, novels, and short stories, and frequently leads to articles not indexed online. (It probably is not necessary for undergraduates to use this index; but grad students who wish to do comprehensive literature reviews should consult it.)

One of the best shortcuts to critical articles on major literary works is through the Prentice-Hall *Twentieth Century Interpretations* series. Look in your library's catalog under the title *Twentieth Century Interpretations of [Title of work]*. (Within the brackets you can enter such titles as *A Farewell to Arms, The Crucible, Doctor Faustus, Gray's Elegy, Julius Caesar, Moby-Dick, Oedipus Rex, Pride and Prejudice*, etc.) There are about ninety volumes like this, each about 120 pages long, and each presents an excellent collection of scholarly analyses.

Another comparable series is Prentice-Hall's *Twentieth Century Views*. These volumes tend to have titles of the format *[Name of author]: A Collection of Critical Essays*. The best entry into the contents of this series is an obscure but useful volume entitled *Reader's Index to the Twentieth Century Views Literary Criticism Series, Volumes 1–100* (Prentice-Hall, 1973). This reproduces the index pages from the end of each volume in the series. It thus offers a way to find articles on particular topics connected with authors (as opposed to particular works), such as "Negative capability in Keats," "Inscape and instress in Hopkins," "Irony in Mann," and "Puritan influences on Hawthorne." (As with published bibliographies, you can in effect do Boolean combinations of "specific topic AND particular author" in a printed source.)

You can easily find either of these series in your library's computer catalog by combining the phrase "Twentieth Century" with either the name of a literary work or the name of the literary author.

Three newer, comparable series published by Chelsea House are *Modern Critical Views* (each volume of which is entitled with the name of a literary author, e.g., *Alice Walker* or *Homer*); *Major Literary Characters* (each with a title such as *Hester Prynne* or *Huck Finn*); and *Modern Critical Interpretations* (each with the title of a particular work such as *Jane Eyre* or *The Scarlet Letter*). These volumes are compilations of critical articles, often more recent than those in the Prentice-Hall series. All three of the Chelsea House series have Harold Bloom as their general editor. This makes computer searching easy: just combine "Bloom" and ([author] or [title] or [character]) to find if there is a volume relevant to your interest.

G. K. Hall publishes several comparable "Critical Essays" series; these can be found by searching for titles of the form *Critical Essays on [name of author]* or *[title of literary work]*.

Ongoing series of biographical and critical articles on authors worldwide are the *Dictionary of Literary Biography* and *Contemporary Authors*, both from Gale. Online versions of both can be found in the subscription database *Literature Resource Center* (Thomson/Gale), which also includes the full texts of the series *Contemporary Literary Criticism, Classical and Medieval Literature Criticism, Nineteenth-Century Literature Criticism, Twentieth-Century Literary Criticism, Shakespeare Criticism, Drama Criticism, Poetry Criticism, Short Story Criticism,* and *Literature Criticism 1400–1800*. Your library may have the latter titles in print format if it does not have the Web subscription.

Perhaps the most important thing for an undergraduate to keep in mind when doing an analysis of a literary work, however, is that quite possibly no research at all is required, or even desired, by the professor. Often the purpose of such assignments is to stretch your analytical powers rather than your research abilities. Another problem with critical articles is that—as most graduate students in English will tell you—much of what you find simply won't be worth reading. (The Prentice-Hall and Chelsea House series, above, are singled out as being noticeable exceptions.) Few things are more frustrating to a student than expending a lot of time reading critical articles and finding they don't give you any particular "keeper" insights; the time involved would often be more profitably spent devising your own analyses.

## Maps

Often the best starting point for map research is the open Internet. Depending on the level of information you need or the depth of historical research you need to do, you may well wish to follow up with printed sources in research libraries. (Viewing large maps formatted to be readable on small computer screens is a convenience consideration for many people, too.) Scholars who are writing works for publication may also wish to cite printed copies of the sheets they have used, if only because their online equivalents may change their URLs, or even vanish entirely, in relatively short order.

Good starting points are the following:

- Maps.com at www.maps.com.
- *The World of Maps* at www.maps.ethz.ch/.

- *Western Association of Map Libraries' Map Librarian's Toolbox* at www.waml.org/maptools.html.
- Multimap.com at www.multimap.com/.
- MapQuest (for driving directions) at www.mapquest.com.
- Map collections at the Library of Congress at www.loc.gov/rr/geogmap/.
- Cartography Associates' Rumsey Map Collection at www.davidrumsey.com/index4.html.

The printed set *Inventory of World Topographic Mapping*, compiled by Rolph Bohme (English language editor, Roger Anson), 3 vols. (London and New York: International Cartographic Association and Elsevier Applied Science Publishers, 1989–93) gives an overview of the history of mapping in each country and also provides a list of current map scales and map series for each. Historical listings may be found in Thomas Chubb's *The Printed Maps in the Atlases of Great Britain and Ireland: A Bibliography, 1579–1870* (Martino Pub., 2004) and *A List of Geographical Atlases in the Library of Congress, with Bibliographical Notes*, 9 vols. (Martino Pub., 1997). A good manual for citing maps is Suzanne M. Clark's *Cartographic Citations: A Style Guide* (American Library Association, 1992).

The *Maps On File, Historical Maps On File*, and *Charts On File* compilations of copyright-free, photocopyable illustrations from Facts On File are also useful (see the above section on Illustrations), and probably can be found in a local library.

## Newspapers

Many newspapers offer current articles on their own Web sites. The best subscription databases for full texts of hundreds of newspapers are *Nexis, Factiva*, and *ProQuest*. *Nexis* offers about 3,000 newspapers, *Factiva*, about 1,500. *ProQuest* comes in different segments. The file *ProQuest Newspapers* provides full texts of over 500 titles internationally, while *ProQuest Historical Newspapers* (a different subscription) can be configured to include any or all of *The New York Times, The Washington Post, The Wall Street Journal, The Christian Science Monitor,* the *Los Angeles Times,* and *The Chicago Tribune.* (Other titles will be added.) In each case, the full retrospective run of the newspaper, back to its very first issue, is completely digitized for full-text keyword searching. An especially useful feature of ProQuest's indexing is that it allows you to search the historical titles by 19 specific formats: article, birth notice, classified ad, comic, display ad, editorial article, editorial cartoon, fire loss, front page, legal notice, letter, lottery numbers, marriage, obituary, photo standalone, real-estate transaction, review, stock quote, table of contents, weather. (The current newspaper files in ProQuest can also be searched by these and other format types.)

The subscription database *Ancestry Library Edition* allows retrospective searching of obituary notices in scores of newspapers, which are not available in the open-Web *Ancestry.com* version.

*Accessible Archives* is another subscription file offering full texts of newspapers, in this case, nineteenth century American titles, including several African American papers.

Many indexes to small town newspapers exist in unpublished form throughout the United States in libraries, newspaper offices, and historical and genealogical societies. The best guide to these is Anita Cheek Milner's *Newspaper Indexes: A Location and Subject Guide for Researchers*, 3 vols. (Scarecrow Press, 1977–82).

To identify the library locations of old newspaper issues the standard *WorldCat* and *RLG Union Catalog* databases are useful (see Chapter 11); but neither supersedes an old printed listing, *American Newspapers, 1821–1936: A Union List of Files Available in the United States and Canada*, edited by Winifred Gregory (H. W. Wilson, 1937; Kraus Reprint, 1967). I've found titles and years of coverage in Gregory that are not mentioned in either online source.

An excellent guide to the literature on American newspapers in general is Richard A. Schwarzlose's *Newspapers: A Reference Guide* (Greenwood Press, 1987).

## Out-of-Print and Secondhand Books

Although the emphasis of this book is on resources available in research libraries, nevertheless, scholars will wish to own personal copies of many important books. There are three Web sites that are particularly good in locating copies of out-of-print books being offered for sale, worldwide:

- Bookfinder at www.bookfinder.com.
- Addall at http://used.addall.com.
- Abebooks at www.abebooks.com.

Each site can be searched by author, by title, or by keywords. Prices and ordering information are given for any works you find.

## Primary Sources

Many term paper assignments nowadays are given out with the specification that students should "include primary sources" in their research. These have been discussed already in the "Archives, Manuscripts, and Public Records" section of Chapter 13. There is, however, a kind of reference librarian's trick for short-circuiting the search for primary sources that eliminates the need to comb through actual manuscripts or archival materials. The important point to remember here is that tens of thousands of primary sources have already been conveniently published in book form; and the fact that they appear within book covers does not change or diminish their nature as primary sources. They are still contemporary or eyewitness accounts of events, original testimony or observations, etc., even if you find them within book covers rather than in files of handwritten manuscripts.

The trick in finding published primary sources is to use several of the standard subdivisions within the *Library of Congress Subject Headings* system (Chapter 2). If you first find the right heading for your topic (e.g., **Civil rights movements; World War, 1939–1945**, etc.), you can then enter it into Boolean combinations with the following *LCSH* subdivisions:

**Sources**
**Diaries**
**Personal narratives** [or just **Narratives** when entered in a Boolean combination]
**Correspondence**
**Interviews**
**Quotations**
**Collections**

When I am doing such searches myself, I usually add the following keywords into the combination:

Document? [to include titles with the words "Documentary" or "Documents"]
Eyewitness?
Oral [to include "oral history" accounts]

Theoretically, documentary histories, eyewitness accounts, and oral histories should already be included under the formal subject subdivisions listed above; but oversights in cataloging are not unknown.

You may find that you cannot combine all of these elements in one Boolean command without overloading your library catalog's search software—e.g. "'**World War, 1939–1945**' AND (**Sources** OR **Diaries** OR **Narratives** OR **Correspondence** OR **Interviews** OR **Quotations** OR **Collections** OR document? OR eyewitness? OR oral)." If you break the search into smaller units of combination, however, you'll still get the results you want. Remember, too, that using *browse displays* of subdivisions under LC subject headings (Chapter 2) is a very effective way to spot most of these terms if you cannot remember them, as well as to notice other standard subdivisions that may be of use (e.g., —**Songs and music**, which can alert you to resources that could be considered primary literature in some contexts).

Another good shortcut to primary sources lies in consulting bibliographies of published diaries. The following are especially helpful:

- *American Diaries: An Annotated Bibliography of Published Diaries and Journals*, 2 vols., by Laura Arksey, Nancy Pries, and Marcia Reed (Gale Research, 1983–87).
- *British Diaries: An Annotated Bibliography of British Diaries Written Between 1442 and 1942*, by William Matthews (P. Smith, 1967).
- *And So to Bed: A Bibliography of Diaries Published in English*, by Patricia Hate Havlice (Scarecrow, 1987).

These all have useful subject indexes that connect the diaries to various historical events or periods.

*Oral History Online* is a subscription database from Alexander Street Press that indexes "oral history collections in English around the world, linking through to full texts where available." A free directory of the top 100 collections, along with further information, is available at http:// alexanderstreet2.com/oralhist/.

An Internet site for full texts of many primary-source documents on American history is maintained by the University of Kansas at www.ukans. edu/carrie/docs/amdocs_index.html.

## Standards and Specifications

A useful source that is readily available in public libraries is *Architectural Graphic Standards* (John Wiley & Sons, revised irregularly); this book provides diagrams and standard measurements of such things as tennis courts, horseshoe pits, swimming pools, door frames, fireplaces, etc. It even diagrams the profiles of major species of trees, listing their average heights and spreads.

If you need to obtain a technical, engineering, industrial, military, or governmental standard, a good overview is provided by the Library of Congress's Science, Technology, and Business Division at www.loc.gov/rr/ scitech/trs/trsover.html#standards. This site provides further links to the American National Standards Institute, the Institute of Electrical and Electronic Engineers (IEEE), the Society of Automotive Engineers (SAE), and Underwriters Laboratory (UL), as well as to the International Organization for Standardization (ISO) and the International Telecommunications Union (ITU-R and ITU-T).

Another good starting point is the National Institute of Standards and Technology at www.nist.gov and its list of national standards bodies all over the world, as well as international standards organizations, at www.nist.gov/oiaa/stnd-org.htm.

## Statistics

The most useful compendium of statistics on all sorts of things is the federal government's annual *Statistical Abstract of the United States*. A large collection of federal statistics online is searchable at the FedStats site (www.fedstats.gov).

Several compendiums are good for historical statistics:

- *Historical Statistics of the United States, Colonial Times to 1970* (U. S. Government Printing Office, 1975). Although this is easier to use in paper format, it is now also online at www2.census.gov/prod2/statcomp/index.htm.
- *International Historical Statistics: The Americas, 1750–2000*, 5th ed., by B. R. Mitchell (Palgrave Macmillan, 2003).
- *International Historical Statistics: Europe, 1750–2000*, 5th ed., by B. R. Mitchell (Palgrave Macmillan, 2003).
- *International Historical Statistics: Africa, Asia & Oceania, 1750–2000*, 4th ed., by B. R. Mitchell (Palgrave Macmillan, 2003).
- *British Historical Statistics*, by B. R. Mitchell (Cambridge U. Press, 1988).
- *Historical Statistics of Canada*, 2nd ed., edited by F. H. Leacy (Statistics Canada, 1983).
- *Australians Historical Statistics*, edited by Wray Vamplew (Fairfax, Syme & Weldon Associates, 1987).
- *The Arab World, Turkey, and the Balkans (1878–1914): A Handbook of Historical Statistics*, by Justin McCarthy (G. K. Hall, 1982).
- *Value of a Dollar: Prices and Incomes in the United States 1860–1999*, 2nd ed., edited by Scott Dirks (Grey House Pub., 1999).
- *The Inflation Calculator* (for U.S. dollars) at http://westegg.com/inflation/.
- *Columbia Journalism Review Inflation Calculator* at www.cjr.org/tools/inflation/.

The most extensive ongoing subject indexes to statistical publications are published by the Congressional Information Service (CIS), a subsidiary of LexisNexis. They are: *American Statistics Index* (or *ASI*, 1974– , with coverage back into the 1960s); *Statistical Reference Index* (*SRI*, 1980– ), and *Index to International Statistics* (*IIS*, 1983– ). All three exist as paper copy sets (annual cumulative volumes with monthly supplements) and as a subscription service called *LexisNexis Statistical* (which is not included in the basic *LexisNexis* coverage). *ASI* is an index to *all* statistics produced by the U.S. federal government. *SRI* covers thousands of statistical publications from nonfederal sources (state and local governments, business and trade associations, institutes, university research centers, private polling organizations, etc.). *IIS* indexes publications of dozens of international governmental organizations, including the United Nations and its subsidiary bodies, the European Union, the Organization of American States. Each of these three is an index by subject or title; and each has an extremely useful Index by Categories that lists sources giving comparative data according to any of a score of geographic, economic, or demographic breakdowns (e.g., By City, By State, By Industry, By Individual Company, By Occupation, By Age, By Race, By Sex, By Marital Status, By Disease Or Disorder, etc.—the *SRI* is especially useful in identifying *rankings* of companies). For each index there is a corresponding microfiche set of the actual documents; and not all of these microfiche texts are available in the online version.

A good database providing direct access to statistical data is a subscription service called Regional OneSource (www.regionalonesource.com), which enables you to combine various search criteria and create customized tables on the fly. As of this writing the service covers annual data from federal sources on the United States, but its coverage will soon greatly expand.

Rankings of various sorts can be found in sources such as these:

*Places Rated Almanac* (John Wiley & Sons, irregular)
*Retirement Places Rated* (John Wiley & Sons, irregular)
*Gale Country & World Rankings Reporter* (Gale, irregular)
*Gale State Rankings Reporter* (Gale, irregular)
*Gale City & Metro Rankings Reporter* (Gale, irregular)
*Educational Rankings Annual* (Gale, annual)

Other good compendiums include the United Nations' *Statistical Yearbook* and its *Demographic Yearbook* and the *UNESCO Statistical Yearbook. Statistics Sources: A Subject Guide to Data on Industrial, Business, Social, Educational, Financial and Other Topics for the United States and Internationally* (Gale, revised irregularly) is an excellent pointer to sources of statistics on more than 20,000 specific subjects.

The Inter-University Consortium for Political and Social Research in Ann Arbor, Michigan, is a nonprofit organization that maintains the world's largest archive of machine-readable data files in the social sciences; both current and historical statistics are available (via subscription) in manipulable formats. Its homepage is at www.icpsr.umich.edu.

## Tabular Data

The Chemical Rubber Company of Cleveland, Ohio, publishes more than fifty handbooks that present tabular data in such fields as chemistry and physics, mathematics, optics, probability and statistics, microbiology, nutrition and food, and so on. The best avenue of access into this bewildering maze of data is the *Composite Index for CRC Handbooks* (CRS Press, revised irregularly). *Handbooks and Tables in Science and Technology* (Oryx Press, revised irregularly) is also useful.

## Tests (Psychological and Educational)

Two excellent sources that outline your options for finding published or unpublished tests are Web sites from the American Psychological Association and the Educational Testing Service.

The first can be accessed at www.apa.org, and its subdivision, www.apa.org/science/faq-findtests.html; the second can be found at www.ets.org, and its subdivision www.ets.org/tests/index.html.

A good overview in book form is *Tests: A Comprehensive Reference for Assessments in Psychology, Education, and Business*, edited by Taddy Maddox, 5th ed. (Pro-Ed, 2003). Also useful is the *Directory of Test Collections in Academic, Professional, and Research Libraries*, edited by Paul G. Fehrmann and Nancy Patricia O'Brien (Association of College and Research Libraries, 2001).

## Translations

The easiest way to find out if a foreign-language book has been translated into English is to look under the original author's name in one of the big online or printed union catalogs of books; these include the *WorldCat* and

*RLG Union Catalog* databases and the printed *National Union Catalog: Pre-1956 Imprints.*

Another source for information on translations of books (not periodical articles) is the *Index Translationum* maintained online by UNESCO, with coverage from 1979 to date; this is freely available at http://databases. unesco.org/xtrans/xtra-form.html. Printed volumes of this title extend back to 1948, with a cumulative index from 1948 to 1968.

For works of a technical nature, the *Consolidated Index of Translations into English* (National Translations Center, 1969) is supplemented by the *Translations Register-Index* (1967–86) and the *World Translations Index* (1987–1997). The *World Index of Scientific Translations* (1967– ) and its successor title *World Transdex* extend through 1986.

In the humanities, a good way to find translations of major foreign authors' works—especially if you want to find what is considered the best English collected set—is to consult the *Reader's Advisor*, a multi-volume set, revised irregularly, from R. R. Bowker. A recent series from Boulevard Books in London is also useful; it includes:

*The Babel Guide to Brazilian Fiction in English Translation* (2001)
*The Babel Guide to Dutch & Flemish Fiction in English Translation* (2001)
*The Babel Guide to Hungarian Literature in English Translation* (2001)
*The Babel Guide to Scandinavian and Baltic Fiction* (1999)
*The Babel Guide to German Fiction in English Translation: Austria, Germany, Switzerland* (1997)
*The Babel Guide to French Fiction in English Translation* (1996)
*The Babel Guide to Italian Fiction in English Translation* (1995)
*The Babel Guide to the Fiction of Portugal, Brazil & Africa in English Translation* (1995)

Good subject headings to look for in library catalogs are of this form:

**[Name or Subject]—Translations into English** [or **French, German,** etc.]

*World News Connection* is a subscription database offering ongoing full-text English-language translations of foreign media sources (broadcast and print) from 1997 forward. It is the continuation of the Foreign Broadcast Information Service (FBIS) series of translations of non-U.S. radio broadcasts, available on microfiche from 1941 to 1996. The best index to the more recent years is provided by the *FBIS Index on CD-ROM* (NewsBank/Readex, 1975–96), which contains 2.4 million citations. *World News Connection* also now includes what used to be called the *Joint Publications Research Service (JPRS)* series of indexes to, and translations of, foreign newspaper articles. Retrospective paper-copy indexes covering the microfiche documents are the *Bibliography-Index to Current U.S. JPRS Translations*, vols. 1–8 (1962–70); *Transdex: Bibliography and Index to United States Joint Publications Research Service (JPRS) Translations*, vols. 9–12 (1970–74); *Bell & Howell Transdex* (1975–83); and *Transdex Index* (1984–1996).

A good list of which journals internationally are regularly translated into English is *Journals in Translation*, 5th ed. (British Library Document Supply Center, 1991).

An Internet site for on-the-fly translations of text blocks up to 150 words in length may be found at AltaVista's Babel Fish Translation page at http://babelfish.altavista.com. Google offers a similar service at www.google.com/language_tools.

# 15

## *Reference Sources: Searching by Types of Literature*

So far we have been concerned mainly to delineate the options for pursuing *research* questions rather than *reference* questions. The former are more open-ended, in the sense of not having definite "right" or "wrong" answers. For example, "What information exists on land reform in seventeenth-century China?" or "What is available on U.S.–Israeli relations after the Six Day War?" are research questions, in the sense that I'm using the term here. Reference questions, in contrast, are those looking for a specific bit of information—for example, "What is the height of the Washington Monument?" "Who won the Oscar for Best Actor in 1932?" The latter have an ascertainable "right" answer.

In dealing with research questions, the overall point of the discussion so far is that there are eight different methods of subject searching:

- Controlled vocabulary subject heading searches
- General and focused browsing of classified full texts
- Keyword searches
- Citation searches
- Related record searches
- Boolean combination searches
- Searches through published bibliographies
- Using people sources[1]

Browsing classified full texts in library bookstacks and using published subject bibliographies are techniques that cannot be done via computers—the texts and bibliographies I'm referring to here are precisely the bulk of library records that are not *on* computers to begin with. (Copyright restrictions preclude the full digitization of most books in the last ninety years; and services such as Google Print restrict access in ways that prevent recognition of texts whose keywords cannot be thought of in advance. Full-text files on the Internet also bury books amid huge retrieval results that are not adequately sorted by keyword relevance-ranking mechanisms.)

Each method of searching is potentially applicable in any subject area; each has distinct advantages and disadvantages (both strengths *and* weaknesses); and each is capable of turning up information that cannot be reached by the other seven. Information that lies in a blind spot to any one method of searching, however, usually lies within the purview of one or more of the other means of inquiry.

A knowledge of these few distinct search techniques—and the advantages and limitations of each—will enable most researchers to increase substantially the range and efficiency of their investigations in any subject area. Most scholars, unfortunately, do most of their research within much more limited frameworks of perception; they too often act as though their research options consist only of (1) doing keyword searches in Google (or other search engines) on the Internet, (2) looking at footnotes in sources they already have, (3) talking to a small circle of acquaintances, and (4) general browsing in library bookstacks. Those in the sciences tend to skip number (4) entirely and inflate (3) excessively. Very few researchers use databases, catalogs, or indexes efficiently because they so frequently search under the wrong terms to begin with (confusing keywords with subject headings, or searching under general rather than specific terms); because they are familiar with only a very small range of the thousands of sources that exist outside the open Internet; and because they are entirely unaware of search methods (citation and related record) that don't rely on direct verbal attempts to specify subjects. Familiarity with the outline of procedures sketched above, however, will enable most researchers to gain a simple overview of the *full range of options* available in any research inquiry, and (I hope) also assist them in achieving a sense of closure in making estimates of what options remain to be pursued.

The framework of techniques available for research questions, however, is not fully adequate to deal with reference questions. A ninth method of searching is usually preferable here:

- Type of literature searches.

This kind of searching is based on the fact that within any subject or disciplinary field, certain distinct types of reference sources can be expected to exist. By "reference sources" I mean those that either point the way into the core literature contained in books, journals, reports, dissertations, etc., or those that summarize, abstract, digest, or review it. Reference sources tend to be those forms of publication that are simply consulted rather than read from beginning to end. These various types of sources form a kind of structure within the literature of any subject area; and a foreknowledge of the existence of this predictable structure can enable you to quickly find the most efficient paths of inquiry, each tailored to answering certain kinds of questions.

Two important qualifications are in order. First, it must be emphasized that the line between open-ended and specific-fact questions is often rather blurry. In general, however, there is a useful distinction here, and as a reference librarian I find that in pursuing research questions it is best to think in terms of the first eight methods of searching, while in pursuing the fact questions it is usually better to think in terms of types of literature. In other words, you can think of two different conceptual frameworks here; or you can regard the "types" framework itself as an additional, ninth method of searching, still within a single "methods" model. (This distinction may be more a concern to instructors who are trying to structure a class on research techniques than to anyone else.)

The other qualification is that some of the traditional types of reference literature, enumerated below, have indeed been superseded in some ways—but not in others—by the Internet. For example, researchers interested in basic information about a company, an organization, a school, etc.—its address, phone number, departments, contact personnel—used to be much more dependent on published *directories*, available in libraries, than is now the case. Today, virtually every organization that deals with the public has its own Web site that provides this kind of information; any inquirer who knows the name of the organization to begin with can find its home page immediately via Internet searching. Similarly, *newsletters* and *catalogs* of commercially available products are now in large part searchable online, without necessary recourse to printed counterparts. The line between which types of literature are best searched online or in print is itself rather blurry, however. For example, if you want basic information about a specific organization such as the American Academy of Forensic Sciences, you can get what you need directly from its Web page. But if you want an overview of the *range* of *all* of the forensic science organizations in the U.S., you will be better off with the *Encyclopedia of Associations*, which is not freely available on the Net, but which can be freely consulted in any public library in the country. The Internet is often preferable for zeroing in on specific facts—the "reference" information I'm talking about—but at the same time it is not as good as published sources in providing overviews of how the specifics are related. (Nor is the Net as good as a conventional library in dealing with most *research* questions. For example, you can readily find current maps, for driving directions, on the Web; but for maps of the configurations of the classical Mediterranean, you're better off with *Barrington Atlas of the Greek and Roman World* [Princeton U. Press, 2000]. Similarly, from the Net you may be able to gather enough information for a high school or undergraduate term paper on the Dead Sea Scrolls; but for in-depth scholarship there is no substitute for a real research library.) Of course the other problem with the Net is the questionable reliability of many of its sources; it spreads misinformation just as readily as good information.

Several sources on the Net are particularly good for finding specific facts quickly:

- BrainBoost: www.brainboost.com
- InfoPlease: www.infoplease.com
- A9.com at: http://a9.com (This site searches, among other sources, full texts of books via Amazon.com's "Search Inside the Book" feature.)
- AskJeeves at: www.ask.com
- Scirus (for scientific subjects): www.scirus.com

Even if the Internet is the first source to which people turn for reference-type facts, it is still very useful for serious researchers to grasp the structure of printed reference sources defined by types of literature[2]; indeed, these "types" can often be found within the Internet itself. You can reasonably expect to find any of these forms of publication within a wide range of very different subject areas:

- ***Almanacs.*** These are fact books and compendiums of miscellaneous information. They are particularly good for answering questions having to do with statistics, awards, brief news or historical data, dates and anniversaries, geography, city or county data, sports, and so on.

- *Atlases.* These are compendiums of maps or tables that graphically display information not just on geopolitical matters, but also on subjects such as crop production, spread of diseases, military power balances, climate variation, ecological conditions, status of women, literacy levels, technological levels, population trends, soil conditions, occupational distributions, area histories, trade patterns, and the like.
- *Bibliographies.* These are compendiums of citations (sometimes with annotations) to books, journal articles, conference papers, dissertations, reports, and so on, on particular subjects. They are especially important in historical or literary research, as they frequently include references to works that are overlooked by computer databases. Their arrangement, too, often provides an overview of the structure of a topic, which cannot be duplicated by computer printouts.
- *Catalogs.* Catalogs provide listings of merchandise, art objects, publications, equipment, and so forth that are located at particular places or that are available in a particular market niche; they often provide descriptive details, specifications, and prices.
- *Chronologies.* These present facts arranged by the time sequence of their occurrence. Often chronologies present parallel listings that display temporal contexts of different areas of study (e.g., politics, arts, technology, religion) simultaneously, so that a reader may correlate the events of one area with contemporaneous, earlier, or later developments in other subject areas.
- *Computer databases* and *Web sites.* These information sources exist in all subject areas and allow interactive searching, always by keywords and often by other methods of inquiry as well.
- *Concordances.* These are word lists associated with particular texts (usually literary or philosophical classics) that enable researchers to determine exactly where any particular word or words appear within the text.
- *Dictionaries.* These reference sources provide an alphabetically arranged list of words with their definitions, pronunciations, etymology, scope of usage, and so on. Often they contain biographical and geographical information. The term "dictionary" is often synonymous with "encyclopedia," referring simply to an alphabetical (rather than a systematic) arrangement of entries, regardless of their length.

- **Directories.** Directories provide information for identifying or locating individual people, organizations, or institutions in various geographical or subject areas. They list names, addresses, telephone and FAX numbers, e-mail addresses, and Web home pages.
- **Encyclopedias.** The purpose of an encyclopedia is to summarize established knowledge in a given subject area and to provide a starting point for more extensive research; it seeks to provide an overview of a subject written for nonspecialists (unlike a review article). (Note that encyclopedias specialized in a particular *subject area* still tend to be written with a nonspecialist *audience* in mind.) An encyclopedia may be contrasted to a *treatise*, which attempts to provide all knowledge on a subject in a systematic (rather than an alphabetical) arrangement, and which may be written for specialists rather than laypeople. Encyclopedias can usually be counted on to have detailed indexes that will reveal more of their contents than can be found through the simple alphabetical arrangement of their articles. (See Chapter 1.)
- **Gazetteers.** These are alphabetical dictionaries of geographic placenames; entries often include descriptions of the history, population, economic characteristics, and natural resources of the places listed. They are also useful for identifying which larger geopolitical units a smaller locale is part of (e.g., they will tell you which county a town is in—often of interest to genealogists).
- **Guides to the literature.** The literature of any subject area may be thought of in terms of different levels. *Primary literature* deals directly with a particular problem or concern, presenting original testimony, observations, or records about it or creative expressions of it. *Secondary literature* generally comprised both scholarly analyses and popularizations of the primary literature. *Tertiary literature* consists of reference works (the various types of literature: dictionaries, encyclopedias, handbooks, etc.) that identify, point out, summarize, abstract, or repackage the information provided by the other two levels. Guides to the literature ideally seek to provide an intellectual structure that orients a researcher to the most important sources at all three levels of literature for a given subject. In practice, however, many such "guides" fall short of this mark, and present instead an overview of only the tertiary reference literature for their field. (See Chapter 9.)
- **Handbooks and manuals.** These are a type of reference source intended to be easily transportable for actual use "in the field" rather

than just in libraries. They are related to encyclopedias and treatises in that they try to provide the principles and important facts of a subject area, and in that they can be arranged alphabetically or systematically. Their major distinction from these other forms is their emphasis on practice, procedures, and other "how to" directions for producing actual results rather than just intellectual understanding. Also, they tend to be much more concisely written, making them easier to carry about in field situations.

- *Newsletters.* These are current sources, providing up-to-date information in fields that tend to develop or change with some rapidity. They appear daily, weekly, or monthly.

- *Review articles.* These should not be confused with book reviews. They are articles that appear in journals, annuals, or essay anthologies that seek to provide a "state of the art" or "state of the situation" literature review and critical assessment or overview of a particular subject. Unlike encyclopedia articles, they are usually written for specialists, and so may assume familiarity with technical or occupational jargon. They also include a bibliography that seeks to be comprehensive rather than merely selective. Review articles, too, tend to place a greater emphasis on the current state of a subject, whereas encyclopedia articles tend to emphasize its historical aspects. (See Chapter 8.)

- *Treatises.* Like encyclopedias, these try to present a comprehensive summation of the established knowledge of a particular subject; unlike encyclopedias, however, they tend to be arranged systematically rather than alphabetically, and they tend to be written for specialists rather than laypeople.

- *Union lists.* These are location devices; they enable researchers who have already identified specific sources to identify which libraries actually own a copy of the desired works. (See Chapter 11.)

- *Yearbooks.* This type of literature seeks to provide an historical record of, and usually an evaluative commentary on, the year's developments in a particular field. Such annuals often provide a more permanent and better-indexed cumulation of the updating information contained in newsletters.

A foreknowledge of the existence of this structure of reference-source options can greatly increase the efficiency of your searches by enabling you to focus your inquiries, to begin with, in the types of literature most likely to answer them.

Many of the commercial indexes to journal articles allow searches by "document type" within their domains; the lists of types can be found on their "Advanced Search" pages. It is advisable to get in the habit of looking for these search features. (See Chapter 10.)

Some types of literature—indexes and abstracts, for example—are geared much more toward research rather than reference questions; so, again, the line between inquiries that can be handled by "methods of searching" and "types of literature" is not hard and fast. Both models of options can sometimes be used for either research or reference inquiries. The "indexes and abstracts" type, however, does not adequately distinguish among those geared toward controlled vocabulary, keyword, citation, or related record searching; so it isn't *enough* to simply think of the type-category "indexes" as a research option. Further distinctions need to be made at a concrete level, and the "methods" framework of options is preferable in such situations.

The overall point here is that if you understand the trade-offs, and the strengths and weaknesses, of all of the different methods of searching and types of literature, then just from this knowledge of the *formal properties* of the several retrieval systems you can ask much better questions to start with, and also have much better expectations of answering those questions, than if you begin with merely a knowledge of a few particular "subject" sources, or a naive faith in the capabilities of keyword searching in Internet engines. You can map out a likely strategy on a formal level before looking at any particular source by making distinctions such as these:

- This question requires overview information of an unfamiliar topic, and so encyclopedia and review articles are desirable.
- This question requires a published bibliography that will enable me to recognize a whole group of citations whose keywords I cannot adequately specify in advance in a computer search.
- This question requires an arrangement of full-text sources in classified order, rather than just a catalog of superficial surrogate records arranged alphabetically by subject headings.
- This question requires an arrangement of full-text sources categorized by subject, regardless of the keywords they use, rather than a ranking

of sources based on the frequency of the few relevant keywords that I can think of.

- This question demands a database or index that allows keyword access rather than just subject heading or descriptor approaches.
- This question requires some kind of categorization of subject-related sources—whether by subject headings or by compilation within a bibliography produced by an expert—rather than keyword or citation searching.
- This question requires citation searches to find subsequent sources in addition to previous sources listed in footnotes.
- This question requires a database that allows citation searching coupled with postcoordinate limitations by keywords.
- This question requires a database that allows limitation to "review" or "literature review" articles.
- This question requires related record searching because there aren't any good subject headings or descriptors, and keyword searching is not adequate to identify variant phrases for the same subject.
- This question requires talking to someone who can get me oriented in the field.
- This question requires use of printed bibliographies, catalogs, and indexes that can reach into the earlier literature not covered by computer databases.
- This question sounds like it could be answered more efficiently by an encyclopedia article than by browsing the bookstacks or Google searching.
- This question sounds like the kind of thing some experts will know about; therefore it requires a directory that will enable me to find such people.
- This question requires a union list or database that will tell me who owns a copy of a particular source that my local library does not have.

It is possible to frame scores of observations like the above examples that entail a combined knowledge of both methods of searching and types of literature—even without knowing in advance the titles or names of particular databases, indexes, encyclopedias, people sources, and so on, that will meet the desired criteria. Simply knowing the *kinds* of sources that exist within *any* subject area will make you more proficient in finding specific instantiations of them geared toward whatever particular inquiry you may be pursuing.

Such knowledge will also enable you to *eliminate* whole areas of options with which you might otherwise waste time (e.g., in trying to use electronic or printed sources when the information you need is most likely to exist in some person's head; in trying to use computer databases rather than classified bookstacks when the needed information is likely to exist only at the page or paragraph level within printed, copyrighted books, and in unknown keywords; in trying to use Google or other Net engines for overview perspectives when encyclopedias or review articles are preferable).

It is this kind of foreknowledge of the formal properties of the several retrieval options that usually makes reference librarians much more efficient in finding information on a subject than even full professors within the discipline.

Students in a particular subject area usually learn its information resources from a particular list they are given to study. The result is that they often learn the individual trees very well without perceiving the arrangement of the forest or the variety of methods available for getting through it, whether by walking, riding, flying over, swinging from branch to branch, or burrowing underneath. The training of reference librarians, on the other hand, is more from the top down than from the bottom up. They first learn the overall arrangement that can be expected in *any* forest—here the analogy is not perfect—and the various ways of moving around in it. They learn the overall *methods of searching* and *types of literature*; and they thereby usually understand the *full range of options* for finding information even—or rather, especially—in unfamiliar subject areas. The librarians may not understand the content of the discipline in which they are searching as well as professors within it; but the librarians probably will have a better grasp of the range of options for *finding* the content, which is a distinct and different skill.

The study of the categorization, arrangement, storage, and retrieval of information is a discipline unto itself; it is called library and information science. Those whose acquaintance with it is minimal should be wary of assuming they are doing fully efficient research "on their own," for there will always be more options in searching than they realize. The moral of the story is brief: the more you know of what your options are, the better the searcher you will be; but remember to ask for help, since the probability is that you will miss something important if you work entirely on your own.

Librarians have four major aids that help them to exploit the internal type-of-literature structure of the information sources within any given field. The first two can be considered the basic sources; the others, updates. They are:

1. *Guide to Reference Books* (Chicago: American Library Association, revised irregularly). This volume is often considered the reference librarian's bible. (A subscription online version is in preparation.) It enables a searcher to look up any subject field and find within it a listing of virtually all its important reference sources arranged according to types of literature. The citations provide full bibliographic descriptions of each source—both current material, in print and online, and time-tested older works—with descriptive annotations. The overall arrangement of the work is by broad subject groups, with an index by authors, titles, and subjects.

2. *Walford's Guide to Reference Material* (London: Library Association Publishing, revised irregularly). This is a multi-volume set comparable to the American Library Association *Guide,* but with more of an emphasis on British sources.

3. *American Reference Books Annual: ARBA* (Libraries Unlimited, 1970– ). Each annual volume in this series presents a listing of all reference books published in the United States in the preceding year. The distinctive feature of this series is that it provides a detailed review of each work listed. Indexes are by author, title, and subject. *ARBA* thus serves as an excellent update of the ALA *Guide* volume. Various five-year cumulative indexes have appeared since the beginning of the series, and these cumulations themselves are major guides to reference books. Some libraries keep them next to their *Guide* volume.

4. The library's own online catalog. Subject headings within the catalog are subdivided by form subdivisions that correspond to the various types of literature; for example:

**[LC Subject Heading]—Atlases**
                             **—Bibliography**
                             **—Case studies**
                             **—Catalogs**
                             **—Charts, diagrams, etc.**
                             **—Chronology**

—Concordances
—Dictionaries
—Directories
—Discography
—Encyclopedias
—Film catalogs
—Guidebooks
—Handbooks, manuals, etc.
—Illustrations
—Indexes
—Manuscripts—Catalogs
—Periodicals—Bibliography
—Periodicals—Bibliography—Union lists
—Periodicals—Indexes
—Photograph collections
—Pictorial works
—Posters
—Quotations
—Statistics
—Tables
—Textbooks
—Union lists
—Yearbooks

The predictability of this kind of "form" cataloging enables librarians to identify quickly new instances of familiar types of literature within any subject area, because the catalog is updated daily.[3]

The above sources enable researchers to find types of literature in monographic or printed-book formats, and on the Internet (since many Web sites are now cataloged by libraries). There are other types of literature, however, that exist "within" journal and report literature; these include such things as book reviews, database reviews, software reviews, hardware reviews, film reviews, editorials, letters to the editor, curriculum guides, bilingual materials, and state-of-the-art reviews (see Chapter 10.) Many online indexes enable you to specify these kinds of formats within the literature they cover; but there is no convenient overall listing of which types are searchable within which databases. Usually, however, there will be "Help" or "Limit" menu options within the individual databases themselves—especially in their "advanced search" screens—that will bring to your attention "document type" search options for whatever file you're in.

In researching any topic, then, it is important to be able to think in terms of the several types of literature as well as of the various methods of searching. You can use the Table of Contents of this book as a good initial checklist of the range of options available to you whenever you have to take on an unfamiliar subject.

Perhaps the most important point overall, however, is the observation with which this book began: if you want to do serious research, you cannot confine yourself to the Internet or online "virtual libraries" alone. The information universe of the future, no matter how its contents may change and grow, is best understood in terms of unavoidable trade-offs among *what*, *who*, and *where* restrictions. The Internet will never include everything in real libraries until such time as human nature itself changes, in the direction of selfless benevolence, and all writers, artists, and creators forgo the advantages of intellectual property to voluntarily contribute their work products to the good of the socialist whole, accepting recompense at levels determined by bureaucratic formulas rather than by marketplace forces of supply and demand. History has not been kind to systems based on the assumption that most human beings will act in this manner. Within the world of learning, however, history has also witnessed the creation of a marvelous mechanism for protecting the rights of authors while also making the universe of knowledge freely available to anyone who will travel to certain locations. I hope this book will lead to a more efficient use, and greater appreciation, of that mechanism: bricks-and-mortar research libraries.

## Notes

1. Other techniques such as original observation and analysis, controlled experimentation, site examinations, and statistical surveying or sampling are beyond the scope of this book.

2. The descriptions given here are derived largely from another book of mine, *Library Research Models* (Oxford U. Press, 1993).

3. A fuller listing of hundreds of form subdivisions used in library catalogs may be found in my *Library Research Models*, Appendix 2.

# *Appendix: Wisdom*

As mentioned in the Preface, there is a hierarchy in learning—from data to information and opinion, to knowledge and understanding. In an earlier edition of this book, I regarded wisdom as the next, and highest, step on the same "ladder"; I would now revise that assumption. Wisdom, I think, actually lies outside this hierarchy because, as conventionally understood, it entails not just intellectual apprehension of the *true* but also a willed practice of the *good in conduct* as well. Indeed, our capacity to seek the moral good, not our intellectual brainpower, is the defining human attribute that we all share in both possession and degree; it forms the basis of human equality.[1] The intellectual component of wisdom, in contrast, can vary from person to person; this variety arises in part from the fact that it is always based on a kind of faith in an ultimate "something": an entity, a process, or non-being itself, whose ultimacy cannot be "proven" definitively.

To come at the problem from another direction, the intellectual aspect of wisdom is concerned with the discernment of ultimate criteria of truth, goodness, and beauty; these criteria themselves require *assumptions* of what "counts" as evidence, or what "counts" as an explanation. Such assumptions must be grounded in some stopping point which, when reached, finally suffices in justifying any sequence of thought. Candidates for this ultimate ground include the Biblical Jehovah, The Trinity, Allah, the Void (or non-being/non-existence), the pantheistic One, the interaction of *yin* and *yang*, endlessly repeated cosmic cycles, fertility cycles, sexual fulfillment, Platonic Forms, Aristotelian form and matter, matter and energy, Darwinian evolution and genetic diffusion, the Hegelian dialectical process, Marxist dialectical materialism, elegance in mathematics, societal conventions based on power relationships, one's own self and will, one's family or tribe/caste, artistic creation, and so on. The acceptance of any one candidate over another, as that which "explains" the overall universe, entails considerations of whether that Ultimate is personal or impersonal; whether it is known by discovery or by revelation (or both); and whether one's connection to it is a matter of "relationship to" or "identity with." *Some* such ultimate ground of meaning is unavoidably assumed, whether consciously or not, in all thinking.[2] The intellectual, speculative component of wisdom strives to grasp which candidate best corresponds to, and coheres with, the widest range of experience.

The ability to grasp such distinctions is facilitated by education, book learning, and degrees of intelligence, which do vary among people; and so cognitive wisdom itself is a variable property that can be, and is, attributed to persons who do indeed assume contradictory cognitive Ultimates as their explanatory stopping points. The moral aspect of wisdom, however, consists in the habit of living, or at least striving to live, according to the virtues. A traditional list of these would include justice, temperance, courage, and prudence, if not faith, hope, and charity as well. It is this ethical aspect that often leads observers to note that many people who have little formal education—and who may also live within widely variant religious, agnostic, or atheist creeds—nevertheless live wisely or sagely, while, conversely, many with great knowledge of particular subjects are nonetheless practically foolish in the conduct of their own lives. Wisdom as a whole, however, does not reduce to virtue; the former, as conventionally understood, also entails the intellectual insight of being able cognitively to discern, again, a reasonably justifiable view of the *ultimate* structure of the "forest" amid the myriad trees—as opposed, at least, to mistaken views assumed by those who are recognizably unwise, short-sighted, or foolish.

It is noteworthy that several of the options for ultimacy are indeed mutually exclusive—that is, they cannot each be the ultimate explanatory "stopping point" in the same universe. If a Schopenhauerian or Buddhistic Void is the final reality, for example, then belief in a Biblical God is false. If belief in a transcendent God ("outside" the universe) is true, then belief in the immanent pantheistic One is false—and vice-versa. If the process of biological evolution, measuring meaning in terms of the successful spread of genes, is the ultimate ground of explanation, then beliefs in either the Void or God are unnecessary or irrelevant. On the other hand, if the Creator God is real and the entire universe has a purposeful beginning and end, then endless cosmic cycles are ruled out as the ultimate explanation of reality, and evolutionary biological success becomes a subsidiary (not ultimate) ground of explanation. In other words, one cannot give equal credence, or equal ranking, to each candidate for ultimacy without intellectual contradiction and incoherence.

Some possible considerations, if not tests, of the wisdom of accepting one ultimate framework in comparison with another might include the following:

- Does the proposed framework explain or account for the universe having a "big bang" beginning?
- Does it admit or deny (as illusory) the experience of human free will?
- Does it account for the correspondence of pure mathematics to physical reality? Does it account for the elegance of that correspondence?
- Does it account for the possibility of conceptual thought?
- Does it account, in quantum physics, for the status of an observer whose own characteristics are not explained by the variables or coordinates of the system observed; and does it also account, in mathematics, for the parallel Godelian insight that a finished mathematical system cannot account for the outside status of its observer, either (whose outside status enables him to discern additional truths *of* the system not provable *within* the system)?
- Does it accord *relationships* (e.g., mathematical, causal, moral) a reality of ontological status comparable to *entities*? (Or does it need to? That is, is a concern for *coherence*, in addition to *correspondence*, a valid indicator of truth? Or is it merely a sign of delusional wishful thinking?[3])
- Does it assume that's one's best connection to the world is an attitude of attention to, exploration of, and engagement with it—i.e., that the universe is *good* and worthy of attention? Or does it assume that one's best response is detachment, renunciation, or transcendence—i.e., that the universe is *hostile or painful* and that the goal is escape from it or extinction of awareness of it? Or does it assume that the universe is entirely *indifferent* to human concerns, and that one can, with equal validity, choose any response to it at all?[4]

- Does it admit or deny a reality of moral obligation prior to conventions?
- Does it provide any basis for choosing among many alternative and conflicting moralities such as "Help your friends and harm your enemies"; or "Avenge all slights to your honor"; or "Forgive—seventy times seven"; or "Might makes right/Survival of the fittest"; or "It is useless to interfere with others' *Karma*"; or "Everything is permitted"— or Kantian universalism, or Existential authenticity, or the Golden Rule?
- Does it assume human nature to be ultimately benevolent (as in Rousseau)? Or does it recognize any inherent tendency in human nature toward violence, self-assertive (not communal) ends, self-destruction, or irrationality—variously labeled Freud's *id*, Christianity's *original sin*, Aristotle's *akrasia*, Dostoevsky's *underground*, Stevenson's *Mr. Hyde*, Plato's *thymos*, and so on? Or does it assume that there is no definable human nature at all—i.e., that we are completely "blank slates" formed entirely by external forces or individual choices?

Wisdom, then, cannot be superficially regarded as "tolerance of contradiction" because some beliefs that are wise from one ultimate standpoint must necessarily be regarded as foolish, short-sighted, and even destructive to human well-being, from another.

As suggested by this list, the intellectual acceptance of one stopping point rather than another can have marked cross-over consequences for morality— that is, each candidate for cognitive "ultimacy" has different implications in necessitating, proscribing, or rendering irrelevant some ethical choices rather than others. The Golden Rule, for example, is not hospitably grounded in all of the above alternatives; nor are justice, charity, or compassion. The moral component of wisdom, as conventionally understood, however, is universally attributed only to those sages whose lives exemplify some mixture of justice, charity, or compassion for others. Those whose morality is defined by Machiavellian, "survival of the fittest," or Nietzschean will-to-power beliefs tend to be labeled "shrewd," "crafty," "clever," "guileful," or "cunning," but generally not "wise." The latter adjective is conventionally reserved to those who attain not just inner peace, but also relationships to others that are at least sympathetic and non-exploitive, if not positively beneficent. Since this ethical component of wisdom, as generally understood, can be achieved even by the unlettered, it thus has a standing independent of the intellectual aspect; and, if this is so, the independent validity of the moral virtues in turn narrows the range of possible intellectual grounds that can be adduced as hospitable to their flourishing. In other words, the implications of the intellectual and the ethical components of wisdom are *mutually* restrictive—at least in theory.

In practice, however, one often comes across an apparent incoherence between the cognitive and moral aspects of wisdom, as the term is commonly understood (or in its common attribution to particular individuals). In other words, it is often the case that, in mysterious ways, moral agents still arrive at intuitive grasps of justice, charity, compassion, or the Golden Rule, in spite of the fact that the ostensible "ground" of their thinking would logically point them, instead, toward an ethic of detached disregard for others; or toward one of "survival of the fittest," or sexual license, or an "us vs. them" group orientation, and so on.[5] The fact that some form of the recognition of "lateral" moral responsibility to others seems inextinguishable in human nature, no matter what the intellectual or cultural grounds in which people find themselves situated, seems to confirm the independence of the moral from the cognitive aspect of wisdom. (One might also adduce the historical failure of reeducation camps, inquisitions, gulags, psychiatric hospitals, and so on, to eradicate basic notions of justice.) While the cognitive aspect may be catalyzed by the reading of great books, the ethical seems to be a capacity derived directly from one's experiential encounters with other people.

One would think that the attribution of what I'll call "full" wisdom would be reserved to those whose intellectual insight and ethical choices had the greatest coherence—that is, the highest wisdom would seemingly be best understood as something like the proper entry in a cosmic crossword puzzle, satisfying both vertical (intellectual) and horizontal (moral) criteria simultaneously. (A third axis, corresponding to aesthetic criteria, might also have a place.) Such a framework would enable one, in Yeats's phrase, to "hold reality and justice in a single vision." In this case, one's ethical choices would be pursued in harmony with, rather than against the grain of, the ultimate ground of one's intellectual beliefs. Such, however, is simply not the way the term "wisdom" is conventionally understood—in common usage it is applied equally to sages whose cognitive groundings, at least, are widely variant and mutually incompatible, even if their ethical orientations may be similar.

Complexities such as these prevent "wisdom" from being regarded as a simple cognitive or intellectual "top step" in the hierarchy of learning. For these reasons it is better viewed as something enveloping (or not) the other stages of learning, rather than as their culmination, simply because those persons at the topmost rung of the hierarchy, that of understanding, are not necessarily *also* wise; and what is regarded as genuine (even if not "full") "wisdom" may still be attained with little or no "academic" knowledge or understanding of its Ultimate ground.

## Notes

1. See John E. Coons and Patrick M. Brennan, *By Nature Equal* (Princeton U. Press, 1999). It is noteworthy that equality cannot be grounded in any characteristic of human beings that is scientifically measurable; *any* such feature will be variable from one individual to another. The tacit recognition of human equality thus also entails a recognition of a valid form of knowledge (the philosophical) that is not reducible to the scientific.

2. See Roy A. Clouser, *The Myth of Religious Neutrality: An Essay on the Hidden Role of Religious Belief in Theories* (U. of Notre Dame Press, 1991).

3. For that matter, the term "wishful thinking" itself is a double-edged sword. It is usually applied dismissively, by strict materialists, to those who think that belief in a benevolent, transcendent God is justified; such belief is regarded as invalid because it can be "explained" as fulfilling a psychological need rather than corresponding to an objective reality. It is arguable, however, that a reverse form of wishful thinking is equally apparent in secular materialism or nihilism. That is, the attraction of these beliefs themselves may be "explained" with equal justice as stemming from a psychological need to avoid the pain of disappointed hopes; if one simply assumes the worst to begin with, one can never be painfully disappointed. Neither the optimistic nor the pessimistic worldview can be proven true by a test of correspondence to some discrete object; if there is any test of correspondence at all, it would have to lie in an agreement of the belief with some broad assessment of the requirements of human flourishing, and an assessment of which belief systems have actually facilitated or impeded that flourishing as their effects work out over time in history. In this regard, even if a verdict (on which systems marshal the greatest evidence of correspondence-to-flourishing) is still regarded as an open question, at the very least some assumptions of Ultimacy may be safely discredited if they have led repeatedly to disastrous human consequences. Regardless of any *correspondence* test, however, the dismissal of any objective source for transcendent moral values may lead to a worldview lacking *coherence*—i.e., a worldview in which one's own values are conceded to have no ultimate and non-

arbitrary justification. (Sartre, for example, assumed to begin with the absurdity of the universe. Hume, too, accepted the basic incoherence of morality and knowledge as simply an unavoidable aspect of reality—which raises the question, noted above, concerning whether a desire for *coherence* is, along with *correspondence*, a valid test of truth, or is itself merely an example of dismissable wishful thinking.) The important point here, however, is that the underlying *motivation* for either belief—that is, the psychological need for "comfort" of either a positive or negative sort—does not in itself establish or disprove the *truth* of either belief.

4. For example, after the Enlightenment deemed God irrelevant to the existence and functioning of the universe (at least, in the minds of many thinkers), a problem remained of how to justify the world as still basically *good*. The subsequent Romantic movement attempted to solve this problem by rooting the notion of the basic benevolence of the universe within Nature itself, which came to be viewed as a kindly nurturer and teacher (as in Wordsworth's lyric poetry). The inadequacy of this ground for the notion of goodness, however, was demonstrated by the widespread abandonment of Romanticism in the latter half of the 19th century; it was effectively killed by the publication of Darwin's *Origin of Species*, which portrayed nature not as a realm of kindly nurturing but rather as an arena of survival of the fittest. Other attempts to portray "the whole" of the universe as fundamentally "good" run into the problem of the myriad genocides and holocausts of human history—are these to be regarded as "good" because of their participation in a larger universe that is simply defined as good to begin with? Certainly they can be regarded as parts of the evolutionary process of survival of the fittest. If, however, that process itself is the measure of "goodness," why are genocides to be regarded as "bad" or "evil"? This dilemma is summarized in Dostoevsky's remark to the effect that if God is dead, "everything is permitted." The Sartrean existentialist position, that the universe is indifferent or absurd and that any "authentic" choice within such a framework is moral, runs into a similar problem–or rather, defines reality in a way that does not recognize that there *is* a such a problem.

5. See James W. Sire, *The Universe Next Door: A Basic Worldview Catalog* (3rd ed.; InterVarsity Press, 1997), 48–50, 72, 90–92, 105–6, 111–12, 128–30, 153, 155–57, 198.

# Index

When multiple page references are listed, page numbers of the major discussion are in *italics*.